CALPU SICU[...]
THE ECLOGUES

Edited with Introduction
and Commentary by
C.H. Keene

Bristol Classical Press

First published by George Bell & Sons, London, 1887

This edition published in 1996
by Bristol Classical Press
an imprint of
Gerald Duckworth & Co. Ltd
The Old Piano Factory
48 Hoxton Square, London N1 6PB

A catalogue record for this book is available
from the British Library

ISBN 1-85399-491-X

Available in USA and Canada from:
Focus Information Group
PO Box 360
Newburyport
MA 01950

Printed in Great Britain by
The Cromwell Press, Melksham, Wiltshire

CONTENTS.

INTRODUCTION.

NAME AND PERSONAL HISTORY OF CALPURNIUS.

ALMOST all authorities give Calpurnius the praenomen
Titus. The praenomen *Caius*, however, is found in VR1.ra
and in one Florentine MS., while several MSS. give no
praenomen. Glaeser says that a Vienna MS. (n. 286) has
at the beginning *Incipiunt buccolica Theocriti Calphurnii
siculi P. cl.*, and at the end *Expliciunt buccolicon Theocriti
Calfurnii poetae siculi*, whence he conjectures that the
praenomen *Titus* originated from the name *Theocritus*, ap-
plied to Calpurnius on account of the style of his poetry.
He also thinks that the praenomen *Caius* originated from
an erroneous repetition of the beginning of the name *Cal-
purnius*, and concludes that we should follow those MSS.
which give no praenomen.

Wernsdorf says that Gyraldus, Fabricius, and Burmann
give our poet the praenomen *Junius*, or *Julius*, doubtless
identifying him with the Junius, or Julius Calpurnius, *qui
ad memoriam dictabat*, mentioned by Vopiscus, in his life of
Carus, chapter 8. On this subject, and also on the mean-
ing of *Siculus*, as applied to Calpurnius, see page 9.
Sarpius, with little probability, as Haupt shows, attributes
the poems to one Calpurnius Serranus, in the time of
Claudius.

As to the personal history of Calpurnius we are left in as much doubt as with regard to his full name, and have, in fact, no information save what may be gleaned from his poems, in which, following the example of Virgil, he speaks of himself under the names Corydon and Tityrus. He had a brother of nearly equal age (IV. 17, 18) devoted, like himself, to poetry. He found the Muses but empty-handed (*inanes*) patrons, and having been reduced to great straits, was on the point of emigrating to Spain, when he attracted the notice of Meliboèus (probably Seneca), who raised him above want, and apparently secured him some office at Rome (IV. 29 sq.).

Date of Calpurnius.

From an examination of Eclogues I.–VII., which alone, to the exclusion of VIII.–XI. (see page 14), are the work of Calpurnius, it appears that the principal conditions to be satisfied in fixing the date of Calpurnius are, that the Emperor during whose reign the poems were written was young, handsome, and himself a poet, that he exhibited splendid games, that his accession was coincident with the beginning of an era of peace and freedom, that the preceding reign had been tyrannical, and that the appearance of a comet was fresh in men's minds. All these conditions seem to point to the beginning of the reign of Nero, and of him alone, as will appear from the following particulars :—

1. The reference in I. 77 sq. seems to be to the comet, which, we learn from Pliny, Suetonius, and Dion Cassius, appeared at the end of the reign of Claudius, and be-

ginning of that of Nero. The words of Calpurnius are :

> Cernitis ut puro nox jam vicesima coelo
> Fulgeat et placida radiantem luce cometem
> Proferat ? ut liquidum nutet sine vulnere plenus ?
> Numquid utrumque polum, sicut solet, igne cruento
> Spargit et ardenti scintillat sanguine lampas ?
> At quondam non talis erat, cum, Caesare rapto,
> Indixit miseris fatalia civibus arma.

Now, we learn from the first lines of the Eclogue that it was in autumn that Corydon and Ornytus found these lines cut on the beech-tree, and we know that it was on the 13th of October, 54 A.D., that Claudius died and Nero succeeded to the empire, at which time a comet is said to have appeared. Suet. Claud. 46: *praesagia mortis ejus praecipua fuerunt, exortus crinitae stellae, quem cometen vocant*, &c. Dion Cassius 60, 35 : οὕτω μὲν ὁ Κλαύδιος μετήλλαξεν (i. e. died), ἐς τοῦτό τε ὅ τε ἀστὴρ ὁ κομήτης ἐπὶ πλεῖστον ὀφθεὶς καὶ ἡ ψεκὰς ἡ αἱματώδης ἔδοξε σημῆναι. Pliny N. H. 2, 25, 92 : *sed cometes nunquam in occasura parte coeli est, terrificum magna ex parte sidus atque non leviter piatum, ut civili motu Octavio consule iterumque Pompei et Caesaris bello, in nostro vero aevo circa veneficium quo Claudius Caesar imperium reliquit Neroni, ac deinde principatu ejus adsiduum prope ac saevum.* It appears from these passages that the comet was visible for a considerable time, and the poet would not hesitate to regard it as an omen of disaster at the close of the despotic reign of Claudius, and as an omen of good fortune during the happy *quinquennium Neronis*. Pliny's statement, that the comet was *saevum*, as well as *assiduum*, during the reign of Nero is explained by his having written when the enormities of Nero's later years had effaced the memory of his early promise, at which time every omen would of course receive a sinister interpretation.

2. Calpurnius speaks often of the youth of the Emperor, and of his beauty. Nero was but seventeen at his accession, and was of handsome appearance, according to Suetonius (51) and to Seneca, the latter of whom compares him to Apollo (de Morte Claudii 4), almost in the same words as Calpurnius uses VII. 83.

3. The Emperor's early eloquence is praised in I. 45 : *maternis causam qui vicit in ulnis.** Now, Nero (Suet. 7) pleaded for the people of Bologna in Latin, and those of Rhodes and Ilium in Greek at the early age of thirteen, which might justify the poet's extravagant eulogium.

4. The Emperor seems to be described as a poet, IV. 87, and we have abundant testimony that Nero posed in that character.

5. In I. 69 sq. Faunus foretells that during the new reign constitutional rights and the authority of the consuls will be respected, and this accords with the promises which Tacitus (A. 13, 4) says Nero made in the senate at the beginning of his reign.

6. The games described in VII. may correspond with those in Suet. Nero 11, and the wooden amphitheatre of VII. 23, 24, answers to that mentioned by Suet. Nero 12 and Tac. A. 13, 31.

7. The revivifying of the tree in IV. 107 sq. answers to Tac. A. 13, 58 : *eodem anno* (A. D. 58) *Ruminalem arborem in comitio, quae octingentos et triginta ante annos Remi Romulique infantiam texerat, mortuis ramalibus et arescente trunco deminutam prodigii loco habitum est, donec in novos fetus reviresceret.*

8. The reference to the cessation of civil war (I. 46 sq.) at the first glance does not seem appropriate, as the reign of

---

* For this remarkable hyperbole cf. Themistius, Oratio Consularis ad Jovianum (Oratio 12 in Paris edition, 1618): τὸν ἐν ἀγκάλαις ὕπατον, τὸν ἐκ τοῦ μαστοῦ πατρόζοντα ἤδη.

Claudius was peaceful, save for a five days' mutiny of the legions under Camillus. It may, however, merely allude to Nero's peaceful succession, as compared with the civil wars of an earlier period, and was perhaps suggested by the speech reported in Tac. A. 13, 4: *ceterum peractis tristitiae imitamentis curiam ingressus, et de auctoritate patrum et consensu militum praefatus, consilia sibi et exempla capessendi egregie imperii memoravit, neque iuventam armis civilibus aut domesticis discordiis imbutam; nulla odia, nullas injurias nec cupidinem ultionis afferre.*

9. The treatment of the senate described 1. 60 sq. corresponds with Seneca's statement, Ludus de Morte Claudii, that Claudius put to death thirty senators.

The description of a false peace in 1. 54–57, also corresponds to the time of Claudius. See Notes 2 on that passage.

Should it be objected that the strictures of Calpurnius on the preceding reign are too severe to be justly applicable to Claudius, a little consideration will show that this is really a strong argument in favour of the Neronian epoch. It is shown on page 12 that in all probability the Meliboeus of Calpurnius was Seneca. The poet would, therefore, naturally adopt his patron's somewhat exaggerated view of the shortcomings of Claudius, and we find a perfect parallel for the disparaging expressions of Calpurnius with regard to the reign preceding that under which he wrote, in Seneca's bitter political satire de Morte Claudii, referred to above, which is commonly known by the title Ἀποκολοκύντωσις.

The evidence here adduced in favour of the Neronian era seems overwhelming, and the reign of no other emperor presents such a number of coincidences. The most weighty argument in support of a later date is that of Professor Maguire, in *Hermathena*, vol. 5, page 139. He points out that Justinian (Inst. 2, 1, 39) tells us that

Hadrian gave (*concessit*) the property in treasure-trove to the finder, and to this law he thinks reference is made in IV. 117 :

> Jam neque damnatos metuit jactare ligones
> Fossor et invento, si fors dedit, utitur auro.
> Nec timet, ut nuper, dum jugera versat arator
> Ne sonet offenso contraria vomere massa,
> Jamque palam presso magis et magis instat aratro.

He therefore regards Calpurnius as the poet of Commodus, and supposes that the legislation of Hadrian, the founder of the Aelian line, is mentioned to glorify Commodus, his lineal representative.

This view, however, involves some serious difficulties, for it makes *nuper*, as Professor Maguire points out, refer to a period some fifty or sixty years previous, and it seems a poor compliment to seek a ground of eulogy in so distant an ancestor, τίς πατέρ' αἰνήσει εἰ μὴ κακοδαίμονες υἱοί. The lines of Calpurnius are sufficiently explained by the fact which we know on the authority of Suetonius (Nero 10), that the *delatores* were not encouraged during the celebrated *quinquennium Neronis*. This view is confirmed by the tale of Herodes Atticus, who, having found a large treasure, and being afraid, no doubt, of the *delatores*, placed it at the disposal of Nerva, who was then Emperor. Nerva told him to use (χρῶ) it himself, and when Herodes Atticus cautiously replied, that it was too great for him to use, said, ' Well, then, abuse (παραχρῶ) it, for the treasure is yours.' The law of Hadrian, of course, was not passed until long after this occurrence, so we see that sometimes, at any rate, the more constitutional Emperors did not enforce their claim to treasure-trove.

The story of Nero's attempt to secure for himself the treasure of Dido, which Caesellius Bassus imagined he had discovered, does not, as Haupt shows, affect the argument, as this occurrence was subsequent to Nero's early years of equitable rule. The words of Calpurnius, moreover, imply a recent reign of terror, and are as appropriate to the time of Claudius as they are inappropriate to that of the 'philosopher in the purple' who preceded Commodus. Professor Maguire also makes the two following valuable suggestions in support of the late date of Calpurnius. Firstly, he remarks that the discovery in the Colosseum of an arrangement for allowing the beasts to rise from underground seems to satisfy the description in VII. 69–72. Secondly, we learn from IV. 36 sq. that Calpurnius had contemplated emigrating to Spain ; and Professor Maguire suggests that such an enterprise was more likely to commend itself after Vespasian had extended the fuller Latin rights (*Majus Latium*, Plin. N. H. 3, 1 ; Gaius, 1, 95) to the whole of Spain. These arguments, however, cannot be taken as conclusive of the late date of Calpurnius, for the stage machinery, if one may so call it, need not have been peculiar to one structure ; and a man who was starving at home, as Calpurnius tells us he was, may well have been willing to try his fortune in a new country, even though it did not enjoy full Latin rights. Moreover, Mr. Purser points out to me that Seneca, who died several years before the building of the Colosseum was commenced, describes scenic effects similar to those mentioned by Calpurnius. See Epist. Mor. 88, 2 : *Machinatores pegmata per se surgentia excogitant et tabulata tacite in sublime crescentia* (Calpurnius says *ab cavernis aurea creverunt arbuta*) *et alias ex inopinato varietates aut dehiscentibus, quae cohaerebant* (Calpurnius says *rupta voragine terrae*) *aut his quae distabant, sua sponte coeuntibus, aut his, quae eminebant, paulatim in se residentibus.*

That Calpurnius belonged to the Neronian period is the view of Hermann Schiller, whose authority on that period is of the greatest weight. He criticises the poet as follows in his Geschichte des Römischen Kaiserreichs unter der

Regierung des Nero, Berlin, 1872, page 617 : Besser (i.e.
than satire) glückten auch dieser Zeit (i.e. the time of
Nero) die kleinere Aufgaben, welche zwischen Erzählung
und Lied in der Mitte liegen, die bei reinlicher Ausführung
es selbst bisweilen zu einem glücklichen Gedanken zu
bringen vermögen. Hieher gehören einige kleine Erzeug-
nisse der höfischen Poesie, die sich unter dem Namen
des Calpurnius und in der Lateinischen Anthologie finden.
In den Idyllen des ersteren ist der dichterische Gehalt und
die poetische Kraft von verschiedenem Werth. Mit be-
lebter Schilderung wechseln langgedehnte und langweilige
Erörterungen, die nichts anderes als versificirte Ackerbau-
und Viehzuchtslehre (Eclogue v.) enthalten, oder die
Gedanken sind so weit hergeholt und gekünstelt oder
auch die bei dem Originale des Dichters noch erträg-
lichen Motive so übertrieben und verunstaltet, dass man
von diesem gemalten Schäferleben zurückgeschreckt wird
(namentlich Eclogue vi.). Die Originalität der Concep-
tion mangelt gänzlich und der Dichter hängt hier ganz und
gar von seinen Vorbildern, den griechischen Bukolikern
und Vergil ab ; aber auch die Sprache entlehnt Vieles von
den Dichtern der augusteischen Periode ; doch ist die
Darstellung sowie die Behandlung des Verses immerhin
gewandt ; nur in der Ueppigkeit des Ausdruckes erkennt
man die Spuren dieser Zeit. In die herrschende Hofsprache
hat sich der Dichter leicht gefunden und die vierte Ekloge
bietet eine so reiche Blüthenlese, dass sie mit den ähn-
lichen Erzeugnissen der Ptolemäerzeit wol zu wetteifern
vermag.*

---

* iv. 93 : Jupiter ipse parens cui tu iam proximus ipse Caesar abes.
107 gens omnis adorat diligiturque deis. 137 iuvenem quem vos (dei)
nisi fallor ab ipso aethere misistis. 142 Tu rogo (Mähly) mutata seu
Jupiter ipse figura Caesar ades seu quis superum sub imagine falsa
Mortalique lates. 158 fer Meliboee deo mea carmina, nam tibi fas est
Sacra Palatini penetralia visere Phoebi und Vgl. vii. 73 sqq.

Friedländer also, in his Sittengeschichte Roms, follows Haupt in placing Calpurnius at the beginning of Nero's reign.

The theory most generally accepted hitherto, and adopted by Wernsdorf, Bernhardy, Gibbon, and others is that Calpurnius wrote in the time of Carus and his sons, i.e. in the latter half of the third century. This view, however, has little to support it, and is open to serious objections, as will appear from the following considerations :—

It is shown on page 14 sq. that, in all probability, the first seven poems are by Calpurnius, the last four by Nemesianus, and that the dedication to Nemesianus is a mere error. Yet this erroneous dedication is almost the sole ground for making Calpurnius a contemporary of Carus and his sons, Carinus and Numerianus ; for that the Junius Calpurnius, mentioned by Vopiscus in his life of Carus, is the same as the author of the poems is little more than a gratuitous assumption, and is inconsistent with the traditional name of our poet, which seems to have been Titus Calpurnius. Calpurnius was a not uncommon name, and the only *rapprochement* between the two persons seems to be that Junius Calpurnius was a Syracusan, while Titus Calpurnius is called Siculus, which epithet, Siculus, Glaeser conjectures, is owing to his poems being in the style of the Sicilian Theocritus.*

The games described in VII. cannot be identified with those in the reign of Carinus and Numerianus (see Vopiscus 30, 18), for such games were exhibited by several of the emperors ; and none of the novelties referred to by

---

* It seems, however, a serious objection to Glaeser's theory, that in the Parma edition, we find not only *Titi Calphurnii Siculi*, but also *ad Nemesianum Karthaginensem* and *Aurelii Nemesiani Poetae cartaginensis*, from which it appears that no more is intended than to indicate the birth or residence of the poets, respectively, in Sicily and Carthage.

Vopiscus (e. g. the *neurobaten, tichobaten, pythaulas,* and *ludum Sarmaticum quo dulcius nihil est*) are mentioned in this poem.

Had Calpurnius lived at the era suggested, it is quite inconceivable that he should have mentioned but one Caesar, and yet there is but one referred to in I., IV., and VII., for it is absurd to allege that the plurals *dei* and *numina* must refer to two princes. It will be sufficient to show this in one case. In VII. 78 we read

Dic age, dic Corydon, mihi quae sit forma deorum.

This merely means that Corydon, in describing the appearance of Caesar, would be describing the appearance of the gods, and this is clear also from the following words, in which Corydon describes *one* person only :—

. . . Utcunque tamen conspeximus ipsum
Longius ac, nisi me visus decepit, in *uno*
Et Martis vultus et Apollinis esse notavi.*

The Eclogues could not have been written while Carus was alive, for such emphasis would not have been laid on his youth, nor would all mention of his sons have been omitted ; nor were they written after the death of Carus while Carinus and Numerianus were surviving, for he would not have mentioned one of them without the other ; nor again in the interval between the death of Numerianus and Carinus, for it would be strange that no mention occurs of the death of father or son ; and the peace so

---

* Professor Maguire, holding that the Emperor referred to is Commodus, thinks that his face (*vultus*) is singled out for description because, as we learn from Aelius Lampridius (Historia Augusta, 7, 13), his person was disfigured by disease. It is, however, to be noticed that Corydon's description is given at the request of Lycotas, who specially mentions the *vultumque habitumque* of the Emperor. See line 77.

often mentioned by Calpurnius could not have been said
to prevail during these reigns, for throughout this period
wars were going on with either the Sarmatians or Persians,
either in the north or against Diocletian. Finally, the
first and fourth Eclogues contain reproaches on the pre-
ceding reigns which are not appropriate to the time of
either Aurelian, Tacitus, Florian, or Probus.

It is noteworthy that the Emperor Carus was more de-
voted to arms than to literature, and Gibbon admits that,
even assuming the poems to have been written in the time
of Carus (which is the opinion of that historian), yet he pro-
bably never read the adulation with which he was honoured.
It is strange that Gibbon did not see how strongly this
admission tells against his theory, that the poems, at least
I., IV., VII., in which the Emperor is praised, were of the
time of Carus, for one can scarcely conceive them as
addressed to any but a warm patron of poetry, and one
who was likely to notice and reward the poet's homage.

Moreover, Gibbon admits that the behaviour of Carus
on his accession was such as to afford no favourable pre-
sage for the future, and could not justify the tone of
Calpurnius' poems. This inconsistency the historian ex-
plains as the result of mere servile flattery; but to the
careful student of the poems that explanation will not
seem satisfactory, for the panegyric does not deal only in
vague generalities, but singles out for praise definite points
in the administration of the new Emperor, and this, if
Gibbon's explanation were correct, could only have been
regarded as the most bitter sarcasm.

The blemishes in language, *naevos recentioris Latinitatis*,
as Wernsdorf calls them, which are adduced to show a
later period, are for the most part either erroneous read-
ings, or occur in the last four poems, which are not from
the pen of Calpurnius. Even from these latter poems
some of the irregularities should be removed : e.g. in

XI. 22 Glaeser gives *perdunt spina rosas,* following the reading of the Neapolitan MS., and therefore admits the unusual form, *spinum* n., instead of *spina* f.; but Haupt, it would seem rightly, thinks we should, in this case, leave the Neapolitan MS., and follow the majority of the codices in reading *perdit. Perdunt,* of the Neapolitan MS., may easily be a dittography from the preceding line, where that form occurs. As to the form *oleastrum,* II. 44, it was probably in use side by side with *oleaster,* for a grammarian quoted by Haupt says:—*oleastrum generis neutri: sed Virgilius foliis oleaster amaris.*

The question as to who is referred to by Calpurnius under the name of Meliboeus is of consequence in fixing the date of the poems; and whether L. Annaeus Seneca, or Calpurnius Piso, who seem to satisfy best the conditions of the problem, be our choice, the reign of Nero is again the period at which the poet wrote.

In IV. 53 sq. Meliboeus is not only described as a poet under the special patronage of Apollo and the Muses, but is also said to be an authority on the winds and weather, and on these latter subjects Seneca treated in his *Quaestiones Naturales,* while the reference to Apollo and the Muses is satisfied by his numerous tragedies written in iambic senarii, and interspersed with choral parts in anapaestic and other metres.

In the work just named he devotes an entire book to meteors and another to comets : and this gives a peculiar propriety to the mention of the comet in I. 77 sq., just before the poet commends the poem to the good offices of his patron :—

> Forsitan Augustas feret haec Meliboeus ad aures.

It is true that Calpurnius Piso is also spoken of as under the patronage of Apollo in the *Laudatio Pisonis,* which Haupt, on account of some peculiarities in its form, attributes to Calpurnius Siculus. But this is, after all, a somewhat vague argument for the identification, while the more definite references to weather and comets seem applicable to Seneca alone.

That both Seneca and Piso were patrons of art appears from Juv. 5, 108 sq. : *Nemo petit, modicis quae mittebantur amicis A Seneca, quae Piso bonus, quae Cotta solebat Largiri.*

Wernsdorf, who places Calpurnius in the time of Carus and his sons, identifies Meliboeus with C. Junius Tiberianus, who held the offices of Magister Officiorum and Praefectus Urbis. His arguments however, drawn principally from internal evidence, tell with almost equal force in favour of Seneca, and, therefore, can hardly be said materially to affect the question. In R2.pβa2.sf2. Barth. an inscription to Nemesianus Carthaginensis is found, whence it has been conjectured that M. Aurelius Olympius Nemesianus is Meliboeus. This is, however, unlikely, as there does not seem to be any sufficient ground for supposing that Nemesianus held office, and he would, therefore, not satisfy the conditions implied by the internal evidence of the poems.

Glaeser places Calpurnius shortly after the time of Carus, but thinks we have no sufficient grounds for deciding who was referred to under the name of Meliboeus. He mentions Petrus Crinitus as arguing in favour of the time of Diocletian and Constantius, and in common with Haupt, censures Sarpius for identifying Calpurnius Siculus with Calpurnius Serranus, a writer of the reign of Claudius, quite unknown, save that Juvenal 7, 80, mentions one Serranus, apparently as a poet, and Quintilian, 10, 1, 89 (if we adopt Sarpius' probable emendation *Serranum* for vulg. *Sed eum*), speaks of him as a poet of great power and taste, who died young. Neither Juvenal nor Quintilian, however, call him Calpurnius Serranus, but simply Serranus.

Merivale places Calpurnius in the time of Domitian, to which Emperor he thinks, apparently however with little ground, that there is an allusion in VII. 84.

Conington says that Greswell believes the Emperor in question to be the youngest Gordian.

NUMBER OF ECLOGUES TO BE ATTRIBUTED TO CALPURNIUS.

It seems to be satisfactorily established that the eleven Eclogues commonly assigned to Calpurnius are really the work of two different authors, the first seven having been composed by Calpurnius, about the beginning of Nero's reign, and the last four being the work of Nemesianus, about A.D. 253–284.

The principal reasons for adopting these conclusions are the following :—

Calpurnius shortens final *o* only in agreement with the usage of the strictest poets.* For *putŏ* (VI. 84), and *nesciŏ* (I. 21), are not alien to classical times.

Ovid A. A. 1, 370 :

> Ut puto, non poteris ipsa referre vicem.

---

* Professor Maguire, in *Hermathena*, vol. 5, p. 140, objects that there are no parallels in the Neronian age for a short vowel before *sp*, as in II. 32 : *gramine sparget ;* or for *ŏ* in the imperative, as in V. 24 : *mittito clausos.* But the readings he quotes, although given in Walker's Corpus and elsewhere, are probably erroneous.

In the valuable Neapolitan MS. we find *mitte reclusos*, and the vulgate *mittito clausos* is probably a mere conjecture of some one who thought *mitte* and *reclusos* to be tautological, both expressing the letting of the flocks out of the pens. The whole line runs thus :—

> Sed non ante greges in pascua mitte reclusos
> Quam fuerit placata Pales.

'Do not let the flocks out of the pens and turn them into the pasture

Tib. 1, 5, 75 :

> Nescio quid furtivus amor parat ; utere quaeso.

But in the last four poems, although *horreŏ* (IX. 43) and *canŏ* (X. 18 and XI. 41) may be justified by classical usage, we must regard as innovations *expectŏ* (IX. 26), *conjungŏ* (X. 14), *concedŏ* (XI. 42), *ambŏ* (IX. 17), and perhaps also *mulcendŏ* (IX. 53), and *laudandŏ* (IX. 80), although Juvenal, 3, 232, has :

> Plurimus hic aeger moritur vigilando : sed illum
> Languorem peperit cibus, &c.

In the first seven poems there are but eight elisions, and all in the first foot, or at the outside eleven, if we admit the three doubtful cases, IV. 40, ib. 134, VII. 77, where the elision is in a foot subsequent to the first. On the other hand, we find thirty-nine elisions in the last four poems. In making this calculation it is necessary to correct some of the vulgate readings. In III. 32, for *te o Lycida*, read *te Lycida;* ib. 7, for *neque enim* read *nec enim;* ib. 24, omit *es;* ib. 71, omit *et;* ib. 95, for *vicina ut saepe* (adv.), read *vicina sepe* (subst.) ; IV. 153, omit *in;* ib. 149, for *quae imparibus*, read *quae paribus;* v. 81, omit *et.* The reasons for these changes of reading will be found in the notes.

until, &c.' In spring the flocks which had been penned up (*claudere*) at the close of the year were let out (*recludere*) and sent to pasture. See v. 103 : *cum pecudes extremus clauserit annus.* In II. 96 we have *reclude canalem,* 'let out the stream.'

The first syllable in *recludo* is common. Virg. A. 7, 617 :

> More jubebatur tristesque recludere portas.

In II. 32 the Naples and the Paris MSS. read respectively *jungit* and *pingit;* and though Haupt, who himself proposes *cingit*, thinks both MSS. corrupt, yet they render it very probable that *spargit* is not the correct reading, but a mere gloss suggested by IV. 68 :

> Quem modo cantantem rutilo spargebat acantho
> Nais, &c.

I. 20, *descripta est;* II. 19, *ausa est;* VI. 7, *credibile est,* are not properly instances of elision, for *est* coalesces with the preceding word. In V. 104 *est* should be omitted, although *nitendumst* would be admissible, just as *descriptast, ausast, credibilest.*

After these corrections are made there remain in the 758 lines of the first seven poems (omitting VI. 54) only the eight following elisions :—

  I. 16 : Prome igitur calamos et si qua recondita servas.
  II. 30 : Ille etiam parvo dixit mihi non leve carmen.
  III. 12 : Mella etiam sine te jurabat amara videri.
  III. 55 : Ille ego sum Lycidas quo te cantante solebas.
  III. 58 : Atque inter calamos errantia labra petisti.
  III. 77 : Saepe etiam leporem decepta matre paventem.
  III. 82 : Qui metere occidua ferales nocte lupinos.
  V. 60 : Verum ubi declivi jam nona tepescere sole.

It thus appears that IV., VI., VII. are without an elision, that I., II., V. have one each, while III. has no less than five elisions ; from which facts Haupt conjectures that III. was written before the other Eclogues, and before Calpurnius had perfected his art. We must also notice that he does not elide a long vowel, and that even a short one is elided only in the first foot, if we except the three cases, IV. 40, ib. 134, VII. 77, referred to above, in which *que* is elided in a foot subsequent to the first, and which may be explained by supposing either that Calpurnius allowed himself special licence in that one word, or that the readings are erroneous, to which second alternative Haupt inclines.

On the other hand, in the 319 verses of the last four Eclogues, we find thirty-nine elisions, one-half of which occur in other feet than the first, and in some of which a long vowel is elided.

The difference of authorship is also supported by the absence from the earlier poems of such an ending, as *montivagus Pan* (X. 17), and by the frequent occurrence of the caesura after the second syllable of a dactyl in the fourth foot (*post quartum trochaeum incisio*) in the earlier poems, which caesura is found only six times in the last four (VIII. 44; IX. 41, 61; X. 55; XI. 11, 14).*

Wernsdorf's argument that Calpurnius would probably write eleven Eclogues, because that is the number of idyls of a strictly pastoral character which Theocritus has left us, is of little weight; for the second idyl of Theocritus, entitled Φαρμακεύτρια, which is counted in the eleven, is by no means purely pastoral; and it might as plausibly be alleged, on the other hand, that seven was the natural number for Calpurnius to compose, since his model, Virgil, has, according to Servius, left only seven Eclogues properly rustic.

The resemblances between the third and ninth Eclogue do not indicate identity of authorship, but a clumsy imitation, for the graceful similes of the first of these poems are exaggerated, and inappropriately introduced in the latter. It is a touch of nature for Lycidas to say that the charm is gone from everything in the absence of Phyllis; but it is an absurd conceit to represent the cattle as neglecting their pasture out of regret for the absence of such a character as Donace. The reference to his wealth is made naturally enough in III. by Lycidas; but probability is violated in IX., where Idas, a boy of fifteen, claims to be master of a thousand heifers.

A difference of authorship is also shown by the marked change in the moral tone and in the subject-matter of the last four poems. Donace, of more than doubtful character, takes the place of the virgin Crotale of II., and receives not only the same vows of affection as that embodiment

---

* This trochaic caesura in the fourth foot, so common in Latin verse, seems to be absolutely excluded from Greek hexameters from the time of Homer to that of Nonnus. See Professor Tyrrell's interesting article on the Bucolic Caesura, in *Hermathena*, vol. 8, page 342.

of rustic virtue, but also the same extravagant adulation which the earlier poet paid to the Emperor, and which, though not offensive to Roman taste when applied to their deified ruler, is little suited to the playfellow of Idas and Alcon.

The objection which Byron raises to Virgil's second Eclogue* holds good against XI., a blot from which the earlier poems are almost free.

While of the earlier poems three at least (I., IV., and VII.) are in glorification of the Emperor, there is no allusion to him in the later poems.

We see from IV. 19 sq. that the Emperor under whom Calpurnius wrote was a patron of poetry, while his predecessor had done little to encourage the poet's art. This well accords with Nero's reign, for that Emperor was *ad poeticam pronus* (Suet. Nero 52), and loved to collect at supper skilful verse-makers who supplied any deficiencies in his own attempts (Tac. A. 14, 16 : *Carminum quoque studium adfectavit, contractis, quibus aliqua pangendi facultas. Considere simul et adlatos vel ibidem repertos versus connectere, atque ipsius verba, quoquo modo prolata, supplere*), but Claudius, his predecessor, was devoted to questions of history and grammar, and doubtless did little to encourage the softer muse.

As a final distinction we may notice that the parenthetic use of *memini* and *fateor* affected in the first seven pieces does not occur in the last four.

The last four poems, then, are by a poet other than Calpurnius, and probably by Nemesianus, for his Cynegetica agree with the last four Eclogues in the very points in which the said four Eclogues differ from the first seven, namely, ŏ in *exerceto* (194) and *devotio* (83), the number and character of the elisions and the infrequent occurrence of

---

* 'But Virgil's songs are pure, except that horrid one
Beginning with *Formosum pastor Corydon.*'

the caesura after the second syllable of a dactyl in the fourth foot. Moreover, *etenim*, which is not very common in the poets, occurs twice in Calpurnius (II. 98 and V. 19), but not in the last four Eclogues, nor in the Cynegetica.

These arguments perhaps only show the possibility of Nemesianus being the author of the poems in question, but its probability is established by the fact that Statius is evidently imitated in both these four Eclogues and in the Cynegetica (cf. X. 23 sq.; Cyneg. 19 ; Stat. Theb. 7, 167 ; VIII. 84 sq. ; Stat. Theb. 12, 812, 818), while no imitation of him is to be found in Calpurnius ; for, as Haupt shows, Wernsdorf is hardly right in comparing IV. 87 with Stat. 5, 1, 11 sq. The unusual expressions *lactis fluores*, moreover, is found in Cyneg. 227, and in X. 68 *fluorem lactis* seems to be the true reading. Little weight can be attached to the fact that Vopiscus, in the Life of Numerianus, mentions the Halieutica, Cynegetica, and Nautica of Nemesianus, but not his Eclogues, for he does not profess to be giving a complete list of the works of Nemesianus, but merely mentions the most important of them.

Having thus proved a marked difference in style between the first seven poems and the last four, and shown the probability that the latter are the work of Nemesianus, let us in the next place inquire to what poet or poets the eleven poems have been attributed in the past. We find that the first five editions attributed the whole eleven to Calpurnius alone. About the end of the fifteenth century, however, Angelus Ugoletus divided them between Calpurnius and Nemesianus, assigning to the latter the last four. This edition was printed at Parma, and has a statement at the end to the effect that it is based on a very old and most correct MS. of Thadaeus Ugoletus, brought from Germany, which presents the following headings over the poems attributed to Calpurnius and Nemesianus, respectively, ' Titi Calphurnii Siculi Bucolicum carmen ad

Nemesianum Karthaginensem incipit', and 'Aurelii Nemesiani Poetae cartaginensis Aegloga prima incipit'. Nor is this the sole MS. authority on which the division rests, for in the Codex Gaddianus (fifteenth century) after the Eclogues 'Calphurnii ad Nemesianum Carthag.', we find 'Aureliani Nemesiani Carthag. ecl. iiii.', and in the codex 'traditionum monasterii Priflingensis', the 'Bucolica Aureliani' are named, and then, after mention of several other books, come the 'Bucolica Calphurnii'. Finally, in the Neapolitan MS., which is of the highest authority, there is indeed no inscription, but we find at the end of the eleventh Eclogue the words 'Aureliani Nemesiani Cartag. bucol. explicit, Deo gratias, Amen.'* It is probable that the inscriptions to Calpurnius and Nemesianus and the subscription to Calpurnius have been omitted through carelessness; but at any rate that Nemesianus is author of some at least of the poems seems made out by these words.

The dedication to Nemesianus, found in the codex of Ugoletus, the codex Gaddianus, and the codex Rehdigeranus, can hardly be genuine, for there is no mention of Nemesianus in the poems, and It is foreign to the usage of antiquity to dedicate a poem to a man, and yet make no mention of him in it. Moreover, if we are agreed that Nemesianus wrote the last four Eclogues we cannot suppose that the first seven, which he has so freely imitated, were dedicated to him. For assuredly it would be mere

---

* *Explicit* and *feliciter* are commonly used in late Latin, to mark the end of a book. *Explicit* is probably a contraction of *explicitus* (*est liber*), 'the book is ended', literally 'unfolded', the book being a scroll, which was unrolled as the reader proceeded. Ignorance of the origin of the expression led to the use of a plural form, *expliciunt*, which is sometimes found.

The pious ejaculation 'Deo gratias, Amen,' also is often found at the conclusion of a work.

barefaced plagiarism to copy whole lines from a collection of poems dedicated to oneself.

It is possible that the poems of Calpurnius ended 'Explicit Calpurnii bucolicon', and those of Nemesianus began 'Aurelii Nemesiani Carthaginensis bucolicon incipit', and from the confusion of these two sentences the spurious dedication may have arisen.

It therefore appears that the first seven poems are by Calpurnius, the last four by Nemesianus, and that the inscription to Nemesianus is a mere error.

It may, however, be of interest to enumerate in one *conspectus* the arguments which have been urged by Wernsdorf, and summarized by Glaeser, to show that the eleven Eclogues should be attributed to Calpurnius. They are as follow. We are not told by any of the ancients that Nemesianus wrote bucolics, nor do we find the Cynegeticon of Nemesianus and Eclogues VIII.–XI. conjoined in any MS. The Middle Age writers, e.g. Jacob. de Cesollis, Franc. Petrarcha, Angel. Politianus, recognize no writer of Eclogues after Virgil, except Calpurnius. The eleven Eclogues are ascribed to Calpurnius in the following MSS. and editions:—PVRı.2.fı.2.rdı.2.nca, and perhaps Dı.2.3.4. From the time of Ugoletus the last four Eclogues have been attributed to Nemesianus, owing to the inscription which Ugoletus said he found in his ancient MS. from Germany. This inscription Wernsdorf thinks arose in the following way:—From I. 94 and IV. 158 some one conjectured that I.–VII. were dedicated to Nemesianus, and then the inscription of VIII. 'Meliboei (= Nemesiani) Ἐπιτάφιος,' was taken to mean that Nemesianus had composed the remaining Eclogues.

The contradiction involved in this latter view, if the dedication of I.–VII. to Nemesianus, and the identification of the said Nemesianus with Meliboeus be also adopted, is justly pointed out by Wernsdorf, for VIII. is a funeral panegyric on Meliboeus, who is presumably dead at the time, and cannot therefore be identified with the Meliboeus (= Nemesianus, according to the hypothesis under consideration) to whom the I.–VII. are dedicated, and yet be at the same time claimed as the author of VIII.–XI.

The style of the eleven Eclogues Wernsdorf considers to be quite uniform, and he considers the opinion held by some, that Theocritus wrote only eleven idyls of a strictly bucolic character, to be a further ground for attributing the entire collection to Calpurnius. It will be observed that most of these arguments have been directly answered in the preceding pages, and I think that any weight they may still possess is fully counterbalanced by the reasons above stated in support of the twofold authorship.

Manuscripts.

1.2.3.4. Codices Dorvilliani a.b.c.d. (D1. D2. D3. D4), four MSS., each containing the eleven Eclogues, and named from J. P. Dorvillius, who collated them. D1. commonly called Neapolitanus, is the best MS. of the poems, and dates from the beginning of the fifteenth century. It was discovered and collated by Dorvillius, in the library of Joann. Carbonarius, at Naples, and is preserved at Naples, in the library of the Museo Nazionale, formerly called the Museo Reale Borbonico. A more accurate collation was made by Conradus Bursianus, of which Haupt has made use. Of D2. D3. D4. little is known beyond the fact that a collation of them was furnished to Burmann by Dorvillius. D2. D3. are of considerable merit, and often agree with other good MSS. D4. is of less value, although Burmann has accepted several of its readings. The collations of D1. D2. D3. Burmann received too late to make much use of them in his Commentary. He has, however, given them along with the collation of D4. in the appendix to his first volume. In his Commentary Dorv., or Dorvil., for the most part represents D4., and Wernsdorf sometimes uses the same vague abbreviation, apparently through error, since, according to the notation of the latter editor, D4. should be represented by Dorv. d.

5. Codex Parisiensis 8049 (Π), of which, according to Glaeser, the first sixteen leaves belong to the eleventh, and the remaining twenty-nine to the twelfth century. Haupt, however, agrees with Wernsdorf in considering it to belong to the thirteenth century. It is written on parchment, in double columns, containing thirty-nine lines each, and contains the Satires of Persius, a fragment of Cicero's 'De Divinatione', the Satires of Petronius Arbiter, and of Calpurnius, Eclogues I., II., III., IV. 1–12, followed by fragments of Seneca.

Except the inscriptions 'Explicit Petronius. Incipit Calpurnius' and 'Incip. Eclogae,' no heading is found in the Eclogues, and they succeed one another without interruption. The MS. is an excellent one, and was collated by Miller for Glaeser, and with more care for Haupt by Conradus Bursianus.

6. Codex Heinsii (H), occasionally quoted by Burmann, often agrees with D1. Haupt considers it identical with the Codex Parisiensis.

7. Codex Rehdigeranus secundus (R2.) in the Bibliotheca Rehdigerana, at Breslau. This MS. belongs to the fifteenth century, is on paper, and carelessly written. It consists of one hundred and fifteen leaves. It assigns the eleven Eclogues to Calpurnius, and is without inscription, save at the beginning. The names of the speakers are not given, except on the first page of the third leaf. A change of persons is sometimes indicated by the mark (") in the margin. The several Eclogues are separated by

the interval of a line. Each page contains twenty-six verses. Glaeser, who himself collated this MS., considers that, in spite of its many faults, it contains some good readings.

8. Codex Rehdigeranus prior (R1.), in the Bibliotheca Rehdigerana, at Breslau. This MS. also was collated by Glaeser, who says that it assigns the eleven Eclogues to Calpurnius, and contains, in addition, the lesser poems of Virgil and of some other writers. It belongs to the fifteenth century, is neatly written on parchment, and consists of one hundred and thirty leaves. The titles and the names of the characters are in red, and each page contains twenty-two or twenty-three verses.

9. Codex Palatinus (P), quoted by Barthius and Gebhard with considerable variations (e.g. I. 30; IX. 40; XI. 17), whence it has been conjectured that there are two Palatine MSS. Wernsdorf considers this MS. the best. It attributes the eleven Eclogues to Calpurnius, and was written before the year 1460.

10. Codex Vossianus (V) attributes the eleven Eclogues to Calpurnius. It begins with the words 'C. Calpurnii carmen bucolicum incipit feliciter,' and ends with the words 'C. Calpurnii bucolicon carmen desinit.' Burmann used it in his Commentary.

11. Codex Gothanus (G), besides the Bucolics, Georgics and Aeneid of Virgil contains the Eclogues of Calpurnius from I. to VII. 65. It is not earlier than the fifteenth century. It ends with the words 'Finis. haec quae de calphurnio inveniuntur.' It was collated for Wernsdorf by Professor Meuselius, of Erfurt.

12. Codex Modii (M), mentioned several times by Modius in his Lectiones Novantiquae, but otherwise unknown.

13. Codices Guidalotti (Guid.), quoted in the Bologna edition.

14. Codices Titii (Tit.), mentioned in the second Florentine edition.

It is difficult to judge of the Codices Guidalotti and Titii. Glaeser thinks that, while they are sometimes really manuscripts, they are in other cases merely printed books.

We also find mention of a very old and correct MS. which Ugoletus brought from Germany, and used in his edition, and Brassicanus refers to an old MS. preserved in the neighbourhood of Tübingen. Of the Codices Martellii, Palmerii, Carrionis, Bartholini, little is known save the names. Glaeser says there are still uncollated one Paris and three Florentine MSS.

Glaeser mentions also a Vienna MS. on parchment of the fifteenth century, containing forty-five leaves. It was collated for him by de Eichenfeld, and this collation he gives in his Introduction. It does not, however, throw much light on the text.

EDITIONS.

The Eclogues of Calpurnius Siculus were much more frequently edited in former times than they have been of late. Glaeser enumerates some twenty-five editions prior to the year 1590, when Pithoeus published at Paris the edition which supplies the basis of the now received vulgate. Of these numerous editions the following are the principal :—

The editio Romana (r), folio, printed at Rome, in 1471, by Sweinheim and Pannartz, is the *editio princeps*, and for the most part, according to Glaeser, follows an inferior MS., although in many readings it agrees with VGR1. P. There is a copy in the Royal Library at Dresden, which was collated by Ulitius, Burmann, and Glaeser. It places the eleven Eclogues under the name of Calpurnius. This book also contains Silius Italicus and a Latin version of Hesiod's Works and Days, by Nicolaus de Valle.

Calphurnii Bucolicon carmen (a), printed at Venice in 1472, folio, along with the Epigrams of Ausonius, Proba's Cento, Ovid's Consolatio, and the Hymns of Publ. Greg. Tiphernus. Glaeser conjectures that this is the true source of certain readings which Dorvillius (at end of Burmann's first volume) denotes by the abbreviation *Ald.*, since these readings agree with neither of the Aldine editions. This edition was reprinted in 1492.

An octavo edition, was printed by the Aldi at Venice in 1534 (a2.). It bore the title 'Poetae tres egregii' (Gratius, Nemesianus, Calpurnius), and has been collated by Ulitius and Glaeser. It is the first edition, to place Eclogues VIII. to XI. before I. to VII.

The first Aldine (a1.) appeared at Venice in 1518.

Two quarto editions (d1.d2.) appeared at Daventry— the first in 1491, following to a considerable extent the *editio princeps*, but somewhat faultily printed ; the second without date, but more accurate.

To the editions Nordheimensis and Coloniensis (n and c), described and used by Wernsdorf, Glaeser attaches but little value. The former is named from Henry de Nordheim, who lived about 1490 ; the latter was printed by Henry Quentell, at Cologne, about the end of the fifteenth century.

The edition (p) printed at Parma by Angelus Ugoletus professes to be based on a very old and correct MS. of Thadaeus Ugoletus, brought from Germany, which assigned the first seven Eclogues to Calpurnius, and the last four to Nemesianus. It is a folio, and though undated, probably belongs to about the year 1500. The earlier Eclogues, which are attributed to Calpurnius, have the following inscription :—' Titi Calphurnii Siculi Bucolicum carmen ad Nemesianum Karthaginensem incipit.'

This edition is followed by Guidalotti in his folio edition, published at Bologna (β) in 1504, but not without valuable readings by Guidalotti himself.

The editio Augustana of H. Stayner, 1534, and the editio Lugdunensis Gryphii. 1537, follow a2.

There were two Florentine editions—the earlier (f1.) of Philip Junta, 1504, of which Glaeser made a fresh collation; and the editio Florentina cum Rob. Titii Comment. (f2.), 1590, which contains the Critical Letters of Hugolinus Martellius. The first of these editions seems to have been the basis of editio Veneta, 1518, editio Viennensis (v), 1519, and editio Tigurina Froschoveri (t), 1537. This editio Viennensis seems to be the same as that to which Wernsdorf assigns the date 1514, and it appears that Vienna (Vienne) is used improperly for Vindobona (Vienna), for it is said to be printed 'Viennae Austriae.'

The editio Parisiensis cum facili commentatione Jodoci Badii Ascensii (a), 1503, attributes the eleven Eclogues to C. Calpurnius, and in the main follows r, though in some places exhibiting bold alterations of the text. Wernsdorf used the collation of it contained in Havercamp and Brucius' edition, Venaticorum et Bucol. Poet. Glaeser made a fresh collation, but does not consider the Commentary of much value.

Glaeser was the first to collate the editio Joann. Alex. Brassicani (b), Hagenouae, 1519. Brassicanus says that he made much use of the MS. referred to on page 25, and he seems also to have known a and β. Glaeser points out that this edition is the basis of the editio Basileensis ex off. Jo. Oporini (o), 1546, which was collated both by himself and Wernsdorf.

The editio Germanica ἄτοπος (ψ) is generally admitted to have been a mere imposition of Barthius, who alleged that he had found it in the ruins of an old convent in the Hercynian Forest, and that, although it bore neither date nor the name of the place where printed, it seemed to be of about 1513. He said it bore the name of Andrea Lotterus, whom, from other books printed in the same, i.e. in the Longobardic character, he conjectured to have lived at Leipzig. He says that it contained the works of Gratius, Nemesianus, and Calpurnius, and this in itself throws doubt on his story, as it has been the usual belief that these authors were first edited together in a2. of the year 1534. Janus Ulitius boldly asserts that this edition had no existence, nor does any writer, save Barthius, bear witness to having seen it. Moreover, we have no mention of an Andrea Lotterus as a printer, although Melchior Lotterus did print first at Leipzig, and afterwards at Magdeburg. Wernsdorf suggests that Barthius may have meant the Parma edition of Ang. Ugoletus, and through an error of memory, quoted it as the Germanica of Andrea Lotterus. Wernsdorf, however, himself points out that this explanation is inconsistent with Barthius' distinct statement, that the edition contained the Cynegetica, and he accordingly abandons the attempt at apology.

In 1590, the same year as the Florentine edition of Titius, there appeared Epigrammata et Poematia vetera P. Pithoei, Parisiis, which edition is the basis of all the succeeding ones, and corresponds in most cases to the Florentine of Junta, but in some cases to the Ascensiana. It for the first time gave the Eclogues in a satisfactory form, and was practically reproduced in the following editions :—Antverpiana ap. Joach. Trognaesium, 1608; Duacensis ap. Alex. Car. Trognaesium, 1632 ; and along with other poets ; Lugduni, 1603; Genevae et Aureliae Allobr., 1611 ; Lugduni, 1616; Genevae, 1627; Aureliae Allobr., 1646; Londini et Hagae Comitum, by Mich. Maittarius, 1713 and 1721 ; Mediolani, 1731. The vulgate text is the outcome of these editions.

After Pithoeus, Casp. Barthius was the first to make any

considerable contributions to the criticism of Calpurnius. His edition (Hanouiae, 1613), which included Gratius and Nemesianus, was, however, censured, on account of the apparently unfounded claims he advanced to having at his command certain old books. The errors of this edition, which were considerable, were corrected by Janus Ulitius, in his Auctores rei venaticae cum Bucolicis Nemesiani et Calpurnii, Ex offic. Elzeviriana, 1645.

Peter Burmann's edition, Poetae Latini Minores, Leidae, 1731, is somewhat severely criticised by Glaeser, who, on the other hand, justly speaks in the highest terms of Wernsdorf's work of similar name (Altenburgi, 1780), save that he thinks he allows too much weight to editions, owing to his having a limited access to MSS.

Beck's edition, Lipsiae, 1803, is founded on Burmann and Wernsdorf. We may also notice the editions of Adelung, Petersburg, 1804, with German notes and translation, Wiss, Leipzig, 1805, and Klausen, Altona, 1807, with German translation.

The text is found in Lemaire's Poet. Lat. Min. Parisiis, 1824; Weber's Corpus, Francofurti ad Moen., 1833, and Walker's Corpus, Londini, 1865.

There is an edition along with the Bucolics of Virgil, by Grauff. Bernae, 1830.

As to Glaeser's edition, see page 41.

IDYLLIC POETRY.

Merivale has described the Georgics of Virgil as the glorification of Labour, and we may perhaps speak of the Eclogues of the same poet as the idealization of rustic Recreation. Both works are modelled on a Greek prototype, and both alike are more artificial and less realistic than the originals from which they are drawn. The didactic character of the Georgics has won for them a higher estimation than the Eclogues enjoy, but the small value of the precepts conveyed must compel a sober critic to esteem them rather for their form than their matter; and the Eclogues will then be found no less worthy of attention, as picturing a side of country life which, though it has found few poets to celebrate its praises, always possesses a charm for lovers of nature and rural pleasures. In Idyllic poetry, as in other branches of literature, the Romans were indebted to Greek inspiration, and indeed almost exclusively to three poets—Theocritus, Bion, and Moschus. The first-named of these poets far surpasses in strength and depth of feeling the other two, but the whole three are much more life-like and realistic than their Roman imitators. What the Latin writers, however, have lost in realistic vividness is perhaps compensated for by their superior purity of subject and treatment, and Virgil and Calpurnius, the principal representatives of this school, are free from the coarseness sometimes found in the Greek poets.

Bion of Smyrna flourished about 280 B.C., and spent the last years of his life in Sicily, where he was poisoned. We have 246 lines by him, the longest piece being a funeral ode on the death of Adonis, expressing sympathy with Venus, who mourns that her divine gift of immortality prevents her from accompanying her favourite to the gloomy realms of Proserpine. With the exception of the poem on the seasons, in which he prays for an everlasting spring (3, 15: εἶαρ ἐμοὶ τριπόθητον ὅλῳ λυκάβαντι παρείη), all his works are of a distinctly erotic character. The concealment of Achilles at the court of Lycomedes is the only mythical tale he treats with any fulness. He alludes, however, to the friendships of Theseus and Pirithous, Orestes and Pylades, Achilles and Patroclus, and to the loves of Galatea and Polyphemus. He makes beauty the crown of womanhood, as strength of manhood (μορφὰ θηλυτέρῃσι πέλει καλόν, ἀνέρι δ' ἀλκά).

Moschus of Syracuse (probably flourished 250 B.C.), who calls himself the heir of Bion's Doric melody, though not of his fortune, has left us 483 lines. His epitaph on Bion is one of his most meritorious pieces. It is modelled on Bion's Ἐπιτάφιος Ἀδώνιδος, and, like that piece, contains a recurring burden. Professor Jebb justly observes that few verses in Greek have more melody or more pathos than those in which this poet sings that the glory of the garden fades to bloom again, but man, when he is once laid in the grave, sleeps an everlasting sleep. These verses are also quoted by Peile as an example of the masterly use which Moschus made of alliteration. The story of Europa he tells at considerable length, and also that of Megara, the wife of Hercules. Among his shorter pieces 'Cupid the Runaway,' in which Venus offers a reward for and gives a description of that truant god, is worthy of notice, and also a description of himself as a fair-weather sailor, and an expression of sympathy for the hardships of a fisherman's life.

The highest ideal in this style of poetry is attained by Theocritus of Syracuse, who flourished about 270 B.C., under Ptolemy Philadelphus. In him we find that perfection of art which holds up the mirror to nature, reflecting all that is fairest and most attractive in country life, and not picturing a merely imaginary state, as was the wont of later bucolic writers. In many passages he shows a perception of that sympathy between mental conditions and natural surroundings which is so often expressed in modern poetry. For example, he describes the feelings of a girl whose lover has proved false in these words :—

ἠνίδε σιγῇ μὲν πόντος, σιγῶντι δ' ἀῆται·
ἁ δ' ἐμὰ οὐ σιγῇ στέρνων ἔντοσθεν ἀνία,
ἀλλ' ἐπὶ τήνῳ πᾶσα καταίθομαι, ὅς με τάλαιναν
ἀντὶ γυναικὸς ἔθηκε κακὰν καὶ ἀπάρθενον ἦμεν.

The sentiment of these lines is much the same as Burns expresses in

> Ye banks and braes o' bonie Doon,
> How can ye bloom sae fresh and fair ?
> How can ye chant, ye little birds,
> And I sae weary, fu' o' care ?

It is specially characteristic of Theocritus that he knows nothing of that affected sentiment, pure innocence and primeval simplicity which later poets and novelists have ascribed to what is known as Arcadian life. He merely gives simple and faithful descriptions of country life, which are aptly called idyls, or little pictures. The Eclogue proper is distinguished from the idyl as being a piece in which shepherds are introduced, while the idyl is merely a piece written in a simple style, but without pastoral interlocutors. According to this definition, many of the twenty-nine poems of Theocritus are not entitled to be called Eclogues, and, indeed, a considerable number of them are not properly pastoral at all ; but he left enough to inspire Virgil, and through him the poets of more modern times, and a comparison of these latter works, with their Greek original, shows that Theocritus is justly to be regarded as the father of this style of verse.

How completely imitative Virgil is in his Eclogues can be fully appreciated only on a careful comparison of his poems with those of Theocritus. Not only does he imitate the Greek poet in style and forms of expression, but the scenery and general outline of his poems are drawn from the same source. His shepherds, though living in Italy, are Sicilians both in name and nature ; the trees under whose shade they sit are native to Sicily, not to Virgil's country, and the sea, which serves as their mirror, is as much out of place in the neighbourhood of Mantua as in Shakespear's Bohemia. These and other incongruities, which have been made the ground for accusing Virgil of being the great corruptor of pastoral poetry, are defended at length by Conington, in his Introduction to the Bucolics, to which interesting essay I must refer the reader, as the full discussion of the question would occupy too much space here, and I wish to point out rather than to justify the important influence Virgil has had on bucolic poetry. I am not, however, to be taken as underrating the grace and the merits of Virgil's Eclogues. I would give them a very high place, and am satisfied with this passing notice only because the following pages contain such frequent acknowledgment of our indebtedness to the Mantuan bard, and because both his poems and those of Theocritus have been so often criticized and reviewed, that they are familiar to most readers.

With the exception of the above-mentioned poets, few bucolic writers have attracted much attention. Calpurnius is commonly spoken of as the only, and he certainly is the most important, later representative of this school. It will be well, however, before considering his poems, to mention a few other idyllic writers whose works are worthy of notice.

Valerius Cato, the gentle-spirited contemporary of the *plagosus Orbilius*, wrote a poem entitled Dirae,* in 183 hexameter lines. The first part of this work contains imprecations on his farm, which had been taken from him and assigned, probably, to some of Sulla's veterans: the latter part laments the loss of his mistress Lydia.

Septimius Serenus (in the third century, A.D.) wrote two works, of which we still have some fragments, viz., *Opuscula Ruralia* and *Falisca.* He is perhaps also the author

---

* Some attribute this poem to Virgil; but Wernsdorf says this was probably owing to the similarity of *Maronis Dirae* and *Catonis Dirae*, and to the lament over his lost farm in the Eclogues of the better-known poet.

of the *Moretum.* This work, however, is usually attributed to Virgil, and it is to be observed that Septimius Serenus does not employ hexameters (the metre in which the *Moretum* is written) in his other works.

Severus Sanctus Endelechius (end of the fourth century, A.D.), wrote an idyl on the rinderpest in asclepiad and glyconic verse, in which a shepherd describes to two of his fellows how he had saved his flock by the sign of the cross :—

> Signum, quod perhibent esse Crucis Dei,
> Magnis qui colitur solus in urbibus,
> Christus, perpetui gloria Numinis,
>   Cujus filius unicus.
> Hoc signum mediis frontibus additum,
> Cunctarum pecudum certa salus fuit.

The works, however, which have reached us from the hands of the above poets are of insignificant extent ; and of the principal remaining writers who may claim our notice, viz. Ausonius, Claudian, Nemesianus, and Tibullus, the two former are bucolic in name rather than reality. Claudian's seven idyls on the Phoenix, Hedgehog, Electric Ray-fish, Nile, Magnet, Hot Springs of Aponus (Bagni d' Albano), and the two brothers who saved their parents at an eruption of Vesuvius, are merely a series of essays on the subjects indicated by the titles, written in smooth flowing rhythm, but lacking all true idyllic colouring either of subject or manner. The first five of these idyls are in hexameter verse ; the last (which in its treatment reminds us of Ovid's *Fasti*) and the second last are in elegiacs.

Ausonius has left us twenty so-called idyls, but they are for the most part mere literary curiosities, e.g. the Griphus Ternarii Numeri, or *jeu* on the number three, the monostichs on the labours of Hercules, the Technopaegnion, or series of hexameter verses, all ending with monosyllabic words of meanings related to the several heads under which the verses are arranged, e.g. de Deis, de Cibis, &c.

Two of his idyls, however, are of superior merit: Rosae, a pretty poem of fifty lines in elegiac verse ; and the Mosella, in 483 hexameters, the most famous piece in the collection, interesting because it describes a journey up the Moselle to Treves, and exhibits a warm appreciation of the beauties of nature.

His Eclogarium has nothing to do with bucolic poetry, but consists (to use Teuffel's words) of a number of astronomical and astrological versifications in epic and elegiac metre, on the names of the stars, days, months, Roman festivals, Greek Agones, &c.

Tibullus, in Teuffel's opinion, possesses the greatest share of the idyllic spirit among the Roman poets ; but he need not detain us, as his poems are distinguished by a very broad line from the school of poetry which we are here considering.

The name of Calpurnius Siculus is perhaps as unfamiliar to most readers as that of any of the authors to whom I have referred, but his works would have gained for him more notice were not the date commonly assigned to him the time of Carus and his sons, a period long subsequent to that which marks the limits of ordinary classical studies. The arguments, however, on page 2 sq. make it highly probable that this date is erroneous, and that his poems belong to the beginning of Nero's reign. But whatever date is assigned to Calpurnius, his most important claim on our attention must be the intrinsic merit of his work ; and we should, therefore, inquire whether he exhibits the true characteristics of bucolic poetry, presenting to us an idealized, but not unreal, picture of rural life, in language which is natural and simple, but, at the same time, dramatic and vivid.

In IV. Calpurnius, under the name of Corydon, professes to take Tityrus, i.e. Virgil, as his model; and the unsurpassed smoothness of his verses goes far to justify his boldness in attempting to vie with the father of Roman idyllic poetry. Meliboeus at first warns him of the presumption of his attempt, but afterwards pronounces a warm panegyric (IV. 150 sq.) on his flowing and honeyed diction; and few critics will hesitate to endorse the judgment which Calpurnius has put in the mouth of his patron. Our poet may, however, claim credit for much more than mere smoothness of versification. Dramatic vividness is no less a characteristic of his amoebean poems, under which title we may include all, except I., V., and VII. The few simple lines in which he describes the silent awe of nature at the name of Caesar are perhaps unsurpassed as a specimen of word-painting.

> *Am.* Aspicis, ut virides audito Caesare silvae
> Conticeant ? Memini, quamvis urgente procella,
> Sic nemus immotis subito requiescere ramis,
> Et dixi, deus hinc, certe deus, expulit Euros :
> Nec mora, Pharsalae solverunt sibila cannae.
> *Cor.* Aspicis, ut teneros subitus vigor excitet agnos ?
> Utque superfuso magis ubera lacte graventur,
> Et nuper tonsis exundent vellera foetis ?
> Hoc ego jam, memini, semel hac in valle notavi,
> Et, venisse Palem, pecoris dixisse magistros.

Scarcely less striking is the celebrated passage in II., beginning *Adfuit omne genus pecudum*, &c., where the rustic deities and all the powers of nature are spell-bound in listening to the praises of the virgin Crotale.

Calpurnius seems to have been a warm enthusiast about the beauties of nature and the charms of country life; and whether he is describing the shady grove, with its moss-lined cave, through whose arched windings is faintly heard the purling of the neighbouring stream, or painting some rustic scene, where 'the village train' (*paganica turba*) applauds the sports held at the cross-roads, he proves himself no mere conventional verse-maker, but a genuine sympathiser with the charms of rustic life and scenery. Though no women are interlocutors in the Eclogues, several are mentioned in the course of the poems. Among these, the most interesting is the unsullied Crotale, whose name supplies a title to II. Her two admirers, Astacus and Idas, however, vie rather in describing their own merits than those of their mistress.

We hear more of Phyllis, who is represented as *mobilior ventis*. She has quarrelled with her lover ; and he tells his friend Iollas of his desire to be reconciled to her. Scaliger pronounces this Eclogue (III.) to be *merum rus, idque inficetum*, an opinion endorsed by Conington. But, in spite of these high authorities, I must say the poem seems to me to possess much delicacy, both of sentiment and expression. It would be difficult to find in classical literature a more chivalrous view of the relation of the sexes than in the advice of Iollas to his friend :—

> Tu prior illi (to her)
> Victas tende manus ; decet indulgere puellae
> Vel cum prima nocet.

The letter of apology also is simply and forcibly expressed. Lycidas first describes his unhappy state since their estrangement, and then, having acknowledged his fault and begged forgiveness, gently reminds her of his former attentions in sending her the earliest lilies and roses. He does not forget to describe the wealth he is ready to place at her disposal, an argument which seems to have had weight in Arcadia, no less than in other countries ; but this plea is given a modest and unobtrusive position, and the letter, both at the opening and close, bases its appeal to Phyllis on the warmth and sincerity of the passions that her charms have excited.

Of the other female characters, Alcippe appears as the confidante of Phyllis ; Petale and Leuce are coy, but not cruel, and Calliroe represents the rich heiress. Nemesianus is much less fortunate in his women. Donace's wildness carries her so far that her parents are obliged to put her under close restraint; Meroe is *immitis, dura,* and *superba,* and Mycale is a witch.

About Calpurnius himself, we learn from his poems that envious poverty often pulled his ear (*vellit saepius aurem*), and bid him mind the sheep-fold, rather than the unmoneyed (*inanis*) Muse, that at first he was inclined to follow this advice, but changed his plans with a change of emperors ; and that, when on the point of leaving for Spain, he was taken up by Meliboeus, a patron, who not only provided for his immediate wants, but conveyed his poems to the Emperor.

Calpurnius devotes three of his Eclogues (i., iv., and vii.) to the praise of the Emperor. He adopts a strain of the most extravagant, and, according to our notions, blasphemous adulation ; but we must remember that a Roman not only believed in the divine right of kings, but held the Emperor to be actually a god.

The angry altercation in vi. finds a parallel in Virgil, E. 3, and the singing match in Sir Philip Sidney's Arcadia (29) entitled Nico and Dorus, reads like a parody on both passages.

The fifth Eclogue has much more of a didactic than bucolic character. It contains the advice of the aged Mycon to his son Canthus on pastoral matters, and is evidently modelled on the Georgics of Virgil.

The seventh Eclogue is that most generally known, and is quoted by Merivale as containing a description of the Colosseum. If Merivale is right in the supposed reference, we could not, of course, place Calpurnius earlier than the reign of Vespasian. See, however, Introduction, page 2 sq., and also the Appendix. The Eclogue consists in the narrative of a shepherd, who describes to his friend Lycotas the spectacles which he had seen during a visit to the metropolis.

There is a lack of direct local reference in Calpurnius; indeed, perhaps, the only such allusions are those to the sheep of Tarentum and to the city of Rome. This omission has an advantage, as that violation of the unities of which Virgil is so often guilty in introducing to Italian scenes the flora and natural features of Sicily, is less distinctly felt when the scene of the poems is not specifically stated.

Pastoral poetry, in a degree beyond any other kind of literature, is marked by a uniformity in both subject-matter and treatment throughout all ages. In the Idyls of Theocritus, the Bucolics of Virgil, Tasso's Aminta, Sir Philip Sidney's Arcadia, and Pope's Pastorals, the same passions are described, the same scenes depicted, and the same mannerisms introduced. It is, therefore, no just cause of offence that Calpurnius follows the (even in his time) traditional usage. A shepherd in search of a lost sheep or heifer meets a brother shepherd, and then in company, forgetting their more prosaic duties, they beguile the noontide hours in singing their mistresses' praises, or in poring over the characters cut in the bark of some neighbouring tree, until the lengthening shadows warn them to water their thirsty flocks, and afford the poet a convenient pretext for concluding his lay. Not unfrequently the love-sick swains engage in a vocal and instrumental contest, some passer-by acting as judge. So common, indeed, were these trials of skill, that the power of song was considered a regular characteristic of Arcadia, as appears from Virg. E. 7, 4, where

Arcades ambo is to be explained, not as in Byron's well-known translation (i.e. blackguards both), but by the words which occur in the next line: *et cantare pares et respondere parati.* Compare also ib. 10, 32 : *soli cantare periti Arcades.* This was, however, probably an idealized conception of Arcadian talent, and more matter-of-fact writers make Arcadia the type of dulness and stupidity. See Juv. 7, 160 : *nil salit Arcadio juveni.*

A brief account of the four pastorals of Nemesianus will suffice, as I have already said something about them, and as they are considerably inferior, both in merit and interest, to the poems of Calpurnius. They contain, however, some passages of much beauty ; and Fontenelle pronounces the third Eclogue (x.), in which Pan celebrates the praises of Bacchus, to be superior in elegance of invention to the sixth Eclogue of Virgil, on which it is evidently modelled.

The funeral ode to Meliboeus (VIII.) is of considerable merit. It bears the strange title of *Epiphunus,* which is a curious mixture of Latin and Greek (ἐπί, *funus*). Timetas, at the request of Tityrus, sings an obituary poem in honour of Meliboeus, in terms which seem to identify him with the Meliboeus of the first seven poems. This is far the strongest internal argument for attributing the last four poems to the same author as the first seven ; and it is strange that it has not, so far as I know, been made use of by those who maintain the unity of authorship. It does not, however, seem sufficient to outweigh the arguments urged above (page 14 sq.) in favour of the separatist theory ; and the poem may, perhaps, be regarded as an imitation of Virgil's *Daphnis,* suggested to Nemesianus by the want he felt of such a patron as had encouraged his predecessor and model, Calpurnius.

The second Eclogue (IX.) contains a curious description of a tame nightingale ; and the fourth (XI.), entitled *Eros,* is remarkable for its abrupt termination, and for being the only one of these poems which contains a recurring burden. Two shepherds sing alternately six verses each, always ending with the words—

Cantet, amat quod quisque : levant et carmina curas.

These four poems are distinguished from those of Calpurnius by the absence of any reference to the Emperor, by the different type of female character which they portray, and by several other peculiarities described on page 14 sq.

Bucolic poetry, unreal and fanciful as has always been its treatment, is based upon one deep-seated feeling, which explains the attraction that this kind of composition possesses: I mean upon the love of nature and country scenes. Hence we can understand the charm of the simple but feeling verses of Calpurnius, and must regret that he is almost the only poet who has helped to perpetuate in Latin literature the pastoral vein introduced by Virgil from a Sicilian source.

I desire to acknowledge my obligations to C. E. Glaeser's valuable edition, Gottingen, 1842, which has been my principal authority for critical purposes. His *apparatus criticus* seemed fuller than was necessary for the present edition, and I have, therefore, only given the more important variations, omitting mere differences in spelling, and such readings as were not of use in determining the true text, or otherwise interesting. His Introduction is the basis of my account of the MSS. and editions, and has been of some help in determining the time when Calpurnius lived, and the number of Eclogues he wrote. On the latter points, however, my principal obligations are to Moriz

Haupt's Essay De Carminibus Bucolicis Calpurnii et Ne-
mesiani (Leipzig, 1854). This is a most able and learned
treatise, and is recognized as such by Teuffel, in his *His-
tory of Roman Literature.* I have adopted the views set
forth in this Essay as to the age and works of Calpurnius,
and the arguments I have given are largely drawn from the
same source. Haupt says he had the advantage of using
Conrad Bursian's collation of the Neapolitan MS. (D1.),
which is much more accurate than that made by Dorvil-
lius, and used by Glaeser. I have given in their proper
places the several readings of this collation, where they
differ from those quoted by Glaeser.

Glaeser's edition is almost exclusively critical, and
Haupt's Essay, although containing several valuable
emendations, is principally devoted to discussing the age
and character of the writings. Far the most satisfactory
notes explanatory of the text are to be found in the
second volume of Wernsdorf's *Poetae Latini Minores* (Alt-
enburg, 1780). His critical notes, however, although at
one time valuable, are now completely superseded by
Glaeser's work. I have also consulted, but without de-
riving much additional help, the editions of Beck (Leipzig,
1803), Adelung (St. Petersburg, 1804), Klausen (Altona,
1807), and Burmann (Leidae, 1731). The notes of all
the editions I have mentioned, except Adelung's and
Klausen's, are in Latin. Klausen gives a translation of
the text in German, and Adelung both notes and a trans-
lation in the same language. Beck's edition contains a
useful glossary. There does not seem to be any English
edition. The references to the *Arcadia* are taken from
Grosart's edition of the Complete Poems of Sir Philip
Sidney (printed for private circulation, 1873).

Though I believe the last four Eclogues to be the work
of Nemesianus, yet, for convenience of reference, I have
numbered consecutively from I. to XI., using Roman

numerals exclusively for referring to these writings, e.g. iv. 3 = the third line of the fourth Eclogue in this edition. My best thanks are due to Mr. L. C. Purser, Fellow of Trinity College, for reading the proofs of this work, and making many valuable suggestions. In some cases I have specially acknowledged my obligations to Mr. Purser. Had I done so in every instance there are few pages on which his name would not appear.

My best thanks are also due to Professor Ridgeway, Fellow of Gonville and Caius College, Cambridge, for much valuable help both in the Appendix and in the notes on Eclogue vii., and to Professor Maguire, Fellow of Trinity College, for several important suggestions.

ABBREVIATIONS.

D1.2.3.4.	Codices Dorvilliani a b c d.
G	Codex Gothanus.
H	Codex Heinsii.
M	Codex Modii.
P	Codex Palatinus.
Π	Codex Parisiensis.
R1.2.	Codices Rehdigerani.
V	Codex Vossianus.
a	editio Ascensiana.
a1.	ed. Aldina prior.
a2.	ed. Aldina altera.
α	Ald. apud Burm. in Excerptis Dorvill.
b	ed. Brassicani.
β	ed. Bononiensis.
c	ed. Coloniensis.
d1.	ed. Daventriensis prior.
d2.	ed. Daventriensis altera.
f1.	ed. Florentina Juntae.
f2.	ed. Florentina Titii.
g	ed. Lugd. Gryphii.
n	ed. Nordheimensis.
o	ed. Oporini Basil.
p	ed. Parmensis.
π	ed. Pithoeana.
r	ed. Romana princeps.
s	ed. Augustana.
t	ed. Tigurina.
v	ed. Viennensis.
ψ	ed. Germ. ἄτοπος.
Barth.	ed. Barthii.
Ulit.	ed. Ulitii.
Burm.	ed. Burmanni.
Wernsd.	ed. Wernsdorfii.
Glaes.	ed. Glaeseri.

In the critical notes c. = conjectures, or conjecture.

Notes 1 = the critical notes.

Notes 2 = the explanatory notes.

ARGUMENTA BUCOLICORUM CALPURNII ASCENSIANA.

———

Primo divini memorantur carmina Fauni.

Inque altro Crotales gemini recitantur amores.

In terno Lycidas canit acres Phyllidis ignes.

In quarto Augustum Corydon laudat Meliboeo.

In quinto genitor dat rustica dogmata gnato.

In sexto sese rivales voce lacessunt.

Ast in septeno spectacula laudat et urbem.

Octavo extincti probitas canitur Meliboei.

In nono Donacen canit Astachus et puer Alcon.

In decimo Bacchi laudes canit, et bona vini.

Undecimo Meroes puerique canuntur amores.

IOANNIS ALEXANDRI BRASSICANI PERIOCHAE.

Ecl. I.

Caesaris Augusti laudes tenet Ecloga prima :
Ornitus, ut summa conscriptas cortice monstrat,
Hinc celebrat docto Saturnia tempora versu,
Proelia dehinc, sperans in cunctis Caesaris aures.

Ecl. II.

Proxima fert Crotales flammas caecosque furores ;
Asthacus atque Idas quam concomitantur amore.
Arbiter at Thyrsus bino quod pignore certent,
Hos iubet, inde pares discedunt iudice Thyrso.

Ecl. III.

Vallibus horrendis vaccam disquirit Iolas,
Quam Lycidas pastor sylvis negat esse canoris.
Tityrus arguta dehinc promit carmina voce,
Phyllida quis gaudet iunctis celebrare cicutis.

Ecl. IV.

Laudibus egregiis Corydon sub nomine vatis
Augustum celebrat, quas cum Meliboeus amicus
Novit, inexplicito subito inflammatur amore
Caesaris, hinc fratrem properato carmine laudat.

Ecl. V.

Non Varro, neque Palladius, Columella, Catoque,
Non ita Virgilius servanda dedere colono,
Quanta brevi hic Canthus sumit praecepta Mycone,
Ordine quo certo possit sibi vivere amicus.

Ecl. VI.

Astylus et Lycidas, quos semper sexus uterque
Sollicitos tenuit, miseris periere periclis.
Arbiter hinc Mnasyllus amat discernere lites,
Sed fugit, ut stulti nimium crudelia tentant.

Ecl. VII.

Hic Corydon ludos varia docet arte Lycotam.
Comprensum circo narrat genus omne ferarum,
Deinde palaestritas multo certasse labore.
Cuncta sinu Augusti sunt concertantia laudes.

Ecl. [I. Nemesiani] VIII.

Tityron in gelido flectentem gramina fiscos
Accedit iuvenis, cupiens, canat ore sonoro.
At negat illa senex, iuveni sunt fortia, dicens,
Membra: decet lapsum tollat super aethera amicum.

Ecl. [II.] IX.

Astacus atque Alcon Donacen coluere puellam :
Multa habuere simul Veneris commercia primae.
Illa ubi rescivit pater, imo carcere natam
Clausit : amans queritur tristi sua damna furore.

Ecl. [III.] X.

Nyctilus atque Mycon, socius quoque pulcher Amyntas,
Arcadiae divo fesso rapuere cicutam.
Qui fugat ut placidum lasso de corpore somnum,
Et genus et Bacchi comites docet ordine certo.

Ecl. [IV.] XI.

Mopsus amat Meroen, miseri formosus Iolas
Ignis edax Lycidae. Qui cum dant membra sopori,
Semper amat Meroen Mopsus, petit alter Iolam :
Sic nulla alta quies, duro qui indulget amori.

———

NOTE.

I have followed Glaeser in printing these Periochae together. In the
edition of Brassicanus, from which they are taken, they are prefixed to
the several Eclogues.

AD LECTOREM.

Prata per et virides reparatis frondibus agros,
  Per nemus umbriferum, per juga celsa simul,
Quid faciat ruris studiis assueta colendi
  Simplicitas, docet hoc, candide lector, opus.

From Vienna edition of HIERONYMUS
VICTOR *and* JOANNES SINGRENIUS.

Divina natura dedit agros, ars humana aedificavit urbes.

VARRO, *Re Rustica*, 3, 1, 4.

God made the country, and man made the town.

COWPER.

CALPURNIUS SICULUS.

ECLOGA PRIMA.

CORYDON, ORNITUS.

THIS Eclogue is inscribed *Delos* in the Juntine and some subsequent editions. Ulitius has conjectured that this title is a misprint for *Deus*, alluding either to Faunus, whose oracle occupies the larger part of the poem, or to the frequent application of the word Deus to the emperor in the course of the poem. Wernsdorf is more likely to be right in his supposition, that the birthplace of Apollo, the great god of oracles, was thought to furnish a suitable title to a poem of oracular character.

The poem seems to be modelled on Virgil's Fourth Eclogue, entitled *Pollio*. As Virgil derives his inspiration from the Sibyl of Cumae, so Calpurnius rehearses a prophetic utterance of Faunus which Corydon and Ornitus discover carved on the bark of a beech tree, while they are sheltering from the noontide heat, near a favourite haunt of Faunus. The hero of this poem is almost as much a matter of dispute as that of the *Pollio;* but all the conditions seem best satisfied in the person of Nero. For the arguments on the subject see Introduction, page 2 sq.

It may be observed that lines 84 sq. indicate distinctly the beginning of a new reign.

E

C. Nondum solis equos declivis mitigat aestas,
Quamvis et madidis incumbant praela racemis,
Et spument rauco ferventia musta susurro.
Cernis ut, ecce! pater quas tradidit, Ornite, vaccae
Molliter hirsuta latus explicuere genista ? 5

In vulg. lines 1–3 are given to Ornitus, 4–7 to Corydon. In fr. π rell.
this Eclogue is inscribed *Delos*, for which Ulit. c. *Deus* and Beck *Faunus*.
1. Heins. c. *declinis*.
2. *Quatinus* VGR1. r. *Quatenus* P. *incumbat* H. *praeda* H11.
4. *et ecce* D2. 4. *vaccas* D4. R2.
5. *Molliter hirsuta* D1. *Molle sub hirs.* vulg.

1. 'Not yet is waning summer
taming the horses of the sun,'
i. e. assuaging the heat. The
names of the sun's horses were
Pyrois, Eous, Aethon, and Phle-
gon, Ov. M. 2, 152.
Declivis. Heinsius, both here
and in v. 60, reads *declinis*, which
might be supported by Lucan,
10, 236 : *donec in autumnum de-
clinet Phoebus.* The adjective
declinis, however, is found in only
two places, viz. Statius Theb.
5, 296 sq. : *Exoritur pudibunda
dies, coelumque retexens Aver-
sum Lemno jubar, et declinia
Titan Opposita juga nube refert;*
and Lucan, 4, 427 : *declinibus un-
dis,* 'ebbing waves'; and in the
latter passage it seems probable
that *declivibus* is the correct read-
ing. The season indicated is early
autumn, before the summer heats
are past.
Mitigat is used of taming ani-
mals in Sen. Ben. 1, 2 : *nec ullum
tam inmansuetum animal est,
quod non cura mitiget. Mollis
hiemps* = 'a mild winter' in
Stat. S. 3, 5, 83.
Virgil G. 1, 312, describes this
season as the time *ubi jam bre-
viorque dies et mollior aestas,*
i. e. 'less oppressive.'

2, 3. 'Although the presses are
squeezing the moist clusters, and
the new wine is fermenting and
effervescing with hoarse whis-
pers.'
Musta, the new, unfermented
wine, was just beginning to fer-
ment (**ferventia**). Cf. Columella,
12, 19, 5 : *cum aliqua jam parte
mustum in se fervebit.*
4, 5. Cernis . . . . ut molliter
. . . . latus explicuere genista,
'do you see how comfortably the
cattle have stretched themselves
on the broom ?'
We would have expected the
subj. instead of the indic. *expli-
cuere;* but, as Roby, § 1761,
remarks, in conversational or ani-
mated language a question is often
put, logically though not gram-
matically dependent on another
verb or sentence. This use is fre-
quent in Plautus and Terence,
even where later writers would
make the question dependent, and
use the subj. Compare the Eng-
lish 'Tell me, where are you ?'
for 'Tell me where you are.' See
Plaut. Bac. 5, 2, 14 : *Viden, limulis,
obsecro, ut contuentur ?* The same
construction is found in VI. 37 :
Aspicis ut fruticat late caput ?
The subj. is used in line 22 sq. :

Nos quoque vicinis cur non succedimus umbris ?
Torrida cur solo defendimus ora galero ?
O. Hoc potius, frater Corydon, nemus, antra petamus
Ista patris Fauni, graciles ubi pinea denset

> **6.** Tit. cites the readings *ulmis* and *umbrae.*
> **8.** *antra p. Ista* D1. *ista p. Antra* vulg.
> **9.** *denset* ΠPVD4. *densent* D1. *densat* vulg.

Aspicis ut virides etiam nunc littera rimas Servet, &c. ?
The difference of mood, however, marks a difference of meaning ; for in the passage last cited the sense is—'some one has only just now cut these letters on the beech tree, and, as a proof of this, do you not see how fresh the incision still is ? '—while in the other passages it is not a reason that is assigned, but vivid attention is called to a matter of fact. 'How the cows stretch themselves, don't you see ?' 'How askance they look at us, don't you see ? ' 'How his head branches with antlers, don't you see ?'

Pater quas tradidit, 'which our father has entrusted to our care.' Cf. Plaut. Most. 2, 1, 59, where the full expression occurs, *in tuam custodiam meque et meas spes trado.*
The name *Ornitus* or *Ornytus* occurs in Virg. A. 11, 677 ; Stat. Theb. 12, 142 and 207.
Molliter is to be taken with *latus explicuere,* 'recline luxuriously on the shaggy broom.' Cf. Cic. de Or. 3, 17, 63 : (*in hortulis*) *recubans molliter.* Ov. Tr. 3, 3, 76 : *Nasonis molliter ossa cubent,* 'lie peacefully.'
With this line, cf. Pervigilium Veneris : *Ecce iam super genistas explicant tauri latus.*
6. Nos quoque, 'we too,' as well as the cattle.

7. 'Why do we shelter our sunburnt faces with only a cap ? '
Torrida. Cf. Pliny, 12, 20, 43, 98 : *color abest ille torridus sole.* It is remarkable that this word also means 'frost-bitten,' e. g. Liv. 21, 40, 9 : *membra torrida gelu,* and v. 107, *torrida hiems,* ' biting,' or rather ' frost-nipped winter.'
The word properly means ' parched up,' and the context must decide whether by the action of heat or cold.
Torrida vox in III. 59 = ' dry, hoarse voice.'
Galero. Nom. *galerum* or *galerus,* properly, as we learn from Servius, ' a priest's cap ' made from the skin of a slaughtered victim, Gr. κυνέη, afterwards used for any cap fitting close to the head like a helmet. The diminutive *galericulum* means 'a wig ' in Suet. Otho, 12 : *galericulo capiti propter raritatem capillorum adaptato et adnexo, ut nemo dinosceret.*
8 sq. 'Let us rather make for this grove, brother Corydon, and those favourite caves of yours (ista), sacred to father Faunus.'
Iste is applied to anything in which the person addressed is interested or concerned.
Hoc shows that the grove is near at hand.
Pater is a constant title of respect for a deity, e. g. *Gradivum patrem,* Virg. A. 3, 35 ; *pater*

Silva comas, rapidoque caput levat obvia soli,　　　　10
Bullantes ubi fagus aquas radice sub ipsa
Protegit, et ramis errantibus implicat umbras.
C. Quo me cumque vocas, sequar, Ornite ; nam mea Leuce,
Dum negat amplexus nocturnaque gaudia, nobis

11. Heins. c. *Palantes.*
13. *sequar* D1. *sequor* vulg.
14. *noct. nasura* D1. Perhaps we should read *noct. munera.*

Lemnius, i.e. Vulcan ib. 8, 454 :
Bacche pater Hor. C. 3, 3, 13 :
pater o Lenaee, i.e. Bacchus Virg.
G. 2, 7 : *pater Silvane,* Hor.
Epod. 2, 21.

Faunus, the son of Picus, and
grandson of Saturn, plays a pro-
minent part in the mythical his-
tory of Latium. He was the patron
god of fields and shepherds, and
was also an oracular divinity. He
was identified with Pan, when the
worship of that deity was intro-
duced into Italy, and as he mani-
fested himself in various ways the
idea arose of a plurality of Fauns,
represented as half men half goats,
just as the Greeks used Πᾶνες of
sylvan deities. See Theocr. 4, 63.

Graciles, &c., 'where the pine
forest spreads thickly its delicate
foliage, and by interposing itself
to the burning sun gives relief to
the head.'

Denset. For the form *denseo*
cf. Virg. A. 11, 650 : *hastilia
denset,* i.e. shoots thickly together.

Rapidus, lit., 'tearing away,
seizing,' is often applied to fierce,
consuming heat, e. g. Virg. G. 1,
92 : *rapidi potentia solis.*

11. Bullantes = *bullas exci-
tantes,* 'bubbling'; besides the
form *bullare* we also find *bullire*
with same meaning.

12. Ramis, &c., 'by the sway-

ing of its branches casts a tangled,
confused, shadow.' For use of
implicat cf. Virg. A. 12, 742 sq. :
*Ergo amens diversa fuga petit
aequora Turnus, Et nunc huc,
inde huc incertos implicat orbes.*

13. Quo . . . cunque. A com-
mon tmesis.

Leuce. Several islands bore
this name, but it is seldom applied
to a woman. Servius, however,
on Virg. E. 7, 61, says that this
was the name of a daughter of
Oceanus, with whom Pluto fell in
love, and who was changed into a
white poplar (λεύκη).

Of the Leuce here mentioned
we of course know nothing, save
what may be gathered from the
context.

14. Dum negat, 'by denying
me.'

Nobis. This word is to be
taken with the following line. It
is readily understood with *dum
negat,* &c., but its expression is
required with the next line to give
a satisfactory sense. 'My Leuce's
coyness has enabled me to fre-
quent the sanctum of the horned
Faunus.'

Nobis after **me** presents no
difficulty. The first person singu-
lar and first person plural are often
used indiscriminately, e. g. Ov.
Trist. 5, 12, 57 sq. : *Ipse mihi*

Pervia cornigeri fecit sacraria Fauni.   15

O. Prome igitur calamos, et, si qua recondita servas :
Nec tibi defuerit mea fistula, quam mihi nuper
Matura docilis compegit arundine Lygdon.
Et iam captatae pariter successimus umbrae.
Sed quaenam sacra descripta est pagina fago,   20

16. Beck suspects that something is lost after this line. In the vulg.
lines 16–21 are given to Or., 22–27 to Cor.
17. *nova fist.* VGR1. rabod2.
18. *Natura* II. *docti* D1. m. sec. Beck c. *docili* or *docilem.*

videor jam dedidicisse Latine;
Jam didici Getice Sarmaticeque
loqui. Nec tamen, *ut verum fa-*
tear tibi, nostra teneri A com-
ponendo carmine Musa potest.
Scribimus et scriptos absumimus
igne libellos, Exitus est studii
parva favilla mei.
So Tullia uses *nostrae = meae*
of herself in Ov. F. 6, 589, but
me in the following line : *Quid*
juvat esse pares, te nostrae caede
sororis, Meque tui fratris, si pia
vita placet ?
15. Pervia fecit, &c. Those
who indulged in the pleasures of
love could not lawfully enter a
shrine.
16. Calamos, 'reed-pipe.'
Si qua recondita, sc. *carmina,*
as in Virg. E. 2, 4 : *Ibi haec in-*
condita solus Montibus et silvis
studio jactabat inani : and ib. 7,
22 : *proxima Phoebi Versibus ille*
facit.
17. Defuerit = *deerit,* but with
a certain modification of sense :
' *You will find* that my pipe will
not fail you.' Cf. Tac. G. 19 : *non*
forma, non aetate, non opibus,
maritum invenerit. Cf. the Greek
use of ἄν with optative for future.
Her. 4, 97 : ἔψομαί τοι καὶ οὐκ ἂν
λειφθείην.

18. Matura, 'full-grown.'
Docilis, 'skilful.' The full ex-
pression would be *docilis compin-*
gendae fistulae, 'apt pupil in
framing a shepherd's pipe.' Cf.
Sil. Ital. 3, 233 : *docilis fallendi,*
'apt pupil in deceit.'
With *compingere fistulam,* cf.
Theocr. 8, 21 sq. : σύριγγ' ἔχω
ἐννεάφωνον· πρῴαν νιν συνέπαξα.
19. Et jam pariter, 'and so
now we also,' sc. as well as the
cattle, 'we in like manner.' See
line 6, where *Nos quoque* corre-
sponds to the *pariter* of this line.
It may, however, merely mean,
' we have together come beneath
the desired shade.' Cf. Virg. A.
2, 205 : *pariterque ad littora ten-*
dunt, and Ov. F. 3, 207 : *O pari-*
ter raptae, 'O ye who were carried
off along with me.'
Captatae . . . umbrae, 'the
shade we were seeking.' Cf. Virg.
E. 2, 8 : *Nunc etiam pecudes um-*
bras et frigora captant.
20. Quaenam . . . . pagina.
Cf. VIII. 29 : *inciso servans mea*
carmina libro, and Virg. E. 6, 12 :
sibi quae Vari praescripsit pagina
nomen.
Sacra. The beech is sacred
because in Faunus' favourite re-
treat.

Quam modo nescio quis properanti falce notavit ?
Aspicis, ut virides etiam nunc littera rimas
Servet, et arenti nondum se laxet hiatu ?
C. Ornite, fer propius tua lumina : tu potes alto
Cortice descriptos citius percurrere versus,   25
Nam tibi longa satis pater internodia largus,
Procerumque dedit mater non invida corpus.
O. Non pastor, non haec triviali more viator,
Sed deus ipse canit : nihil armentale resultant,

24. *altos* D2.
25. *ertius* P, whence Barth. c. *percurrere certius orsus.* Kempfer
cites *visus* as occurring in some editions.
28. *tibi vili* D1. m. sec. *rivali* o. *sacerdos* R1. *mole viatur* R2.
non hoc vulg.
29. *resultant* D3. *resultat* vulg.

21. Modo. He judges that the words have only just been cut from the freshness of the marks ; see next line. **Nesciŏ,** cf. Tib. 1, 75 : *Nescio quid furtivus amor parat : utere quaeso.* **Properanti.** The words were hastily and roughly cut. The praise in lines 28–30 refers to the matter of the inscription, not its execution. **22 sq.** 'Do you notice how the letters still keep the incisions fresh, and do not yet open out with sapless rift ?' **Se laxet.** Cf. Juv. 6, 144 : *se cutis arida laxet,* probably describing the enlarged pores, and the coarseness of a withered skin. **25. Percurrere,** 'run over,' 'glance through.' Cf. Liv. 9, 18, 12. **26. Internodia,** 'legs' : properly the space between two knots or joints, either of a plant, e. g.

Plin. 7, 2, 2, § 21 *internodia harundinum ;* or of the leg, e. g. Ov. M. 6, 256 : *Mollia nervosus facit internodia poples.* **Largus,** 'liberal, unstinting,' corresponding to *non invida* in the next line. The father of Ornitus transmitted to him limbs of liberal proportions. **27. Non invida,** 'ungrudging.' **Prŏcērum.** Distinguish *prŏcĕrum.* **28.** 'These are no commonplace shepherd's or traveller's verses.' **Trivialis** prop. means of or belonging to the cross-roads, hence commonplace. Ov. Trist. 4, 1, 5 sq. describes a shepherd, and Hor. S. 1, 5, 16, a *viator,* solacing himself with song. **29. Nihil armentale resultant,** 'they do not ring of the cattle stall.' Cf. IV. 5 : *Carmina jamdudum, non quae nemorale resultent, Volvimus,* &c.

Nec montana sacros distinguunt iubila versus.   30
C. Mira refers : sed rumpe moras, oculoque sequaci
Quam primum nobis divinum perlege carmen.
O. Qui iuga, qui silvas tueor, satus aethere, Faunus
Haec populis ventura cano : iuvat arbore sacra
Laeta patefactis incidere carmina fatis.   35
Vos o praecipue nemorum gaudete coloni,
Vos populi gaudete mei : licet omne vagetur

30. *Nec* D1.2.Vrabo. *Non* vulg. P, according to Barth., gives *distingunt;* according to Gebhard., *destingunt. destringunt* D4. *distinguit* R1. Heins. c. *destringunt sibila. iubilia* Π. *nubila* D4. R2.
32. Gud. c. *praelege.*
35. *fagis* vulg. Heins. and Ulit. c. *fatis.* See notes 2.

30. 'Nor do the upland halloos separate, mark the pauses of, the sacred verses.' The mountaineers' cries were often introduced into shepherds' songs, and served to divide the verses as in some of the Swiss songs at the present day.
Distinguunt. In II. 25 *distinguere cantus* is used of singing an amoebean strain, and Quint. 1, 8, 1 uses the same verb of marking the pause at the end of a verse: *superest lectio : in qua puer ut sciat, ubi suspendere spiritum debeat, quo loco versum distinguere, ubi claudatur sensus, unde incipiat . . . demonstrari nisi in opere ipso non potest.*
Jubila, plural of *jubilum* 'the shepherds' cry,' is found again in VII. 3 : *tua moerentes expectant jubila tauri.* Heinsius proposes to read *sibila* in both passages after Ov. M. 13, 784 : *pastoria sibila,* but *sibila* were made with the *fistula, jubila* apparently with the voice. Compare the German *jodeln,* 'to sing in the Swiss Tyrolese style.'

31. Rumpe moras, 'break off, end delay.' Cf. Virg. G. 3, 43, et passim.
Oculo sequaci . . . perlege, 'trace out with your eye.' Cf. Statius Theb. 3, 499 sq. : *Postquam rite diu partiti sidera, cunctas Perlegere animis oculisque sequacibus auras.*
33. Satus aethere, 'heaven sprung.' Faunus was grandson of Saturn. Mountains and woods were under his protection.
34. Juvat impers. sc. *me,* 'it is my pleasure to carve verses of good tidings on the sacred tree, and so disclose the future.' The reading *patefactis fagis* = cutting open the bark of the beech-trees, would be tautological after *arbore sacra incidere.*
36. Nemorum . . . . coloni, 'denizens of the woods,' viz., shepherds who fed their flocks in *saltus,* i. e. woodland pastures.
37 sq. Licet omne, &c., 'the whole herd may stray without the herdsman being anxious, and the shepherd need not close the pens at night with wattles of ash-wood.'

Securo custode pecus, nocturnaque pastor
Claudere fraxinea nolit praesepia crate.
Non tamen insidias praedator ovilibus ullas　　　　40
Afferet, aut laxis abiget iumenta capistris.
Aurea secura cum pace renascitur aetas,
Et redit ad terras tandem squalore situque
Alma Themis posito, iuvenemque beata sequuntur

42. This line is wanting in D1. Burm. c. *sincera cum.* Friesemann
c. *Aurea Saturni.*

40. Tamen, 'notwithstanding,'
i. e. although the shepherd takes
no precautions. *Praedator* is a
man, not a wolf, as appears from
the following line.
41. Laxis . . . **capistris,**
Wernsdorf and Adelung explain
'at full speed,' 'giving them
the reins,' equivalent to *immissis
habenis.* This, however, seems an
unauthorized use of *capistrum,* and
we should surely translate 'loos-
ing, taking off the halters.' Such
cattle-lifters are called *abigei* in
the Digest.
42. 'The golden age returns
once more with undisturbed
peace.' *Sincera* has been con-
jectured instead of *secura,* on
account of *securo* having occurred
in line 38, but the change lacks
MS. authority, and the repetition
of *securus* is not inappropriate in
describing the reign of peace.
Seneca says of Nero in the
Ludus de Morte Claudii 4 : *Aurea
formoso descendunt secula filo.*
For a description of the Golden
Age see Ov. M. 1, 89 sq., and
Theocr. 12, 15 : ἦ ῥα τότ᾽ ἔσσαν
χρύσειοι πάλαι ἄνδρες.
Renascitur, 'is born again.'
Cf. v. 21 : *viridisque renascitur
annus.*
43. Themis is here represented

as returning to earth after escap-
ing from some foul prison. The
poets usually imply that heaven
was her abode while banished
from earth. Cf. Virg. E. 4, 6
sq. : *Jam redit et Virgo,* &c.
Squalore situque . . . **posi-
to,** 'casting off foulness and de-
cay.'
44 sq. **Juvenemque,** &c.,
'and ages of happiness will at-
tend the young prince, who won
a cause while still in his mother's
arms.' The allusion is to the
early forensic attempts of Nero.
Wernsdorf, who assigns a late
date to Calpurnius, thinks the
reference is to Numerianus, of
whom Vopiscus (30, 11) says that
he was *eloquentia praepollens,
adeo ut puer publice declamaverit.*
Juvenem, as in IV. 137, and
VII. 6. So Augustus is called
juvenis in Virg. G. 1, 500 ; Hor.
C. 1, 2, 41 : id. S. 2, 5, 62.
Wernsdorf reads *lusit,* which he
explains 'essayed,' 'practised,' as
in IV. 21, not of childish sport, as
Burmann does, who compares
Suet. Nero 35 : *ludere ducatus et
imperia.*
Maternis . . . **in ulnis.** For
the hyperbole, cf. Themistius,
Oratio Consularis ad Jovinianum
(Oratio 12 in Paris edition, 1618):

Saecula, maternis causam qui vicit in ulnis. 45
Dum populos deus ipse reget, dabit impia victas
Post tergum Bellona manus, spoliataque telis
In sua vesanos torquebit viscera morsus,
Et modo quae toto civilia distulit orbe,

45. Burm. c. *caussas.* *curam* D4, R2. *vicit* D1. HΠ. Glaes. also gives *ludit* as occurring in D1.2. *lusit* vulg. *in ulnis* D1. f1. va1. boπ. *Iulis* PVD2.3. GR1.2.rd2.apβa2.sf2. *vilis* Π. *lusit i* . . . D4. Wernsdorf suggests that *Iulis* might allude to the Basilica Julia, but observes that *maternis* would then be difficult to explain. Adelung reads *in ulmis*.
46. *vinctas* vulg. *victas* D1.2.3. abo Barth. *iunctas* pβ (Guid. in commentary *vinctas*) a2.sf2.
48. *vesano. morsu* D1.

τὸν ἐν ἀγκάλαις ὕπατον, τὸν ἐκ τοῦ μαστοῦ πατρώζοντα ἤδη. Manilius I, 795 : *matrisque sub armis* (from *armus*, not *arma*, according to Wernsdorf) *Miles Agrippa suae.* Petron 4 : (*parentes*) *eloquentiam pueris induunt adhuc nascentibus.*

Adelung, reading *in ulmis*, explains the line 'who already in his mother's grove trained himself for a prince,' and thinks there is a reference to some anecdote of Numerianus' youth.
46 sq. Deus. The title is often given to the emperor by the bucolic poets, cf. Virg. E. I, 6 : *O Meliboee, deus nobis haec otia fecit. Namque erit ille mihi semper deus,* where the god spoken of is Octavianus.

Ipse, 'the god himself,' the true sovereign deity as contrasted with the weaker and conquered goddess of war.

Dabit victas Bellona manus is for the more usual *dabit victa Bellona manus,* and **post tergum** is an awkwardly introduced reminiscence of Virg. A. I, 295 sq. :

(*Furor*) *centum vinctus aenis Post tergum nodis.* The epithet **impia** was doubtless borrowed from ib. 234. 'The unholy goddess of war will submit (and suffer her hands to be bound) behind her back.' The vulgate reading *vinctas* for *victas* is doubtless due to a remembrance of the passage in Virgil, quoted above, and to a misunderstanding of the pregnant construction of *post tergum. Manus dare* or *dedere* is a regular phrase for 'to give up,' 'yield,' 'surrender.'

48. Torquebit morsus. Cf. Virg A. 7. 112 : *vertere morsus Exiguam in Cererem penuria adegit edendi.*

49 sq. 'And will wage with herself the wars which lately she spread among fellow - citizens throughout the world.'

Distulit. Cf. use of *diffundo* in line 57, and Caes. B. C. 2, 14 : *hunc* (sc. *ignem*) *distulit ventus.*

Wernsdorf, in the Addenda to his fourth volume, suggests another explanation, viz., 'continuit, vel cessare fecit.'

Secum bella geret. Nullos iam Roma Philippos   50
Deflebit, nullos ducet captiva triumphos.
Omnia Tartareo subigentur carcere bella,
Immergentque caput tenebris, lucemque timebunt.
Candida pax aderit, nec solum candida vultu,
Qualis saepe fuit, quae, libera Marte professo,   55

51. This line is wanting in PVD2.3.4. R1.2. rd1.2.a.
52. *subiguntur* Π. *subdentur* VGR1.ra. Ulit. c. *claudentur*.
55. Burm. c. *Quali*. Barth. Heins. Burm. c. *quam* (so also in next
line). Beck *quum* (so also in next line). *matre* P. *profuso* β[1.2.
a2.sψ.

50. Jam, i. e. when this time,
the golden age, has come.
Nullos, &c. ' Rome will have
no civil wars to lament.'
The battle of Philippi, B. c. 42,
in which Octavian and Antony
defeated Brutus and Cassius, is
taken as a type of civil war. ' No
such battles as Philippi.' On the
curious error of the Roman writers
in representing the battles of Phar-
salia and Philippi as fought on
the same spot, see Merivale,
vol. 3, note at end of chap. 26.
Some think that by *Philippos*
are meant Philippus, emperor, A.D.
244–249, and his son of the same
name, in whose time Rome suf-
fered much. This is of course
impossible, on the supposition of
Calpurnius being a contemporary
of Nero, but in any case the ex-
planation given above is more
probable.
51. Nullos ducet, &c., ' will
celebrate no triumphal proces-
sion in which she herself is the
captive.' Under many of the
emperors Rome was but the slave
of the ruler whose triumphs she
celebrated. We may compare as
an inverse parallel Hor. Ep. 2, 1,
156: *Graecia capta ferum victorem
cepit.*

52. Cf. the description of the
prison of the winds in Virg. A.
1, 54, and of the closing of the
temple of Janus, ib. 293 sq.
54. Nec solum candida vultu,
'and not fair in appearance alone.'
Candida vultu corresponds to
simulatae pacis in line 58.
55 sq. ' Such as it (peace) often
was, which though free from open
war, and though the enemy at a
distance were subdued, yet, amidst
the license of arms spread public
discord with secret sword.'
Libera, ' free from,' with abl.
as in Cic. Fin. 1, 15 : *animus
omni liber cura et angore.*
Professo, ' open, confessed.'
Cf. Ov. Am. 3, 14, 6 : *Non peccat,
quaecunque potest peccasse negare;
Solaque deformem culpa professa
facit.*
Grassari is specially used of
rioting, e. g. Liv. 3, 13, 2 : *se in
juventutem grassantem in Sub-
ura incidisse. Grassator* is ' a
footpad' in Juv. 3, 305.
Discordia. This is the plural
of *discordium* a neuter form of
discordia, found here only. Uli-
tius, with less probability, regards
it as neut. pl. of adj. *discors*
agreeing with *publica,* which he
considers equivalent to *respublica.*

Quae, domito procul hoste, tamen grassantibus armis,
Publica diffudit tacito discordia ferro.
Omne procul vitium simulatae cedere pacis
Iussit, et insanos Clementia contudit enses.
Nulla catenati feralis pompa senatus   60
Carnificum lassabit opus, nec carcere pleno
Infelix raros numerabit curia patres.
Plena quies aderit, quae, stricti nescia ferri,

56. Heins. c. *cessantibus. crassantibus* VGD3.R1.2.rd1.2.
57. *diffugit* VGR1.r. Herm. c. and Haupt approves *Iubila.* On account of the apparent contradiction in saying that peace spreads discord, on account of the unusual form *discordium,* and the apparent contradiction in *grassantibus armis* and *tacito ferro,* Beck thus alters lines 55-57 : *quum* (i.e. quando) *lib. Marte prof. Quum, dom. . . . armis Publica* (i. e. civilia) *diff. tacito* (or *tacite*) *Discordia bella.* The apparent contradictions, however, constitute the point of the passage, the peace spoken of being fictitious and unreal.
59. *dementia* PGD3.R2.raf1.vbo. *condidit* vulg. *truderit* D1.
61. *laxabit* ΠPD4. and also D1., but the latter has *lassabit* from a second hand.

Hermann's conjecture, approved of by Haupt, viz. *jubila* for *publica* has no MS. authority and hardly gives a suitable sense, as it properly means *shepherds'* cries.

For double forms similar to *discordium* and *discordia,* cf. *oblivio* and *oblivium, contagio* and *contagium.* For *spinum* and *oleastrum* see notes on XI. 22, and II. 44.

With lines 54–57 cf. what Merivale (General History of Rome, p. 464) says of the principate of Claudius :— ' There had been disturbances in the city, occasioned apparently by the turbulent spirit of the Jewish element in the population. On the other hand, the arms of Rome had been crowned with success in Britain and in Germany ' (*domito procul hoste*).

59. Clementia. Clemency is personified, as often. She had a temple at Rome. Stat. Theb. 12, 482 : *mitis posuit Clementia sedem.*

60 sq. ' No funereal procession of the fettered senate will make the executioners' task a weary one.' The reading *laxabit* could hardly be translated 'shall extend, increase the executioner's work,' and ' shall lighten, abate,' would not suit the context. For **Carnificum opus,** cf. *Pacis opus,* line 67.

61 sq. Nec carcere, &c., 'nor will the luckless senate - house count but a senator here and there, while the prison is crowded.'

63. Plena quies, ' complete, perfect peace.' Cf. Cic. Off. I, I, 2 : *oratio plenior.*

Altera Saturni referet Latialia regna,
Altera regna Numae, qui primus ovantia caede　　65
Agmina, Romuleis et adhuc ardentia castris,
Pacis opus docuit, iussitque silentibus armis
Inter sacra tubas, non inter bella sonare.
Iam nec adumbrati faciem mercatus honoris,
Nec vacuos tacitus fasces et inane tribunal　　70

64. *revocet* vulg. *referet* Dr.
70. Burm. c. *vanos. nec inane* dr.2. *etiamne* D2.4.R1.VGra.

64 sq. 'Will bring back once again the reign of Saturn in Latium, once again the reign of Numa, who was the first to teach the pursuits of peace to bands exulting in bloodshed, and still full of fiery spirit from the camp of Romulus.'
64. The reign of Saturn was traditionally the golden age of Italy.
65. To Numa was attributed the establishment of the religious and civil institutions of Rome, as her military system was attributed to Romulus. Cf. Vopiscus Hist. Aug. 30, 2: *quid Numam loquar? qui frementem bellis et gravidam triumphis civitatem religione munivit.* Lactantius Instit. Div. 1, 22, says of Numa : *Novi populi feroces animos mitigavit, et ad studia pacis a rebus bellicis avocavit.*
66. **Agmina.** This term was more appropriate than *populus* for the warlike people of Romulus.
Romuleis . . . castris, i. e. the city of Rome, which during the reign of Romulus was like a camp in the midst of the enemy.
Ardentia, sc. *bellandi ardore.* Cf. Florus 8: *quid Romulo ardentius.*
67. **Pacis opus.** Such works

as can only be done in time of peace, e. g. the making of laws, establishing religious institutions, &c. Livy, 1, 42, uses the expression in reference to the census : *aggreditur inde pacis longe maximum opus.*
Silentibus armis, 'war being hushed,' opposed to *grassantibus armis,* line 56.
68. The *tuba* was commonly used not only for military purposes, but also at religious festivals, games, and funerals.
69. **Adumbrati,** 'counterfeit,' lit. 'represented merely in outline.' Cf. Plato Rep. 583 : ἐσκιαγραφημένη ἡδονή, 'unreal pleasure,' opposed to παναληθής, καθαρά. Cic. de Leg. Agr. 2, 12 : *comitia curiata ad speciem per triginta lictores adumbrata.* Id. Verr. 3, 33: *Pippae vir adumbratus.*
70. **Vacuos . . . fasces,** 'fasces that are but an empty name, worthless.' Cf. Tac. H. 1, 30: *si respublica et senatus et populus vacua nomina sunt.*
Tacitus. The consul was silenced and could no longer administer justice or consult the senate, all power being transferred to the emperor. Cf. Lucan, 3, 107 : *vacuaeque loco cessere cur-*

Accipiet consul, sed legibus omne reductis
Ius aderit, moremque fori vultumque priorem
Reddet, et afflictum melior deus auferet aevum.
Exsultet, quaecumque Notum gens ima iacentem
Erectumque colit Boream, quaecumque vel ortu   75
Vel patet occasu, mediove sub aethere fervit.
Cernitis, ut puro nox iam vicesima coelo
Fulgeat, et placida radiantem luce cometem
Proferat ? ut liquidum nutet sine vulnere plenus ?

72. Barth. Adv. 44, 15, cites *legemque* for *vultumque*.
73. This line is wanting in D3. *afferet* D1. HΠ.
74. D1. gives *in tua* for *ima*.
75. *Ereptumque* D1. HΠ. Heins. and Kempfer c. *Evectumque*.
76. *servit* PGD2.3.4.R1.2.rd1.2.apβa2.sgf2.bo.
78. *Fulgeat ? ut placidum radianti* vulg. *et placida radiantem* D1. 2. 3.
79. *nitidum* V. *nutat* Pd1.2.pβf1.va1.tψ. *mutet* D3. *mutat.* D1.4. *mittat* ΠR2.π. Barth. c. *nictet.* Ulit. c. *niteat. plenus* D1. HΠ (sc. *cometes*). *sidus* vulg. Burm. c. *lumen.*

ules ; Omnia Caesar erat. Sen. Ludus de Morte Claudii 4 : *felicia lassis Secula praestabit legumque silentia rumpet,* where Nero is the subject of the sentence.
72. Vultum priorem, 'the former appearance of the courts,' is opposed to *adumbrati faciem honoris*, line 69. For *vultus* applied to inanimate objects, cf. Virg. A. 5, 848 : *salis placidi vultum*, and the similar use of *frons*, Lucan 9, 207 : *Nec color imperii nec frons erit ulla senatus.*
73. Melior, 'kinder, more favourable.' Cf. Ov. M. 1, 21 : *Hanc deus et litem melior natura diremit.*
Auferet, ' will dispel' the age of mourning : or perhaps will carry off for himself, appropriate, cf. Ov. F. 4, 949 : *aufert Vesta diem.*
74, 75. The classical writers speak of the south as being de-

pressed (**jacentem**), and the north as being elevated (**erectum**) because the Pole star sinks towards the horizon as the observer travels south, and rises high in the sky as he travels north.
The same idea is expressed by Virg. G. 1, 240 sq. : *Mundus, ut ad Scythiam Rhipaeasque arduus arces Consurgit, premitur Libyae devexus in austros.*
76. Mediove sub aethere, ' or under the middle (i. e. torrid) zone.' The heavens are supposed to be divided into zones corresponding to those of the earth, and *aether* is used here as *caelum* is in Virg. G. 1, 233 : *quinque tenent caelum zonae.*
77 sq. **Nox vicesima.** Cf. VII. 1. See Introduction, page 2 sq.
79. Nutet. Wernsdorf thinks this word is used of a star which does not blaze fiercely, but seems

Numquid utrumque polum, sicut solet, igne cruento   80
Spargit, et ardenti scintillat sanguine lampas ?
At quondam non talis erat, cum, Caesare rapto,
Indixit miseris fatalia civibus arma.
Scilicet ipse deus Romanae pondera molis

80. There are several readings of the beginning of this line, e.g.
Dumquid, Non quod, Non per. The text, however, seems to be correct, and requires *Spargit* in the next line, where D1. and Heins. give
Pergit, and Nodell reads *Spargitur ardenti scintillans lumine.*
83. *Induxit* D3.a1.   *fatalis* d1.
84. Glaes. c. *Sed Deus, ipse Deus*.   *Scilicet* D1.

to move and burn with a calm
light. Cf. Manil. 2, 14 : *tituban-*
tia sidera.

Liquidum nutet, 'twinkles
brightly.' *Liquido* and *liquide*
are the usual forms of the adverb.

Sine vulnere, i. e. without pre-
saging bloodshed. Comets were
commonly thought to forebode
disaster.

Plenus, sc. cometes.

82. This and the following line
refers to the portents which ac-
companied the death of Julius
Cæsar, as described in Virg. G.
1, 487 sq.: *Non alias coelo cecide-*
runt plura sereno Fulgura, nec
diri totiens arsere cometae. Ergo
inter sese paribus concurrere telis
Romanas acies iterum videre Phi-
lippi.

84. 'Aye, for a very god will
take on his strong shoulders the
weight of the Roman empire,
so unshaken that neither will
a thundering crash be heard as
the world passes to its new
ruler, nor will Rome (i. e. the
Roman senate) decree that the
dead should be deified in ac-
cordance with their deserts, be-
fore that the beginning of the
new reign can look back on the
close of the last.' This is merely

an oracular and obscure way of
saying that the new emperor was
to succeed the old one without
interregnum and without disturb-
ance.

If the translation which, follow-
ing Wernsdorf, Klausen, and
others, I have given of this most
difficult passage be correct, it is a
strong additional proof that Cal-
purnius wrote under Nero. Sue-
tonius (5, 45) tells us that the
death of Claudius was kept secret
until all arrangements were com-
pleted for his successor taking up
the reins of government (*mors*
ejus celata est donec circa succes-
sorem omnia ordinarentur), and
that Nero was saluted as emperor
on the very day when the death
of Claudius was made public (id.
6, 8). One of Nero's first acts
was to have his predecessor in the
imperial office deified (id. 6, 9 :
orsus hinc a pietatis ostentatione,
Claudium apparatissimo funere
elatum laudavit et consecravit.
Id. 5, 45 : (*Claudius*) *funeratus*
est sollemni principum pompa et
in numerum deorum relatus.

Wernsdorf thinks that the *ipse*
deus of line 84 is Carus, but there
is a fatal objection to this, inas-
much as Probus, the predecessor

Fortibus excipiet sic inconcussa lacertis,   85
Ut neque translati sonitu fragor intonet orbis,
Nec prius ex meritis defunctos Roma penates
Censeat, occasus nisi quum respexerit ortus.

87. *emeritis* R2.   *et meritis* D2.3. pd1.2.   See notes 2 on this and
the following line.
88. *Sentiat* D2.3.

of Carus, does not seem to have
been deified, and therefore lines
87 and 88 would be unintelligible.
If *sentiat* were read instead of
censeat, Wernsdorf might per-
haps reconcile these verses with
his hypothesis; but he retains
censeat, and indeed specially com-
ments on its use.

Romanae   pondera   molis.
Perhaps suggested by Virg. A. 1,
33 : *Tantae molis erat Romanam
condere gentem.*

Compare Ovid's words describ-
ing the accession of Numa after
the death of Romulus, M. 15,
1 sq. : *Quaeritur interea, qui
tantae pondera molis Sustineat,
tantoque queat succedere regi.*

85. Excipiet . . . lacertis. As
lacertus, ' the upper arm,' and
not *humerus,* 'the shoulder,' is
used, Wernsdorf thinks the allu-
sion is not to Atlas or Hercules
bearing the heavens, but to the
representation sometimes found
on coins of an emperor holding in
his hands a ball representing the
earth.

87. Ex meritis. Cf. Tac. H.
4, 50 : *quosdam punivit, alios
praemiis adfecit, neutrum ex me-
rito.*

Defunctos, sc. *vitâ,* ' the de-
ceased emperor.' The plural re-
ferring to one person is used here
the more naturally on account of
penates, which is found only in the
plural.

The expression *penates censere*
is explained by the following pas-
sages :—Capitolinus, Hist. Aug.
3, 3, 5 : *somnio saepe monitus est
dis penatibus ejus Hadriani simu-
lacrum inserere,* and ib. 4, 18, 6 :
*denique hodieque in multis domi-
bus Marci Antonini statuae con-
sistunt inter deos penates.*

88. Occasūs is acc. pl.; **ortŭs**
nom. sing.

For use of **respexerit,** cf. Ov.
F. 4, 677 : *sed jam praeteritas
quartus tibi Lucifer Idus Respi-
cit.*

For **occasus,** cf. Cic. Ac. 1, 2,
8 : *post L. Aelii nostri occasum.*
For **ortus,** cf. Cic. Leg. 3, 8, 19 :
tribuniciae potestatis ortus.

Barthius and others take the
words as a prayer for the long life
of the emperor : ' May Rome not
perceive the death of her tutelary
gods until the west looks back on
the east, i. e. never.' In fact,
' O king, live for ever ! '

Haupt (Hermes, vol. 8. p. 251)
reads: *Nec prius emeriti defunctos
Roma parentis Sentiat occasus
nisi cum suspexerit ortus.*

Nec prius . . . nisi. Cf. Gr.
οὐ πρότερον . . . εἰ μή or ἢν μή,
and Juvencus, 3, 336 : *Nec prius e
prono vultus sustollere casu Aude-
bant, sancto Christi nisi dextera
tactu Demulcens blandis firmasset
pectora verbis.*

Gronovius (Observationum, 3,
18), from the MS. reading *nisi*

C. Ornite, iamdudum velut ipso numine plenus
Me quatit, et mixtus subit inter gaudia terror.　　　90
Sed bona facundi veneremur numina Fauni.
O. Carmina, quae nobis deus obtulit ipse canenda,
Dicamus, teretique sonum modulemur avena :
Forsitan Augustas feret haec Meliboeus ad aures.

89. Barth. and Burm. c. *plenum.*
90. *querit* D1.
93. Werns. c. *teretisque sono modulemur avenae,* comparing Virg.
E. 10, 51 : *Carmina pastoris Siculi modulabor avena.*

quom for *nisi cum,* conjectures:
*Nec prius emeriti defunctos
Roma parentis Sentiat occasus,
gnati quam aspexerit ortus,* i. e.
nec fore, ut Roma videat eme-
riti et defuncti parentis occasus
(per hypallagen) prius quam ali-
cujus ex eadem domo (i. e. of
Carus, according to Gronovius)
ortum viderit.

90. Mixtus, &c., 'awe (at the
presence of the deity) mingled
with joy (at his kindly words)
steals upon me.'

91. Bona = *benigna, propitia,*
'kindly.' Cf. Virg. A. 12, 647 :
vos o mihi Manes, Este boni.

92. Deus obtulit ipse. Cf.
line 29.

94. Meliboeus is probably Se-
neca. See Introduction, p. 12.
Augustas . . . aures, 'the
ears of Augustus.' For Augus-
tus = of or belonging to Augus-
tus, cf. Virg. A. 4, 552 : *cineri
. . . Sychaeo,* 'the ashes of Sy-
chaeus.'
Conington, on Virg. E. 1, 6,
says the name Meliboeus is ex-
plained by Servius, ὅτι μέλει αὐτῷ
τῶν βοῶν, a plausible and obvious
etymology, but unsupported by
analogy, which would rather point
to μέλι as the first part of the com-
pound. Perhaps the name was
suggested by the geographical
Meliboea, and adopted simply
from its connexion with βοῦς.

ECLOGA SECUNDA.

IDAS, ASTACUS, THYRSIS.

THIS Eclogue, inscribed Crotale, from the mistress whom Idas and Astacus praise, is amoebean, and is modelled on the seventh Eclogue of Virgil, in which, as well as in this, four lines are alternately sung by each of the rivals. Thyrsis acts as judge, and each of the swains describes his wealth and personal attractions, while all nature listens to their song. Lines 1–27 are introductory. The contest of the shepherds begins at line 28. Line 98 is spoken by the poet, not by the interlocutors.

Intactam Crotalen puer Astacus et puer Idas,
Idas lanigeri dominus gregis, Astacus horti,

*Explicit prima Aegloga Incipit II*ᵃ. *Pastores duo Astacus et Idas Emuli. Poeta incipit R*1. rd2. *In hac Aegloga pastores duo Astacus et Idas contendunt: primum tamen loquitur poeta* a. Inscribed *Crotale* in fi. π.

1. *Crocalen* D3. 4. d2. pa2.f2.

1. **Intactam.** Perhaps not only chaste, but also hard-hearted, unkind to her lovers. Cf. Propert. 2, 6, 21 : *Tu rapere intactas docuisti impune Sabinas.* Hor. C. 1, 7, 5 : *intactae Palladis. Integer* is used in the same sense, Hor. C. 3, 4, 70 : *Notus et integrae Tentator Orion Dianae.*

Crotale. The form *Crocale* is found in Ov. M. 3, 169, as the name of a nymph attending on Diana. The name Κροκύλος is found in Theocr. 5, 11.

Idas is repeated by the figure called παλιλογία or ἀναδίπλωσις. Cf. Virg. E. 7, 2 and 3 : *Compulerantque greges Corydon et Thyrsis in unum, Thyrsis ovis, Corydon distentas lacte capellas.*

F

Dilexere diu, formosus uterque, nec impar
Voce sonans.   Hi cum terras gravis ureret aestas,
Ad gelidos fontes et easdem forte sub umbras   5
Conveniunt, dulcique simul contendere cantu
Pignoribusque parant: placet, hic ut vellera septem,
Ille sui victus ne messem vindicet horti:
Et magnum certamen erat sub iudice Thyrsi.
Adfuit omne genus pecudum, genus omne ferarum,   10

---

3. All the books give *sed impar.* Mod. and Ulit. c. *nec impar*, which has been accepted since Burm.

4. *Hi cum terras* D1.   *Terras hi cum* vulg.

5. *ulmos* vulg.   *umbras* D1.

8. Heins. c. *venditet horni.*

9. *Thyrso* GR1.rβf1.a1.vbod2.

---

3. Diligo, distinguish *deligo.*

Nec impar Voce sonans, 'and not unequally matched in singing.' The reading *Nec impar* seems established as against the vulgate *sed impar* by line 99: *este pares*, and also by Virg. E. 7, 5: *cantare pares*, as the introduction of this Eclogue seems modelled on the seventh Eclogue of Virgil.

4. Gravis, 'oppressive.'

5. Forte, 'as it chanced.'

6. Dulcique, &c., 'and they prepare to contend together in sweet song and for a stake.'

For *contendere pignoribus* cf. Catullus, 44, 4: *Quovis Sabinum pignore esse contendunt.*

7. Placet, &c. 'It is agreed that the one (Idas), if defeated, should surrender all claim to seven fleeces, the other (Astacus) to the crop of his garden.'

Placet is a *vox propria* for making a bargain or stipulation. Cf. Ter. And. 1, 1, 75: *placuit: despondi: hic nuptiis dictust dies.*

Vellera is usually explained = *oves*, as in Ov. M. 7, 244: *cultrosque in sanguine velleris atri Conjicit;* but perhaps *vellera* should be taken in the literal sense—Idas staking the fleeces, not the sheep, as Astacus stakes a year's crop, not his garden. This latter explanation is also supported by line 78 sq.

Ne vindicet = *ut alteri concedat nec jure domini in eam utatur.* Wernsdorf.

9. Magnum certamen. Cf. Virg. E. 7, 16: *Et certamen erat, Corydon cum Thyrside, magnum.*

Sub judice, 'before Thyrsis as judge.' Cf. Hor. A. P. 78: *Grammatici certant et adhuc sub judice lis est.*

Thyrsi. Nom. *Thyrsis*, gen. *Thyrsis.* Virgil makes the gen. *Thyrsidis.* Several MSS. here read *Thyrso* from *Thyrsus.*

10 sq. Cf. Theocr. 15, 118: πάντ' αὐτῷ πετεηνὰ καὶ ἑρπετὰ τεῖδε πάρεστι.

Et quaecumque vagis altum ferit aera pennis.
Convenit umbrosa quicumque sub ilice lentas
Pascit oves, Faunusque pater, Satyrique bicornes.
Adfuerunt sicco Dryades pede, Naiades udo,
Et tenuere suos properantia flumina cursus.   15
Desistunt tremulis incurrere frondibus Euri,
Altaque per totos fecere silentia montes.

11. Ulit. c. *quodcunque.* R2. and several editions read *alitum* instead of *altum.* Of this Wernsdorf seems to approve, but retains *altum.* *Alitus* seems to have been principally used in the post-Augustan period as a form of the participle, for the sake of distinction from the adjective *altus.* Barth. c. *avium.* Beck seems to think *alitum* must be from *ales*, in violation of the metre.
12. Tit., from an old copy, gives *laetas.*
14. *Adfuerant* D1.d1.2.vψ.
16. *fontibus* D2.
17. Burm. c. *egere.*

11. Quaecunque (sc. avis), &c., 'whatever bird strikes the air on high with roving wings.'
12. Lentas, 'lazy, slowly-walking.' Cf. Ov. M. 3, 15 : *Incustoditam lente videt ire juvencam.*
13. Satyrique bicornes. The Satyrs are represented with two small horns growing out of the top of the forehead. They are beings of Greek mythology, but the Roman poets confound them with the Italian Fauni, as Pan is confounded with Faunus.|
14. Adfuěrunt. For this short penult, cf. Virg. A. 2, 774 : *Obstupui, stetěruntque comae, et vox faucibus haesit.* See Roby, vol. i. § 577.
Sicco Dryades pede, because they frequent the groves ; **Naides udo,** because they frequent the moist river-banks.
15. Tenuere . . . cursus, 'checked their course.' Compare Caes. B. G. 1, 39 : *neque interdum lacrimas tenere poterant.* Cf.

Milton's Comus : *Thyrsis, whose artful strains have oft delayed The huddling brook to hear his madrigal.*
This line seems to confirm the traditional explanation of *requierunt* as active, in Virg. E. 8, 4 : *Et mutata suos requierunt flumina cursus,* where *cursus* might be explained as acc. of respect with *mutata*, but tradition says it is governed by *requierunt ;* and a similar use is found in Calvus ap. Serv. : *Sol quoque perpetuos meminit requiescere cursus.* Ciris, 233 : *(tempore) quo rapidos etiam requiescunt flumina cursus.* Calpurnius, who probably had the passage of Virgil in his mind, considered *requierunt* to be active, and expressed it by *tenuere.*
16. ' The east wind ceases driving against the quivering leaves.'
17. The breezes are said to cause the silence which they leave undisturbed, as the wind is said to cause the smoothness of the

Omnia cessabant, neglectaque pascua tauri
Calcabant: illis etiam certantibus ausa est
Daedala nectareos apis intermittere flores.   20
Iamque sub annosa medius consederat umbra
Thyrsis, et, O pueri me iudice pignora, dixit,
Irrita sint, moneo : satis hinc mercedis habeto,
Si laudem victor, si fert opprobria victus.
Et nunc alternos magis ut distinguere cantus   25

18. *neglectaque pascua tauri Calcabant* and *etiam* are omitted in
PVD3. 4.GR1.2.rd1.2.aβbo.
19. *cantantibus* D3.
20. *intervisere* VR1.ra.   *intermisere solis* G.
21. *annosa m. c. umbra* D1.Π.   *umbrosa* PVrapβf1.2.vbo. *arbo-
rea* D4.   *sub herbosa* D3.   *umbra* PD2.3.R2.d1.2.   *ulmo* vulg.
23. *satis hic* D1. whence Glaeser c. *hinc. hoc* vulg.   *habento* D2.
habete d2.

sea in Virg. A. 5, 763 : *placidi
straverunt aequora venti,* where
we would say, 'the wind left the
sea unruffled.' Cf. Id. G. 4, 484 :
vento rota constitit. Id. A. 1, 66 :
mulcere fluctus et tollere vento.
Conington thinks these passages
are conscious imitations of Soph.
Aj. 674 : δεινῶν δ' ἄημα πνευμάτων
ἐκοίμισε στένοντα πόντον.
Montes, often used of the
haunts of shepherds, e. g. Virg.
E. 5, 8 : *Montibus in nostris solus
tibi certat Amyntas,* and IV. 63,
88, 153.
18 sq. 'Everything was idle,
came to a standstill, and the
cattle neglected and trampled
under foot their pasture: while
they contended, even the la-
borious bee ventured to neglect
the nectar-yielding flowers.'
20. Daedala. This epithet is
applied to Minerva by Ennius,
and to Circe by Virgil. It ex-
presses fertility of resource and
unremitting industry, and is here

a substitute for the bees' constant
epithet, *sedula.* Lucretius uses
it in an active sense both of na-
ture and of the tongue. It is also
found in a passive sense, e. g.
Lucr. 1, 7 : *daedala tellus,* 'the
variegated earth.' Mr. Purser
suggests that the epithet *daedala*
is applied to the bee from its
flitting from flower to flower, and
thus resembles the epithet αἰόλος,
which is applied to wasps in Hom.
Il. 12, 167.
Intermittere flores. For the
construction, cf. Caes. B. G. 3, 5 :
paulisper intermitterent proelium.
21. Sub annosa . . . umbra,
'under the shade of an aged tree.'
22 sq. In VI. 3, on the con-
trary, the contest is for a stake :
judice me, sed non sine pignore.
23. Irrita, &c., 'I advise that
stakes should count for nothing.'
Satis, &c., 'let him have
sufficient reward from this, if,'
&c.
25. This line is difficult. The

Possitis, ter quisque manus iactate micantes.
Nec mora ; decernunt digitis ; prior incipit Idas.
I. Me Silvanus amat, dociles mihi donat avenas,
Et mea frondenti circumdat tempora taeda.
Ille etiam parvo dixit mihi non leve carmen :   30

26. Burm. c. *Possimus.* *terquinque manus iactante* R2. *iactare*
ΠGRι.dι.2.
27. *discrevit digitus* D3.pβa2.f2. *decernunt digitis* Dι.Hdι.2. *dis-
cernunt digitis* VGRι.rafι.aι.vboπ.
29. For *taeda* Heins. c. *taenia ;* Burm. c. *pinu,* on which he thinks
taeda was a gloss. Gronov. defends *taeda* from Plin. N. H. 16. 10.
30. *parvo hoc dixit* vulg. Dι. omits *hoc.*

meaning seems to be—'that you may the better mark off in order your alternate verses, each of you three times raise your hands suddenly, like a flash.'
Distinguere seems to be equivalent to *referre in ordine* (Virg. E. 7, 20), *vicibus reducere carmen* (IV. 80), and *invicem dicere* (XI. 30), and the game of *morrà* was used to decide which should begin. *Distinguere* means ' to mark off, separate ' the parts of a song in I. 30 also.
26. The order of the singing is decided by the game of *morrà,* as the Italians call it, which is still in use in Italy on similar occasions, just as we are in the habit of *tossing up.* The two players simultaneously raise any number of fingers they choose, at the same time crying a number. If the number so cried by one of the players proves to be the sum of the number of fingers raised by both, that player scores a point. If both are right or both wrong, it counts for nothing. On this occasion the victor was whoever scored most out of three trials.

Dignus est quicum in tenebris mices, Cic. Off. 3, 19, 77, is proverbial of an honest man, as it would be easy to cheat in the dark. Marius is said to have invented the game to amuse his soldiers during a tedious siege.
28. Silvanus. The god of cattle and of the country. Virg. A. 8, 600 sq.
Me . . . amat. Cf. Theocr. 5. 80 : ταὶ Μῶσαί με φιλεῦντι. Virg. E. 3, 62 : *et me Phoebus amat.*
Dociles . . . avenas, ' pipes easily taught ' what I wish to play. Cf. Ov. A. A. 3, 343 sq. : *Deve tribus libris, titulus quos signat Amorum, Elige quod docili molliter ore legas.*
29. Taeda. The pine was sacred to Silvanus, and the badge of his votary.
30. Parvo . . . mihi, ' to me while yet a boy.'
Non leve, ' of no slight importance,' with a play on the ' slender pipe,' *levis fistula,* in the next line.
Carmen. This word is often used of a divine utterance or prophecy.

Iam levis obliqua crescit tibi fistula canna.
A. At mihi Flora comas pallenti gramine cingit,
Et mihi matura Pomona sub arbore plaudit.

31. *crescat* D1.Π.   Haupt and Glaes. think the sense requires
crescit.
32. *Et mihi* PVD2.4.GR1.2.rd2.apβa2.f2.bo.   The same MSS. and
Πr give *flore*.   *pienti* D4.   Rooy Spicil. crit. c. 17, p. 111, c. *pal-
lenti.* Heins. c. *ridenti, varianti, vernanti, roranti.* Glaes. thinks
we should read some epithet agreeing with *mihi. parienti* vulg.
iungit D1., according to Glaes.; but Haupt says D1. has *pingit*, and H
also, if it is right, as Haupt thinks it is, to identify H with Π. Glaes.,
however, cites *iungit* from H and *pingit* from Π. *spargit* vulg. Haupt.
c. *pallenti gramine cingit.*
33. *mihi matura* bo.   *matura mihi* vulg.   *matuta mihi* a.   *poma*
D1.   *pemmena* R2.   *peramoena* D2.Gd1.2.na.   Haupt c. *plaudit* for
the vulg. *ludit.*

31. 'A slender pipe of the
sloping reed is now growing up
for you.'
Obliqua denotes a particular
kind of dwarf reed: see Pliny,
16, 36: *est et obliqua arundo, non
in excelsitatem nascens, sed juxta
terram fruticis modo se spar-
gens.* Some think that the words
obliqua crescit canna simply
describe Pan's pipes, which were
made of several reeds, gradually
increasing in length and calibre,
and which are described by Ov.
M. 8, 192 sq. : *sic rustica quon-
dam Fistula disparibus paulatim
surgit avenis.* The meaning would
then be merely ' I have a sloping
Pan's pipe for you,' which does
not exhibit much oracular profun-
dity. It is a different thing to
say, ' boy though you are, a reed
pipe is already growing up (*cre-
scit*) for you.'
32. I have adopted Haupt's
emendation of this and the follow-
ing line. It is to be observed that
in each case Astacus takes up the
idea started by Idas, and tries to
improve upon it. This 'follow-
ing suit' in fact forms the very

essence of the contest. Accord-
ingly, as Idas says that Silvanus
is his patron, presents him with
the shepherd's pipe, and wreaths
his temples with luxuriant pine
leaves ; so Astacus replies that the
goddess Flora encircles his hair
with pale-green grass, Pomona
applauds his song under the ripen-
ing fruit-tree, and the Nymphs
signify their approval by supply-
ing abundance of water for his
garden.
Wernsdorf's reading and ex-
planation ignore this parallelism
in the replies of Astacus. He
reads, *At mihi Flora comas pari-
enti gramine spargit, Et matura
mihi Pomona sub arbore ludit,*
and explains : But Flora, for my
sake, scatters the luxuriant flow-
ers *(comas)* on the fertile *(pari-
enti)* grass, and ripe apples (lit.
Pomona, goddess of fruit-trees)
play (i. e. fall and rebound from
the earth) beneath the trees.
There would thus be no refer-
ence to poetic skill, to which Idas
lays claim, and to which accord-
ingly Astacus should advance his
counter-claim.

Accipe, dixerunt Nymphae, puer, accipe fontes:
Iam potes irriguos nutrire canalibus hortos. 35
I. Me docet ipsa Pales cultum gregis, ut niger albae
Terga maritus ovis nascenti mutet in agna,
Quae neque diversi speciem servare parentis
Possit, et ambiguo testetur utrumque colore.
A. Non minus arte mea mutabilis induit arbos 40
Ignotas frondes et non gentilia poma.
Ars mea nunc malo pira temperat, et modo cogit

34. *fontes* D1.2.3.4. ΠPR2. *fontem* vulg.
35. *Jam potes* D1.H. *Nam potes* vulg. *irriguos* D1. *irriguis*
vulg. *mutare* D2.R1.2.rd1.2.apβa2.f2.bo. *ortus* D1. *Ortus* is used
of the source of a river in Ov. M. 11, 139; *donec venias ad fluminis
ortus,* but is unsuitable here, as the source would feed the canals, and
not *vice versa.*
37. *mutat* D4.
40. *mirabilis* Π.
41. *genitalia* D1.R1.2.Πraf1.va1.boπ. The rest from Burm. read
gentilia.

35. Irriguos, 'well-watered':
if *irriguis* be read it will be active
= *irrigantibus,* as in Virg. E. 4,
34: *irriguumque bibant violaria
fontem,* and line 49.
36 sq. Cultum gregis, 'the
breeding of cattle.' Cf. Virg. G.
1, 3: *qui cultus habendo sit pecori.*
Ut niger, 'how a black ram
mated with a white ewe changes
the fleece of a lamb at its birth,
which is both unable to retain the
appearance of its sire, who differs
from its dam, and bears witness
to both its parents by its variety
of colour.' Cf. Virg. G. 3, 387 sq.:
*illum . . . Nigra subest udo tan-
tum cui lingua palato, Rejice, ne
maculis infuscet vellera pullis
Nascentum.*
40 sq. 'In like manner the tree
transformed by my skill clothes
itself with unfamiliar leaves, and
fruits not of its own species.'
Mutabilis corresponds to *mu-
tet* of line 37, the change pro-

duced in trees by grafting being
contrasted with that produced in
sheep by cross-breeding. *Muta-
bilis* means liable to or capable
of change, and is perhaps used
because only some trees admit of
grafting.
Gentilia seems a preferable
reading to *genitalia,* from compa-
rison with Virg G. 2, 82: *novas
frondes et non sua poma.*
42. 'My art now grafts apples
on pears (lit. modifies pears by
apples), and now forces engrafted
peaches to steal upon, supplant,
the early plums.'
Nunc . . . modo = *modo . . .
modo.* Cf. XI. 8, 9.
For grafting cf. Propert. 4, 2,
17: *Insitor hic solvit pomosa vota
corona, Quum pirus invito stipite
mala tulit.* Virg. G. 2, 32 sq.: *Et
saepe alterius ramos impune vide-
mus Vertere in alterius mutatam-
que insita mala Ferre pirum, et
prunis lapidosa rubescere corna.*

Insita praecoquibus subrepere Persica prunis.

I. Me teneras salices iuvat aut oleastra putare
Et gregibus portare novis, ut carpere frondes 45
Condiscant, primoque recidere gramina morsu,
Ne depulsa vagas quaerat foetura parentes.
A. Et mihi cum fulvis radicibus arida tellus

43. *praecocibus* aob.
45. *novis, ut* D1.4.R2. Ulit. *novas ut* vulg.
46. Voss c. *condiscat.*
47. *Nec* R2.abo. *vagos* vulg. Scaliger and Voss c. *vagas.*
48. Burm. c. *furvis* or *vulsis. altera tellus* PVD4.GR1.2.rabod2.

Praecoquibus. There are three forms of this adjective : *praecox*, gen. *praecocis, praecoquis*, and *praecoquus.* The early plums of summer are distinguished from those which ripen in autumn.

Subrepere. Cf. Tib. 4, 3, 21 : *quaecunque meo furtim subrepet amori.*

Persica, *Persicum*, n. a peach : *persicus*, f. a peach-tree. Mommsen says the peach was probably introduced into Italy 150 years before Christ.

44. Oleastra. *Oleastrum* = the wild olive-tree, is peculiar to Calpurnius ; elsewhere we find *oleaster.* The word, however, is not without analogy, e. g. *siliquastrum*, 'pepperwort,' and that it was in use appears from a passage quoted by Haupt from a grammarian : *oleastrum generis neutri : sed Virgilius foliis oleaster amaris.*

Putare, 'prune, lop boughs from.'

45. Gregibus novis, 'the young flocks': expressed in line 47 by *depulsa foetura.*

46. Primoque, &c., 'and to begin cropping the grass.'

47. 'That the weaned lambs may not seek their straying dams.'

Depulsa, sc. *a matribus.* Cf. Virg. E. 3, 82 : *Dulce satis humor, depulsis arbutus haedis.*

Vagas. Cf. Hor. C. 1, 17, 6 : *deviae Olentis uxores mariti.*

Foetura. In concrete sense, as in Ov. M. 13, 827 : *Sunt foetura minor tepidis in ovilibus agni.*

48 sq. 'And I, when I plant the parched ground with tawny roots, drench the flower-bed with a soaking flood, and saturate it with water, lest perchance the slips, drooping from the change of soil, may miss their former moisture.'

Burmann suggests *furvis* or *vulsis*, and explains the latter of herbs pulled up for transplanting to another place, whence he thinks we should read *altera*, not *arida tellus.* The latter reading might readily arise from the next line, *irriguo perfunditur area fonte*, in which not only the sense suggests the mention of the dry ground, but the very form of the word *area* suggests *arida.* The words *mutata terra* also, in line 51, support *altera.*

Pangitur. Cf. Prop. 3, 17, 15 : *Ipse seram vites, pangamque ex ordine colles.*

Pangitur, irriguo perfunditur area fonte,
Et satiatur aqua, succos ne forte priores   50
Languida mutata quaerant plantaria terra.
I. O si quis Crotalen deus afferat, hunc ego terris,
Hunc ego sideribus solum regnare fatebor.
Decernamque nemus, dicamque : sub arbore numen
Hoc erit; ite procul, sacer est locus, ite profani.   55

49. *Pangitur* D1.f1.va1. *Panditur* vulg.

52. In R1., instead of *deus*, &c., we find *si quis mea vota deorum*, which was introduced by the copyist from line 56, doubtless on account of *Crotalen* occurring in the same position in both lines.

54. *Dicam namque* PVD4.GR1.2.rapβf1.2.a1.2.bo. Gronov. Obss. 3, 13, c. *Secernamque.* Glaes. c. *Discernamque. Decernamque* π Barth., Ulit., Burm., Wernsd.

55. All the books give *Hoc erit.* Ulit. c., with much probability, *Hac* δεικτικῶς.

Irriguo (see note on line 35), active, as in Virg. G. 4, 32 : *irriguumque bibant violaria fontem.*
Area = a bed or border in a garden. Cf. Columella, 10, 152 : *Aggere praeposito cumulatis area glebis Emineat.*
51. Quacrant, ' seek for something missing, miss.' Cf. Stat. Theb. 4, 702 sq. : *deceptum margine ripae Stat pecus atque amnes quaerunt armenta natatos.* Astacus uses *quaerant* to correspond with *quaerat*, used by Idas in line 47.
Plantaria, from *plantare*, as appears from Juv. 13, 122 sq. : *non Epicurum Suspicit exigui laetum plantaribus horti.* It seems, however, to occur only in plural. *Plantarium* = a nursery-garden.
52. Afferat, ' bring me.' The lover thinks a god only can perform so difficult a task.
Terris . . . sideribus . . . regnare. Similarly, Virg. G. 1, 27,

describing Caesar as a god, says : *Auctorem frugum tempestatumque potentem.*
54. *Dicam namque*, which has most authority on its side, can hardly be right, on account of the following *dicam*, unless we adopt Wernsdorf's theory, that the poet purposely makes the rustic speak in an uncouth style. It seems best to adopt *decernam* or *discernam.* Gronov. 3, 13, reads *secernam* in same sense as Livy, 10, 23, uses *excludere : in vico Longo, ubi habitabat, ex parte aedium, quod satis esset modico sacello, exclusit, aramque ibi posuit.*
Nemus. A grove was the shrine of a rural deity. Cf. 1., where *sacraria* of line 15 corresponds to *nemus* of line 8.
Distinguish *dico* and *dico.*
Profani, ' ye uninitiated.' Cf. Virg. 6, 258 : *procul, o procul este profani, Conclamat vates.*

A. Urimur in Crotalen : si quis mea vota deorum
Audiat, huic soli, virides qua gemmeus undas
Fons agit et tremulo percurrit lilia rivo,
Inter pampineas ponetur faginus ulmos.
I. Ne contemne casas et pastoralia tecta :   60
Rusticus est, fateor, sed non et barbarus Idas.
Saepe vaporato mihi cespite palpitat agnus,

56. Kempfer c. *quisquis mea.*
57. *huic similis* D2.4.R2.d2.pβa2.f2.   Gronov. c. *hic similis* or
hic solus. Burm. c. *huic soli lucus, qua.*
58. *praecurrit* G.
61. *sed non et* D1.2.   *sed non est* vulg.

56. ' I burn with love for Cro-
tale.' Cf. Virg. E. 2, 68 : *me
tamen urit amor.* Id. A. 4, 68 :
uritur infelix Dido. So ὀπτάω
(in partic. ὀπτεύμενος) is used of
the fire of love by Theocritus, e. g.
7, 55 : αἴκεν τὸν Λυκίδαν ὀπτεύμενον
ἐξ ᾿Αφροδίτας ῥύσηται; and 23, 34 :
ἁνίκα τὰν κραδίαν ὀπτεύμενος ἅλμυ-
ρὰ κλαύσεις.
57. Gemmeus . . . fons. Cf.
Scott's Marmion, 6, 30 : *Water
clear as diamond spark.*
Soli, dat. of solus. Cf. line
53 : *hunc solum.* To him alone
shall be offered a beech-wood
bowl. **Faginus** = *scyphus fagi-
nus.* Beech-wood bowls were
often staked by rustics : see Virg.
E. 3, 36 : *pocula ponam Fagina.*
Gronov. suggests *hic solus* for
huic soli. Cf. Hor. Sat. 2, 3 :
*Latus ut in Circo spatiere, aut
aeneus ut stes.* He also sug-
gests *hic similis ponetur faginus*
= *hujus effigies ponetur e fago.*
Cf. Stat. Sil. 5, 1, 1 : *si manus aut
similes docilis mihi fingere ceras,*
' likenesses in wax.'
For such rustic acts of worship,
cf. Virg. E. 5, 67 : *Pocula bina
novo spumantia lacte quotannis*

*Craterasque duo statuam tibi pin-
guis olivi.* Tib. 1, 10, 8 : *faginus
adstabat cum scyphus ante dapes.*
Faginus in this passage is
commonly explained as a statue
of beech-wood, in which case
similis is read instead of *soli* in
line 57, or as simply equivalent to
fagus; but Wernsdorf's explana-
tion, given above, seems prefer-
able.
58. Et tremulo, &c., 'and flows
among the lilies with rippling
stream.' For **tremulo,** cf. Mil-
ton's Comus: *By dimpled brook.*
59. Pampineas . . . ulmos,
' vine-clad elms.' In Italy the
vines were trained to elms. Juv.
8. 78, calls the *ulmi,* when without
vines, *viduae.*
60. Cf. Virg. E. 11, 28 : *O tan-
tum libeat mecum tibi sordida
rura, Atque humiles habitare
casas.*
Pastoralia tecta. Cf. VII.
22 : *pastoralis Apollo.*
61. ' Idas is a countryman (pro-
vincial, clownish), I admit ; but
he is not also a savage.'
62. Vaporato . . . cespite,
' on the smoking altar of sods.'
Palpitat, ' struggles in its

Saepe cadit festis devota Palilibus agna.

A. Nos quoque pomiferi Laribus consuevimus horti
Mittere primitias et fingere liba Priapo,   65
Rorantesque favos damus et liquentia mella :
Nec fore grata minus, quam si caper imbuat aras.

I. Mille sub uberibus balantes pascimus agnas,
Totque Tarentinae praestant mihi vellera matres.

---

63. In d1.2.nc this line is omitted and the following given in its
place : *Perfundens aras divorum sanguine largo.*
65. Other readings for *fingere* are *figere*, *fundere*, and *farrea*, of
which *fundere* has most MS. authority. *vina*, instead of *liba*, is found
in D4, which also gives *fondere* for *fingere*.
66. *Portantesque favos* d1.2.n. *Rorantes fagos* pβa1.2.vf2. *atque
liquentia* d1.2.n.
67. *Nec fore* is found in D4.R2. and many editions, and is defended
by Barth. *Nec sunt* D1.Π. Glaes. c. *stant.* Heins. c. *Nec fors.*
Burm. c. *Nec fert* (sc. Priapus). *Nec fere* VD2.GR1.rd2. *Nec fero*
Maπ. Barth.
68. *palantis* R1.rf1. *pallentes* D4.d1.2.

---

death-pangs.' Idas commends
himself to the love of Crocale by
showing that he is observant of
religion, and therefore probably a
favourite of the gods. Cf. Hor.
C: I, 17, 13 : *di me tuentur, dis
pietas mea . . . cordi est.*
63. The feast of Pales, the shep-
herd festival, was celebrated on
the 21st of April, the anniversary
of the foundation of Rome.
64. Laribus . . . horti, i. e.
Flora, Pomona, and Priapus.
65. Mittere, 'to offer.' Cf.
Virg. A. 6, 380 : *Et statuent
tumulum, et tumulo sollennia
mittent.*
Primitias, 'the first-fruits.'
Fingere liba Priapo. Cf.
Virg. E. 7, 33 : *haec te liba, Pri-
ape, quot annis Expectare sat est.*
66. ' Dripping combs and trick-
ling honey.' The tautology cor-
responds to the repetition of
agnus and *agna* in lines 62 and 63.

Liquentia, from *liquor,* inf.
liqui: distinguish *liquo* and *liqueo.*
67. Fore. This infinitive de-
pends on *spero, credo, puto,* or
some similar word understood.
Cf. Virg. A. 1, 444 : *sic nam fore
bello Egregiam, et facilem victu
per saecula gentem.* Hor. C. 3,
16, 7 : *fore enim tutum iter et
patens, Converso in pretium deo.*
The Neapolitan MS., however,
reads *sunt* for *fore.*
68. Idas boasts of his wealth,
as above, line 62, of his piety.
Mille, for a large number, as
in IX. 35, and Virg. E. 2, 21. Cf.
Sir P. Sidney's ' Arcadia,' 6,
117 sq. Thyrsis and Dorus: *Who
is an heir of manie hundreth
sheepe, Doth beauties keepe which
never sunne can burne Nor
stormes do turne : faireness serves
oft to wealth.*
69. The Tarentine sheep were
celebrated for their wool. See

Per totum niveus premitur mihi caseus annum :   70
Si venias, Crotale, totus tibi serviet hornus.
A. Qui numerare velit, quam multa sub arbore nostra
Poma legam, citius tenues numerabit arenas.
Semper olus metimus, nec bruma nec impedit aestas ;
Si venias, Crotale, totus tibi serviet hortus.   75
I. Quamvis siccus ager languentes excoquat herbas,
Sume tamen calathos nutanti lacte coactos.
Vellera tunc dabimus, quum primum tempus apricum
Surget, et a tepidis fiet tonsura Kalendis.

71. Burm. c. *totum tibi serviet hornum* or *foetus tibi serviet hornus.*
ortus aβ.   *hortus* bo.   *annus* D4.R2.d2.pa2.f2.g.
73. *aristas* vulg.   Burm. c. *avenas.*
74. R2. omits this line.
77. *Sume terra calathos* D1., whence Glaes. c. *Interea calathos*
(omitting *sume*, and understanding *damus* from the following *dabimus*)
nutanti, &c.   *mutanti* P.   Burm. c. *nutantes* or *sudantes lacte coacto.*

Virg. G. 2, 196 sq : *sin . . . magis studium . . . tueri . . . ovium fetum . . . Saltus et saturi petito longinqua Tarenti.*
Tarentinae . . . matres, 'Tarentine ewes.'
70. 'I am making snow-white cheeses the whole year through.'
Cf. Theocr. 11, 36 sq. : τυρὸς δ' οὐ λείπει μ' οὔτ' ἐν θέρει οὔτ' ἐν ὀπώρᾳ, οὐ χειμῶνος ἄκρω· ταρσοὶ δ' ὑπεραχθέες αἰεί.
71. Venias. A *vox propria* of a mistress favouring her lover. Cf. 111. 53, 96.
Totus . . . hornus, sc. *caseus*, 'all this year's cheese.'
Serviet, 'will be at your command.' Cf. Ov. M. 13, 820 : *omnis tibi serviet arbor.*
72. Cf. Hor. C. 1, 28, 1 : *numero carentis arenae Mensorem.*
73. Tenues . . . arenas, 'fine sand.'
76 sq. 'Although the parched field is drying up the drooping

grass, yet accept (i. e. in spite of the drought I will be able to give you) the curdled pails of shaking milk': i. e. the pails of curdled milk which trembles and shakes as jelly does.
77. Calathus is also used of a vessel for carrying milk in Virg. G. 3, 402.
Nutanti, &c.   Cf. 111. 69 : *nullo tremuere coagula lacte.*
78. Cum primum tempus apricum, 'as soon as the first sunny weather,' &c.
79. A tepidis, &c., 'sheepshearing begins from the warm kalends.'
Tepidis = moderately warm, which kind of weather is recommended for shearing by Varro, 2, 11, 6. The season therefore is either April or May, or, as the contest between Idas and Astacus takes place in the hot weather (see line 4), September or October.

A. Et nos, quos etiam praetorrida munerat aestas, 80
Mille renidenti dabimus tibi cortice Chias,
Castaneasque nuces totidem, cum sole Decembri
Maturis nucibus virides rumpentur echini.
I. Num, precor, informis videor tibi ? num gravis annis ?
Decipiorque miser, quoties mollissima tango 85
Ora manu, primique sequor vestigia floris
Nescius, et gracili digitos lanugine fallo ?
A. Fontibus in liquidis quoties me conspicor, ipse
Admiror toties : etenim sic flore iuventae
Induimur vultus, ut in arbore saepe notavi 90

81. *renitenti* GR1.2.rapβa2.sf2.bo, which violates the metre if from
reniteo, and is alien to the sense if from *renitor*. *tillas* D3. whence
Guid. c. *telas*.
82. *sole Decembri* D1. *sole Novembri* vulg.
84. *Nunc precor* II.
85. *Decrepitusque miser* VGR1.rabod2.
87. *fragili* VR1.rabod2.
88. *Montibus* D2. *esse* IID2.3.GR2.rpβa2.f2.bo. Burm. c. *ecce*.
90. All the books give *Induimus*. Heins. c. *Induimur*. Cf. IX.
77 : *nulla tegimur lanugine malas.*

80. 'I too, whom even the
scorching summer presents with
gifts.'
81. 'I will give you a thousand
figs of Chios, with glistening
skin.'
Chias, sc. ficus. The Chian
figs were of peculiar excellence,
and Martial, 7, 25, 8, contrasts
the insipid (*fatuae*) *mariscae*.
82 sq. **Cum sole**, &c., 'when
the nuts ripen with the December
sun, and the green husks burst.'
Cf. Ov. Nux 67 : *At cum matu-
ras fisso nova cortice rimas Nux
agit*.
Decembri, adjective, as in Hor.
C. 3, 18, 10 : *Nonae Decembres;*
id. Sat. 2, 7, 4 : *libertate Decem-
bri.*

83. **Echini**, usually sea ur-
chins ; here the prickly husks of
the chestnuts.
85 sq. 'And am I so unhappy
as to be deceived when I touch
my soft face with my hand, and
unconsciously trace out the marks
of the first bloom, and beguile my
fingers with the slender down ?'
Nescius. Cf. Ov. M. 2, 57 :
*Plus etiam, quam quod ;uperis
contingere fas est, Nescius affectas.*
88. **Fontibus in liquidis**. For
this rustic mirror, cf. IX. 74-77,
and Ov. M. 13, 767.
89. **Flore juventae**, 'the
bloom of youth, the first down.'
Sic . . . ut, with indic., 'so . . .
as.' Cf. Cic. Att. 4, 6, 1 : *de
Lentulo sic fero ut debeo.*

Cerea sub tenui lucere Cydonia lana.
I. Carmina poscit amor, nec fistula cedit amori ;
Sed fugit, ecce! dies, revocatque crepuscula vesper.
Hinc tu, Daphni, greges, illinc agat Alphesiboeus.
A. Iam resonant frondes, iam cantibus obstrepit arbos,   95
I procul, i Doryla, plenumque reclude canalem,

92. *sistit amori* VGR1. rd2.   *Carmina nec poscit nec fistula sistit amori* a.   *Carmina spernit amor neque fistula flectit amorem* bo. Haupt unnecessarily c. *sordet.* He is certainly not right in saying that *cedit* is unintelligible.   See notes 2.
94. *agit* s.   *vocet* D3.   *vocat* PVD2.4.R̈1.2.rd2.a.
95. *cratibus* VGR1.rd2.
96. *Hic procul et dorila* Π.   *I procul, o Doryla,* Glaes.   *I procul ydorila* D1., whence Haupt c. *I procul, i Doryla.*   *plenumque* is Haupt's conjecture for the vulg. *primumque,* which gives no satisfactory sense.   Perhaps the true reading is *Hinc procul, i Doryla.*   *Hinc* would be written *hic,* and so account for *hic* of Π, and the lengthened form in which *I* is written in MSS. would account for *I procul* sup-

91. 'Wax-like quinces glisten under the delicate down.'   Cf. Martial, 10, 42, 3 : *Celantur simili ventura Cydonia lana.*

Quinces derived their name *Cydonia* from the town Cydonia, now Khania, on the north-west coast of Crete, whence they were first brought to Italy.

92. 'Love calls for song, nor does the pipe vail to love.'   The shepherd's pipe is not hushed out of deference to love, but, on the contrary, love is an incentive to song.   It is not love that silences our pipe, but want of time to sing, *sed fugit ecce dies.*

Haupt strangely says '**Cedit** sane non potest intelligi.'   It is to be explained from the well-known passage in Cic. Off. 1, 22, 77 : *Cedant arma togae, concedat laurea laudi,* i. e. 'military merit must vail to civil.'   Cf. Ov. F. 1, 698 : *cedebat taurus arator equo,* 'the ploughing ox gave place to the horse.'

Haupt's conjecture, *sordet* for *cedit,* is not as happy as his suggestions generally are.

93. Crepuscula, 'twilight': from the adj. *creper,* 'dark,' hence 'obscure, doubtful.'   *Diluculum* is used of the morning twilight.

94. Daphnis, Alphesiboeus, and Dorylas are doubtless farm servants, as Tityrus in III. 19.

The concluding stanzas consist of three lines each, instead of four, just as in the comedians a change of metre often marks a change of thought or subject-matter.

95. Resonant, 'rustle.'

Obstrepit, &c., 'the trees drown the sound of our song.'   Adelung is wrong in supposing that this refers to the noise made by the cicadae in the trees, as appears from VIII. 30: *vento garrula pinus obstrepat.*

96. 'Go off, go, Dorylas, and open the full channel.'

I for *O* before *Doryla,* and **ple-**

Et sine iamdudum sitientes irriget hortos.
Vix ea finierant, senior cum talia Thyrsis:
T. Este pares, et ob hoc concordes vivite, nam vos
Et decor et cantus et amor sociavit et aetas.   100

planting *Hic procul. O* would then be substituted for *i* before *Doryla*,
in order to avoid the repetition.   *Procul* is often found with particles
of place, as *hinc, inde istinc,* &c.
98. R1.raob add *Poeta.*
99. Burm. c. *Ite pares. ab hoc* (= *abhinc*) VR1.

num for *primum* are Haupt's
corrections. On the other hand,
Virg. E. 3, 111, says: *claudite jam*

rivos, pueri: sat prata biberunt.
100. **Amor,** i. e. love for Cro-
tale.

ECLOGA TERTIA.

IOLLAS; LYCIDAS.

SCALIGER'S criticism on this Eclogue, *merum rus, idque inficetum*, is known to everyone, but will be endorsed by few. It seems to be based on the treatment of Phyllis by Lycidas in lines 29 and 30; but those who have read Todhunter's *Laurella* will be able to understand, although perhaps not to justify, the episode, and the chivalrous advice of Iollas, and the graceful apology of Lycidas, redeem the poem from the clownish character which Scaliger endeavours to affix to it. A very similar love-quarrel is described by Ovid, Am. 1, 7, 47 sq.

On account of certain metrical peculiarities (see Introduction, page 16), Haupt considers this Eclogue to have been written before the others, and when Calpurnius had not yet matured his art.

Iollas, in search of a lost heifer, meets Lycidas, who tells him where the heifer may be found. Tityrus is despatched to bring her back, while Iollas listens to the tale of Lycidas' love-quarrel, and undertakes to bear a letter of apology to the offended Phyllis. Just as the letter is finished, and copied out on the bark of a cherry-tree, Tityrus reappears with the heifer, which is taken as an omen of the reconciliation of the lovers.

Tityrus is one of the servants whom the shepherds of Arcadia seem to have had at their command, to do the dirty work, and give their masters leisure for piping love ditties.

The Eclogue is inscribed *Exoratio*, and is an imitation of Virg. E. 7, and Theocr. 3, 14, and 23.

I. Numquid in hac, Lycida, vidisti forte iuvencam
Valle meam ? solet ista tuis occurrere tauris,
Et iam paene duas, dum quaeritur, eximit horas ;
Nec tamen apparet.   Duris ego perdita ruscis
Iamdudum nullis dubitavi crura rubetis   5
Scindere, nec quidquam post tantum sanguinis egi.
L. Non satis attendi nec enim vacat.   Uror, Iolla ;
Uror, et immodice : Lycidan ingrata reliquit
Phyllis, amatque novum post tot mea munera Mopsum.

Desinit certantium emulatio et conciliatio incipit. Ecloga III^a.
Interlocutores duo Iollas et Lycidas R1.r.   *Aegloga tertia in genere*
dramatico Interlocutores duo Iollas et Licydas a.   This eclogue is in-
scribed *Exoratio* in f1.π and the other editions until Wernsd.
 1. *valle juvencam Forte meam* D4. V.
 2. *ista* D1.   *illa* vulg.
 5. *et nullis* vulg.   *et* is omitted in πVR1.2.raπ Barth. Ulit. Heins.
c. *nullus.*
 7.   Haupt considers *nec enim,* which he says is found in D1., to be
the true reading.   Glaes. says *nec enim* is found in R2.
 8.   Barth. connects *immodice Lycidan ingrata.*
 9. *mea vulnera* VD4.GR1.2.abod2.

1. **Numquid** = *num,* and is
seldom found except in direct in-
terrogations. The *quid* is accusa-
tive of respect, ' did you at all, by
any chance?'
2. **Occurrere,** 'go to meet.'
See Virg. E. 8, 86 sq.
3. **Eximit,** ' wastes.' Cf. Cic.
Q. Fr. 2, 1, 3 : *Clodius rogatus*
diem dicendo eximere coepit; Id.
Phil. 6, 3, 7 : *horam eximere*
ullam in tali cive liberando sine
scelere non possumus; Livy 1,
50: *quia ea res exemisset illum*
diem.
4. **Ruscis,** ' butcher's broom.'
Nom. apparently both *ruscum*
and *ruscus.* Pliny 23, 9, 83,
166 : *Castor oxymyrsinen myrti*
foliis acutis, ex qua fiunt ruri
scopae, ruscum vocavit, ad eos-
dem usus. Colum. 10, 374 :

hirsuta sepes nunc horrida rus-
co.
5. **Rubetis,** from *rubeta, orum,*
a neut. pl. ' bramble-thickets';
formed from *rubus,* ' a bramble-
bush,' after the analogy of *querce-*
tum, myrtetum, &c. Though his
legs had already suffered from the
broom, he did not hesitate to tear
them with the brambles. *Et,*
which the vulgate exhibits before
nullis, is omitted by Glaeser on
good MSS. authority.
6. **Nec quidquam,** &c., ' nor
did I effect anything after losing
so much blood.' In Theocritus'
Fourth Idyl the herdsman suffers
similar inconvenience from the
thorn bushes.
9. **Novum,** ' a new admirer.'
Post tot mea munera, ' after
all my presents.'

I. Mobilior ventis o! femina: sic tua Phyllis? 10
Quae sibi, nam memini, si quando solus abesses,
Mella etiam sine te iurabat amara videri.
L. Altius ista querar, si forte vacabit, Iolla:
Has pete nunc salices, et laevas flecte sub ulmos.
Nam cum prata calent, illic requiescere noster 15
Taurus amat, gelidaque iacet spatiosus in umbra,
Et matutinas revocat palearibus herbas.
I. Non equidem, Lycida, quamvis contemptus abibo:

10. *est femina* D4.
13. *si quando* vulg. *vacabis* D4.R2.pβa2.boπ Ulit. *vocabis* v. *va-
cabit* VGR1.rad2.
16. *spatiosus* D1. H. *spatiatus* vulg. Heins. c. *satiatus.*
18. *contentus* PD1.3.4.R1.2.d1.2.b Barth. Burm. c. *quum sis
contemtus* or *quamvis non tempus.*

10. ' O woman more change-
able than the wind !' Cf. the
song in Rigoletto ; *La donna è
mobile qual piuma al vento,* and
Scott's Marmion : *O woman, in
our hours of ease Uncertain, coy,
and hard to please, And variable
as the shade By the light quiver-
ing aspen made.*
Sic tua Phyllis? ' Is that
the way with your Phyllis?' *Sic*
in such expressions is equivalent
to *talis.* Cf. Cic. Rosc. Am. 30,
84 : *sic vita hominum est.*
11. Solus, ' if you alone were
absent.'
13 sq. I will tell you my troubles
more fully when you have leisure,
but will not now detain you, and
merely wish to say that you will
probably find your heifer under
the elms on the left.
14. Flecte, 'turn aside,' neuter,
as in Livy 28, 16, 3 : *Hasdrubal
ad Oceanum flectit.*
16. Jacet spatiosus, ' reclines
his immense bulk.'

17. ' And chews the cud after
his morning's grazing.'
Palearia, properly the dew-
lap, or skin that hangs down from
the neck of an ox, is here used for
the throat. Cf. Ov. Am. 3, 5,
17 : (*taurus*) *lente revocatas ru-
minat herbas.*
18 sq. Iollas refuses to obey
Lycidas' order to depart (line 14),
but sending Tityrus to seek the
heifer, himself remains to hear
the story of Lycidas' love-quar-
rel.
In like manner, in Theocr. 3,
1 sq., Tityrus looks after the flocks
while his master amuses himself
with love and song : Κωμάσδω
ποτὶ τὰν 'Αμαρυλλίδα· ταὶ δέ μοι
αἶγες Βόσκονται κατ' ὄρος, καὶ ὁ
Τίτυρος αὐτὰς ἐλαύνει. Τίτυρ'
ἐμὶν τὸ καλὸν πεφιλαμένε, βόσκε
τὰς αἶγας, καὶ ποτὶ τὰν κράναν
ἄγε, Τίτυρε, κ. τ. λ.
Quamvis contemptus, refer-
ring to the cool reception he got
from Lycidas in line 7.

Tityre, quas dixit, salices pete laevus, et illinc,
Si tamen invenies, deprensam verbere multo   20
Huc age ; sed fractum referas hastile memento.
Nunc age dic, Lycida : quae vos tam magna tulere
Iurgia ? quis vestro deus intervenit amori ?
L. Phyllide contentus sola, tu testis, Iolla, es,
Calliroen sprevi, quamvis cum dote rogaret.   25
En sibi cum Mopso calamos intexere cera
Incipit, et puero comitata sub ilice cantat.
Haec ego cum vidi, fateor, sic intimus arsi,

19. *laetus* HVD1.4.Gf1.boπ Barth. *solus* D2.3.R2.Πd2.pβa2.f2. *solus pete solus* Ulit. Perhaps we should read *illam* for *illinc*, which is found in all the books. IVVENC., i. e. *iuvencam* would be a natural gloss on *illam*, and would closely resemble ILLINC. *Deprensam* in the next line is hardly satisfactory unless the noun or pronoun be expressed.
23. Tit. mentions a reading *vestrum d. intervertit amorem.* Ulit. c. *vestros deus intervertit amores* or *vestro dolus intervenit amori.*
24. *es* is omitted in D1.Π, and these authorities Haupt would follow.
26. *En ibi* D1. Burm. c. *tibi.* Heins. c. *rogaret Me sibi : cum, &c.*
28. *Hoc ego cum* vulg. *Haec ego dum* D1.

20. Si tamen invenies, ' if indeed you find her.' *Si tamen* = *si modo,* as in Ov. Trist. 3, 14, 24 : *Nunc incorrectum populi pervenit in ora ; In populi quicquam si tamen ore meum est.*
Deprensam, sc. *juvencam.* See lines 1 and 98.
Verbere multo, ' with many a blow.' Cf. Ov. M. 14, 300 : *Percutimurque caput conversae verbere virgae.*
21. Fractum, &c. This is one of the simple touches which the bucolic poets are fond of introducing, to give vividness to their narrative, as in Theocr. 3, 25 ; 8, 24, &c.
Hastile is generally used for a

spear-shaft or spear ; here it is a shepherd's staff or crook.
22. Quae vos, &c., ' what was this great quarrel that carried you away ? '
23. Intervenit, ' interrupted,' ' interfered with.'
26. En indicates an unexpected and unwelcome occurrence. ' Lo and behold.'
27. Puero comitata, ' in company with the boy.' Cf. Cic. Cael. 14, 34 : *(mulier) alienis viris comitata.*
28. Sic intimus arsi, ' such inly fire of passion did I feel.' For *intimus* cf. Two Gentlemen of Verona, Act 2, sc. 7 : *Didst thou but know the inly touch of love.*

Ut nihil ulterius tulerim: nam protinus ambas
Deduxi tunicas, et pectora nuda cecidi.   30
Alcippen irata petit, dixitque: relicto
Improbe, te, Lycida, Mopsum tua Phyllis amabit.
Nunc penes Alcippen manet, ac ne forte vagetur,
Ah vereor: nec tam nobis ego Phyllida reddi
Exopto, quam quod Mopso iurgetur anhelo.   35

29. *alterius* d1. Victor Vigil. c. *amba* (sc. *manu*).
30. *Diduxi* d1.2.ab. Barth. Ulit. Burm. Wernsd. *recidi* HVD2.3.4.
GR1.2. rd1.2. abo.
32. *theliocida* Π, whence Glaes. c. *te, o Lycida*. Haupt approves of
te, Lycida, and thinks *o* in *theliocida* of Π is due to the copyists' habit
of writing the interjection over vocatives. *amabat* D3.
33. *negetur* HΠ.
35. *iungetur* D4.GR2.f1.va1.t Ulit. Heins. c. *quam ne Mopso iun-*
gatur. Burm. c. *quam quo.*

29. 'That I put up with it no
longer.' Cf. Hor. C. 3, 14 : *non
ego hoc ferrem calidus juventa.*
Ambas tunicas, sc. *interio-
rem et exteriorem.* See Var. in
Non. 542, 24 : *postea quam binas
tunicas habere coeperunt, institue-
runt vocare subuculam et indu-
sium.* A man's under-garment
was called *subucula,* a woman's
indusium.
30. Deduxi, 'stripped off,' in-
stead of *diduxi,* 'tore open,' is
supported by Ov. Am. 1, 7, 48,
and Id. M. 3, 480. Cf. Theocr.
14, 34 : τᾶμος ἐγών, τὸν ἴσᾳς τύ,
Θυώνιχε, πὺξ ἐπὶ κόρρας ἤλασα.
33. Penes, 'in the house of.'
Cf. Ter. Ad. 3, 3, 34 : *isthaec jam
penes vos psaltria 'st ?*
Vagetur, 'pass from one love to
another.' Cf. Prop. 1, 5, 7 : *Va-
gae puellae,* 'inconstant in love.'
Lucr. 4, 1071 : *volgivaga Venus.*
34, 35. Nec tam, &c., 'nor
do I so much desire that Phyllis
should be restored to me as that
she should quarrel with the broken-
winded, wheezy Mopsus.'

Anhelo is probably adjective
not verb, for the verb *anhelo* de-
notes fear, grief, or anxiety, not
desire (which latter is the meaning
required here, if the word is a verb),
and the adjective *anhelus* corre-
sponds with the reproaches heaped
on Mopsus in other passages :
*torrida Mopsi Vox et carmen
iners : et acerbae stridor avenae*
(line 59); *risisti calamos et dissona
flamina Mopsi* (VIII. 16) : it de-
notes a voice deficient in the *sos-
tenuto.*
There is of course a difficulty in
the two different constructions,
infinitive *reddi* and *quod jurgetur,*
depending on *exopto,* and the lat-
ter construction instead of *ut* is
rare, although it may perhaps be
justified by Ov. Trist. 5, 1, 16 :
*praemoneo numquam scripta quod
ista legat,* if we can rely on the
reading in that passage.
For the dative with *jurgari* or
jurgare cf. Ammianus Marcellinus
28, 5, 11 : *Burgundii salinarum
finiumque caussa Alamannis saepe
jurgabant.*

I. A te coeperunt tua iurgia. Tu prior illi
Victas tende manus ; decet indulgere puellae,
Vel cum prima nocet. Si quid mandare iuvabit,
Sedulus iratae contingam nuntius aures.
L. Iamdudum meditor, quo Phyllida carmine placem. 40
Forsitan audito poterit mitescere cantu ;
Et solet illa meas ad sidera ferre Camoenas.
I. Dic age, nam cerasi tua cortice verba notabo,
Et decisa feram rutilanti carmina libro.
L. Has tibi, Phylli, preces iam pallidus, hos tibi cantus 45

37. *vinctas* pfı.βa2.tf2. Guid. and Tit. cite *iunctas.*
38. *nocent* PVD4. Rı.2.r.pfı.βa2.sgtψ, whence Glaes. c. *decet in-
dulgere, puellae vel cum prima nocent,* comparing Grat. Fal. Cyneg.
25, where some take *prima* as an adverb = *primo.*
41. Burm. c. *miserescere.*
43. Dı. gives *nunc* for *nam.* Hπ give *mea* for *tua. ceras* VGRı.r.
notato Dı.
44. Heins. c. *Atque incisa,* to which of course the elision is an objec-
tion.

36 sq. A te coeperunt, 'it
was with you the quarrel began.'
Cf. Quint. 9, 4, 23 : *at si coepisset
a toto corpore, non bene ad latera
faucesque descenderet.*
Tu prior, &c., 'do you be the
first to surrender to her at discre-
tion.'
Tendere manus is probably
a mere variety for *dare* or *dedere
manus,* to give the hands to be
bound : cf. line 71 sq. Some read
vinctas in this passage ; if *victas*
be retained it is simply a variety
for *tu victus :* Nep. Ham. 1 : *doni-
cum aut certe vicissent, aut victi
manum dedissent.*
Indulgere. Cf. Nemes. Cyn.
192 : *Nec semel indulge catulis
moderamine cursus.*
38. Vel cum prima nocet,
'even when she is the aggressor.'
Si quid, &c., 'if you wish to
send any message.'
39. Sedulus . . . contingam,

'I will make it my business to
gain access to.' Cf. Ov. M. 1,
211 : *Contigerat nostras infamia
temporis aures.*
41. Forsitan with indicative is
not found in Cicero, and for the
most part occurs only in poetry or
post-Augustan prose.
Mitescere, 'be appeased.'
42. Meas . . . Camoenas, 'my
poetic skill.'
44. 'And I will cut off and carry
with me the verses in the red
bark.'
Rutilanti describes the ap-
pearance of the freshly-cut bark.
Adelung inclines to think tablets
of cherry-wood are meant, because
it is hard to imagine that forty-
seven verses were cut on the bark
of a tree off-hand. *Decisa* and
rutilanti, however, favour the
common explanation.
45. Jam pallidus, sc. with
grief and remorse. Cf. IX. 41.

Dat Lycidas, quos nocte miser modulatur acerba,
Dum flet, et excluso disperdit lumina somno.
Non sic destricta marcescit turdus oliva,
Non lepus, extremas legulus cum sustulit uvas,
Ut Lycidas domina sine Phyllide tabidus erro.   50
Te sine, vae misero, mihi lilia nigra videntur,
Nec sapiunt fontes, et acescunt vina bibenti.
At si tu venias, et candida lilia fient,

46. *modulatus* Π Barth.   Tit. mentions the reading *amara*.
47. *excluso disperdit* Di.HΠ.   *excusso dispergit* vulg.   Scaliger c.
distergit.   Heins. and Kempfer c. *detergit. limina* D2.
    48. *destricta* Di.H.   *districta* fi.vai.t\pid2.   *destructa* VD2.3.4.GR2.
rd2.pβa2.sgf2.bo.   *marcescit* Di.2.   *macrescit* vulg.
    49. *Ut lepus* D4. R2. *unus* R2.   Burm. c. *herbas.*
    50. *turbidus* pβa2.f2.bo.
    52. *et dulcia vina bibenti* VD4.GRi.r.   *nec acescunt vina bidenti*
D4.   *nec crescunt vina* R2.

46. Dat. This is a *vox propria*
for sending a letter. Lycidas
sends you this poem to be de-
livered by Iolas.
    Nocte . . . acerba, 'the weary
night.'
    47. Excluso disperdit, &c.,
'ruins his eyes by loss of sleep.'
    Dispereo is used as passive of
disperdo.
    If the reading *excusso dispergit*
be adopted instead of *excluso dis-
perdit* the meaning is ' shakes off
sleep, and turns his eyes hither and
thither in search of his mistress.'
    48. Wernsdorf says thrushes
are particularly partial to olives.
    Destringere is a *vox propria* of
gathering berries with the hand.
    49. Legulus, ' gleaner.' Es-
pecially used of one who picks up
fallen olives in opposition to *stric-
tor,* who plucks them from the
tree.
    50. Tabidus, 'pining, love-
sick.'

Domina, ' Queen of my heart.'
This title is hardly suitable in
bucolic poetry, and is not found
in Virgil's Eclogues. The word
is used for a sweetheart in Tib.
I, I, 46: *et dominam tenero deti-
nuisse sinu,* and, id. 2, 6, 47 sq. :
*Saepe, ego cum dominae dulces a
limine duro Agnosco voces, haec
negat esse domi.*
    For the following passage cf.
IX. 44 sq., and Ausonius Epist.
24, 99 sq. : *Te sine sed nullus
grata vice provenit annus ; Ver
pluvium sine flore fugit : Canis
aestifer ardet.*
    52. Nec sapiunt fontes, ' the
springs lose their relish.' Cf.
Juv. 11, 121 : *nil rhombus nil
dama sapit.*
    Acescunt, &c., ' wine sours
when I drink.'
    53. Cf. Virg. E. 7, 59 : *Phylli-
dis adventu nostrae nemus omne
virebit.* Theocr. 8, 41-44. See
II. 71.

Et sapient fontes, et dulcia vina bibentur.
Ille ego sum Lycidas, quo te cantante solebas   55
Dicere felicem, cui dulcia saepe dedisti
Oscula, nec medios dubitasti rumpere cantus,
Atque inter calamos errantia labra petisti.
Ah dolor, et post haec placuit tibi torrida Mopsi
Vox, et carmen iners, et acerbae stridor avenae ?   60
Quem sequeris ? quem, Phylli, fugis ? formosior illo
Dicor, et hoc ipsum mihi tu iurare solebas.
Sum quoque divitior : certaverit ille tot haedos
Pascere, quot nostri numerantur vespere tauri.
Quid tibi, quae nosti, referam ? scis, optima Phylli, 65

54. *vina bibenti* R1.rd2. cf. line 52.
58. This line is omitted in D4. R2.
59. *post hoc* vulg. Heins. c. *torpida.*
60. *iners* D1. *inops* vulg. *et crebrae* D1.
62. *jurare* Π. *narrare* vulg. Cf. IX. 79.

58. Inter calamos errantia labra, 'lips straying over the reed-pipe.' Cf. IX. 39, and Claud. Epithal. Pall. et Celer. 36: *Maenaliosque modos et pastoralia labris Murmura tentabat relegens.*

59. Ah dolor. Cf. IV. 44.
Et, introducing an indignant question as in Ov. M. 13, 6, and often.

Post haec. This reading, found also in IX. 69, is preferable to the vulgate *post hoc.* 'After these great proofs of affection.'

Placuit tibi, 'found favour with you.'

Torrida vox, 'dry, hoarse, harsh, voice,' opposite to *liquidas voces* 'soft, clear notes,' Virg. G. 1, 410. *Aridus* is used of a dry crackling sound ib. 357: *aridus altis Montibus audiri fragor.* Cf. the Homeric αὖον ἀϋτεῖν, Il. 13,

160, and elsewhere. Cf. VI. 23.
The expression here may be due to a misapprehension of Theocr. 7, 37 ; Καὶ γὰρ ἐγὼ Μοισᾶν καπυρὸν στόμα, κἠμὲ λέγοντι Πάντες ἀοιδὸν ἄριστον. Καπυρόν, properly 'dried,' 'parched,' in this passage means 'loud,' 'clear-sounding,' and is a term of approbation.

60. Carmen iners, 'spiritless song.' Cf. Hor. A. P. 445 : *Vir bonus et prudens versus reprehendet inertes.*

Acerbae stridor avenae. Cf. Sidney's Arcadia 10, 517 : 'Out, shreaking pipe, made of some witchèd tree.'

63 sq. : Certaverit, 'let him try to pasture as many kids as there are bulls of mine counted at eventide.' For the counting of the flocks, see Virg. E. 3, 34 ; 6, 85.

Quam numerosa meis siccetur bucula mulctris,
Et quam multa suos suspendat ad ubera natos.
Sed mihi nec gracilis sine te fiscella salicto
Texitur, et nullo tremuere coagula lacte.
Quod si dura times etiam nunc verbera, Phylli,   70
Tradimus ecce manus : licet illae et vimine torto
Scilicet et lenta post tergum vite domentur,
Ut mala nocturni religavit brachia Mopsi
Tityrus, et furem medio suspendit ovili.
Accipe, ne dubites, meruit manus utraque poenas.   75

---

67. *suas. natas* D4. R2.   Ulit. c. *ab ubere.*
68. *gracili* d2.pβa2.sgf2., which Glaes. thinks is perhaps the true reading.
69. *nullo* ΠPdι.2.π.   *nulla* VD4.GRι.2.rapfι.βa2.tf2.boψ Beck. *lacte* Ππ.   *lactis* PVD4.Rι.2.rd2.apfι. βa2.tf2.boψ Beck. Burm. c. *molli, mundo, puro, multo t. c. lacte* or *nullo t. c. fisco, nulla t. c. cista, corbe* or *Texta nec in calathis t. c. lactis.*   Glaes. c. *nulla t. c. lacte.*   Wernsd., in his Addenda, approves of *nulla tremuere coagula lactis,* the last syllable of *nulla* being lengthened by the caesura and the two following consonants.
71. Haupt says *et* is omitted in Dι. Π. Glaes. says it is omitted also in PVD4.Rι.2.rpfι.ad2.a2.sf2.bo.
72. Werns. quotes *Si licet* from Doru. (by which Glaeser thinks he means D4). Heins. c. *Quin licet.* Burm. c. *Si libet.*
73. *Vi mala* R2. pfι. v.   Glaes. c. *ut male.*
74. *furem medio* Dι.   *medio furem* vulg.
75. *dubites* Dι.   *dubita* vulg.

---

66. 'You know how many heifers are milked into my pails.'
This use of *numerosus* is post-Augustan ; in earlier times it meant ' rhythmical.'
67. Multa sc. *bucula.*
68. Cf. Virg. E. 10, 71 : *Dum sedet et gracili fiscellam texit hibisco ;* and VIII. 1. Theocr. 11, 73 : αἴκ᾽ ἐνθὼν ταλάρως τε πλέκοις.
71. Tradimus . . . manus. Cf. line 37.
Et. Haupt says this word is not found in the Neapolitan and Paris MSS.

Vimine torto, 'twisted withes.'
Lenta . . . vite, 'pliant, tough, vine twigs.'
73. Mala, ' thievish.' Cf. Tib. 3, 5, 20 : *Quid fraudare juvat vitem crescentibus uvis ? Et modo nata mala vellere poma manu ?*
Nocturni, 'who steals by night.' Cf. Hor. S. 1, 3, 117 : *qui nocturnus divum sacra legerit.* Lycidas takes pleasure in telling of the disreputable adventure of his rival.
75. Accipe: sc. *manus.*

His tamen, his isdem manibus tibi saepe palumbes,
Saepe etiam leporem, decepta matre, paventem
Misimus in gremium ; per me tibi lilia prima
Contigerunt, primaeque rosae : vixdum bene florem
Degustabat apis, tu cingebare coronis.   80
Aurea sed forsan mendax tibi munera iactat,
Qui metere occidua ferales nocte lupinos
Dicitur, et cocto pensare legumine panem :
Qui sibi tunc felix, tunc fortunatus habetur,

76. *his idem* P. *his inquam* ad1.2.pf1.2.vβa2.boπ Barth. Ulit.
77. This line is omitted in D4.R2.
78. *in gremium* d1.2.aboπ. *gremio* Π. *misimus in gremio*
HPVD4.GR2.rpβa2.sf2. *misimus, in gremio per* f1.va1.ψ. *primo* d2.
79. *Contigerant* vulg. Burm. c. *Contigerunt.*
80. Heins. c. *Degustarat.*
81. *iactas* D1. m. prim.
82. Barth. gives *falce.*
83. *et tecto* D1. Glaes. c. *et secto.* *legumina* and *pane* are found
in VGR1.raβbod2.

76. Cf. the presents offered to
Galatea by Polyphemus, Ov. M.
13, 831 sq.
77. **Paventem** 'timid,' 'frigh-
tened.'
78. **Misimus in gremium,**
'threw into your lap.'
Prima, 'earliest,' and there-
fore most valued. Cf. Mart. 4,
28, 4.
79. **Contigerunt tibi,** 'you
had the good luck to get.' The
short penult -*ĕrunt* is found ap-
parently first in Lucretius, oc-
casionally in Virgil and Horace,
e. g. *annuĕrunt, dedĕrunt, stetĕ-
runt*, and often in Ovid.
Vixdum bene, &c., 'scarcely
had the bee well sipped of the
flower before you were wreathed
with chaplets.'
82. **Occidua . . . nocte,** 'when
night is far spent, is waning,' i. e.

just before dawn when the silence
is greatest. Cf. Stat. Theb. 3,
33 sq. : *Ecce sub occiduas versae
jam noctis habenas, Astrorumque
obitus, ubi primum maxima
Tethys Impulit Eoo cunctantem
Hyperiona ponto,* &c.
Ferales . . . lupinos. Cf.
Virg. G. 1, 75 : *tristis lupinus,*
where, however, *tristis* probably
means 'bitter.' Lupines were
served at funeral banquets to the
dead and were often carried off by
the very poor. See Tib. 1, 5, 53 :
*Ipsa fame stimulante furens her-
basque sepulchris Quaerat,* &c.
They were principally used as
food for cattle like the 'husks
which the swine did eat.'
83. **Cocto,** &c., 'to make up
for want of bread by boiled vege-
tables.' Cf. IV. 141 ; *nolit pensare
palatia coelo,* and V. III.

Vilia cum subigit manualibus hordea saxis.　　　　85
Quod si turpis amor precibus, quod abominor, istis
Obstiterit, laqueum miseri nectemus ab illa
Ilice, quae nostros primum violavit amores.
Hi tamen ante mala figentur in arbore versus :
Credere, pastores, levibus nolite puellis ;　　　　90
Phyllida Mopsus amat, Lycidan habet ultima rerum.

85. Scaliger c. *hordea sulcis.*
86. *cujus* for *turpis* H. *quae abominor* D1. *quod abominor* vulg.
quae can hardly be right. Perhaps the meaning of *abominor* was mis-
understood, and *quas* read, referring to *precibus.* As *quas* would not
scan, *quae* might have been substituted in an attempt to patch up the
metre.
87. *innectemus* VGD2.3.4.rabo.
88. *nostros primum* D1. H. *primum nostros* vulg.
89. *Hic* Hg. *Ni* D3. *fingentur* PR2. Heins. c. *signentur.*
91. Tit. and Barth. c. *Mopsus habet.* Mod. c. *Mopsum Phyllis
amat. Lycidan habet* D1. *Lycidas habet* vulg. Barth. c. *Lycidas
amat.* Heins. c. *Lycidas obit.* See Notes 2.

85. 'When he grinds cheap
barley with a hand-mill.' A two-
fold reproach : he uses inferior
grain to make bread, and grinds
it with his own hand like a slave.
For **subigit saxo**, cf. Manil,
5, 281 : *subdere fracturo silici
frumenta.* Such hand-mills were
called *molae manuariae.*
Hordea. Plural as in Virg.
E. 5, 36, and G. 1, 210. Servius
says the poet Bavius ridiculed this
use in the words : *Hordea qui
dixit superest ut tritica dicat.*
Quint, 1, 5, 16 : *scala et scopa con-
traque hordea et mulsa, non alio
vitiosa sunt, quam quod pluralia
singulariter, et singularia plura-
liter efferuntur.* Pliny 18, 7, 10,
56, uses the plural, perhaps owing
to the example of Virgil.
86. Quod abominor, 'which
may God avert.' A common ex-
pression for deprecating anything
as an ill omen, e.g. Ov. P. 3, 1, 105.

87. Cf. Theocr. 3, 9 : ἀπάγξασ-
θαί με ποιησεῖς. Virg. E. 2, 7 :
mori me denique coges.
88. Ilice. See line 27. The
oak was the cause of the quarrel,
as having been the trysting-place
of the new lover.
89. Ante : sc. *quam nectemus
laqueum.*
Mala, 'ill-omened, accursed.'
Cf. *arbor infelix,* and *mala crux.*
90. Levibus, 'fickle.'
91. Ultima rerum : If the
reading of the Neapolitan MS.
given in the text be adopted
ultima is nom. sing., and is to be
explained from Hor. Ep. 1, 16,
79 : *mors ultima linea rerum est.*
It is, however, perhaps better to
read *Lycidas* and regard *ultima*
as neut. pl. **Habet ultima rerum**
is a modification of the common
gladiatorial expression *hoc habet.*
'Lycidas has received the fatal
thrust.' *Rerum* adds emphasis to

Nunc age, si quidquam miseris succurris, Iolla,
Perfer, et exora modulato Phyllida cantu.
Ipse procul stabo, vel acuta carice tectus,
Vel propius latitans vicina saepe sub horti.   95
I. Ibimus : et veniet, nisi me praesagia fallunt.
Nam bonus a dextra fecit mihi Tityrus omen,
Qui venit inventa non irritus ecce iuvenca.

93. *Praefer* G. *Profer* Pbo. *Perfert* (omitting *et*) d1.2. *Pestifer
ore suo modulator Phyllida* D4. *et ore tuo modulabor* pβ. *Postifer
ore tuo modulabor phillida* R2. *ore tuo modulator Ph. nanque* d1.2.
(in the latter with the additions *exora* and *cantu*, and correction *modu-
lato*).
95. *ut* is omitted in PVGD2.3.R1.2.rd2.apf1.2.βa2.bo. *ut saepe*
π rell. *sub ora* d1.2. (in the latter *ara* is added). *sub orti* D1.
Π, whence Glaes., after Oudendorp, c. *vicina* or *vicini sepe sub
horti.* Ulit. c. *vicina sepe sub aram* or *vicinae sepibus arae.* Kempfer
c. *sub aram.* Haupt says D1. Π give *vicina saepe sub orti* (without
ut).
96. *venies* PVGD2.3.ΠR1.2.rd2. Glaes. c. *Ibimus : eveniet.*
97. *dextra* GR1.raβf1.2.va1.boπd2. *dextro* D3. 4. vulg. Ulit.
c. *en dextrum.* See Notes 2.
98. *venit* D1.2.3.4. HΠR1.2.rad2. *redit* vulg.

the superlative, and does not affect
the gender of the adj. as in Hor.
S. 1, 9, 4; *dulcissime rerum*, and
often.
For *ultima* = final event, the
end, cf. Cic. Fam. 7, 17, 2 : *per-
ferto et ultima exspectato.*
93. Perfer, sc. *carmen meum.*
Exora, 'appease, prevail upon.'
Cf. Ov. Trist. 2, 22 : *exorant
magnos carmina saepe deos.*
Modulato cantu, 'harmonious
singing.'
94. Carice, 'sedge.' Cf. Virg.
E. 3, 20 : *tu post carecta latebis.*
Priap. 87, 2 : *villulamque palus-
trem, Tectam vimine junceo cari-
cisque maniplis.*
95. ' Or lurking nearer, under
the neighbouring hedge of the
garden.' The text gives Haupt's
reading, which follows the Nea-
politan and Paris MSS. Werns-

dorf follows the vulgate *vicina, ut
saepe, sub ara,* and thinks the re-
ference is to a mound of turf used
either as a boundary mark or as
an altar.
96. Veniet. See line 53.
97. Bonus, ' honest, trusty,'
opposed to *malus* line 73.
He augurs the return of Lycidas'
mistress from the return of the
heifer, perhaps with a play on
juvenca and *juvencus* being ap-
plied to human beings as well as
to cattle.
A dextra. These words pre-
sent a difficulty as Tityrus had
gone off to the left (laevus), see
line 19. Perhaps Ulit. is right in
conjecturing *en dextrum* agreeing
with *omen. Dextrum* would be
written DEXTR$\overline{\text{V}}$ whence DEX-
TRA or DEXTRO might easily
arise.

ECLOGA QUARTA.

MELIBOEUS, CORYDON, AMYNTAS.

THIS Eclogue, entitled *Caesar*, is devoted to the praises of the
Emperor, which are sung in amoebaean strains by Corydon and Amyn-
tas in presence of their patron Meliboeus. The extravagant adulation
of the latter part of the poem is too common in the writers of the
empire to interfere with the reader's enjoyment of its many beauties.
The long and irrelevant introduction is more justly to be censured
from an artistic point of view, but may well be excused, on account of
its biographical interest.

As to the name of the Emperor whose praises are sung, and as to
the patron referred to under the name of Meliboeus, see Introduction,
pages 2 sq. and 12.

Meliboeus finds Corydon composing a strain in honour of the Em-
peror, and twits him with having formerly advised his brother, Amyntas,
to abandon the poetic art. This gives Corydon an opportunity for
describing his early life and acknowledging his obligations to the
patronage of Meliboeus. They are then joined by Amyntas, and the
brothers sing how the Emperor has conferred peace, happiness, and
prosperity on the world. Meliboeus having expressed approval of
their song, is requested to convey it to the ears of the Emperor, and
the poem is concluded in the orthodox way by the approach of evening
and an admonition to water the flocks.

M. Quid tacitus, Corydon, vultuque subinde minaci,
Quidve sub hac platano, quam garrulus adstrepit humor,
Infesta statione sedes? iuvat humida forsan
Ripa, levatque diem vicini spiritus amnis?
C. Carmina iamdudum, non quae nemorale resultent,   5

Interlocutores sunt Corydon et Meliboeus amici pastores Vra. Inscribed *Caesar* in f1.π rell.
2. *qua* f2. *cui* bo. *obstrepit* f1.va1.ta.
3. *Inseta* D1.2.3. *Insecta* GR2.r. *In secta* R1. *Intecta* d2. *Infecta* PV. *Iniecta* D4. Heins. c. *Insueta,* which Glaes. thinks may be the true reading. Salmas. c. *In festa.* Burm. c. *In certa* or *lecta.* *statio esedes* R1. *statice pedes* P. *iuva h. formâ* R2. *formam* D4.
4. *levatve* Barth.

1. **Tacitus . . . vultuque subinde minaci,** 'in deep meditation, and with an expression that from time to time bodes something.'
Tacitus. Cf. Hor. S. 1, 3, 65: *ut forte legentem Aut tacitum impellat.*
Subinde has two meanings— 1°, 'just after,' ' thereupon,' e.g. Hor. Ep. 1, 8, 15 : *primum gaudere, subinde Praeceptum auriculis hoc instillare memento;* 2°,'from time to time,' 'now and then,' e.g. Suet. Calig. 30 ; *tragicum illud subinde jactabat ; Oderint dum metuant.* The second meaning seems most appropriate here ; Corydon seems every now and then to be on the point of speaking.
Minaci. Cf. ἀπειλεῖν, ' to promise boastfully,' and also Hor. S. 2, 3, 9 : *Atqui vultus erat multa et praeclara minantis.*
2. **Quam garrulus,** &c., 'against which the prattling water purls.'
Adstrepit with acc., as in Plin. Pan. 26, 2 : *irritis precibus surdas principis aures adstrepebant,* where, however, Keil reads

obstrepebant. It usually takes a dat., e.g. Auson. Mosel. 167 : *adstrepit ollis Et rupes et silva tremens et concavus amnis.* The word sometimes means ' to applaud,' e. g. Tac. A. 11, 17 : *adstrepebat huic alacre vulgus.*
3. **Infesta,** ' unfavourable' to meditation, on account of the noise of the stream. The Neap. MS., however, reads *inseta,* whence Heinsius conjectures *insueta.*
Statione sedes. For the phrase cf. Plin. Ep. 1, 13, 2 : *plerique in stationibus sedent tempusque audiendis fabulis conterunt.*
4. **Levatque,** &c., ' and does the breeze from the neighbouring river assuage the noon-tide heat ?' *Dies* is used for ' the heat of the day,' as elsewhere for ' the *light* of the day.' Cf. Ov. M. 7, 411 : *contraque diem radiosque micantes Obliquantem oculos.*
5 sq. 'I have long since been pondering verses, not such as ring of the grove, but in which the golden age might be celebrated.' Cf. l. 29.
Nemorale resultent. This use of the accusative is found not

Volvimus, o Meliboee, sed haec, quibus aurea possint
Saecula cantari, quibus et deus ipse canatur,
Qui populos urbemque regit pacemque togatam.
M. Dulce quidem resonas, nec te diversus Apollo
Despicit, o iuvenis, sed magnae numina Romae   10
Non ita cantari debent, ut ovile Menalcae.
C. Quidquid id est, silvestre licet videatur acutis

8. *urbemque* D4.R2.d2.p. rell. *urbesque* Gf1.va1. π Barth. Ulit.
urbisque VR1.rabod2. *rogatam* P. Ulit. c. *orbemque regit plebem-*
que togatam.
   10. *Respicit* πGD2.3.R1.2.rd1.2.boπ, which makes good sense :
'nor does Apollo look on you with unfriendly glance.' Burm. c.
Respuit. munera VGR1.2.rd2.apf1.βa2.f2.boψ. Tit. c. *moenia.*
   12. *inest* pβf1.a2.f2. *quidque quod idem silvestre* D1. π ends with
this line.

only with the neuter of adjectives
but also with substantives. Cf.
Virg. A. 6, 50: *Nec mortale sonans.*
Ib. 1, 328 : *nec vox hominem sonat.*
   7. Deus ipse. The Emperor
Nero. Cf. 1. 46, and see Intro-
duction, page 2 sq.
   8. Pacemque togatam. The
toga was the garb of peace, the
sagum of war, hence *saga su-*
mere, 'to prepare for war.' The
sagum was assumed as a symbol
of preparation for war, even by
those who were not going to the
field. The *paludamentum* was 'a
general's cloak.'
   Wernsdorf and Adelung con-
sider *pacem togatam* equivalent to
pacem Romanam, and quote Virg.
A. 1, 282 : *Romanos . . . gen-*
temque togatam, which passage,
however, would equally support
the other explanation : 'the race
that wears the toga,' and 'peace
that wears the toga.' Their ex-
planation derives more support
from Stat. Silv. 2, 7, 52 sq.: *Tu*
carus Latio, memorque gentis
Carmen fortior exseres togatum.

   9. Diversus, 'hostile,' 'in-
imical,' like *aversus.* Cf. Tac. A.
13, 57 : *victores diversam aciem*
(the hostile army) *Marti ac Mer-*
curio sacravere.
   10. Numina. That the plural
does not necessarily imply more
than one person, and that there-
fore it cannot be argued from this
passage, that the Eclogue refers
to Carinus and Numerianus ap-
pears from VII. 80 and 83, where
he describes *mea numina* as being
a single individual.
   11. i. e. the praises of Caesar
should not be sung in the pastoral
style, but in the loftier heroic verse.
Menalcas is a shepherd mentioned
in Virg. E. 2, 15, and 5, 4.
   12 sq. Silvestre, &c., 'it may
appear boorish to critical ears,
and worthy of mention only in
my own village.' *Acutus* is op-
posed to rusticity also in Hor.
Sat. 1, 3, 29 : *Iracundior est*
paulo? Minus aptus acutis Nari-
bus horum hominum? Rideri
possit eo quod Rusticius tonso
toga defluit?

Auribus, et nostro tantum memorabile pago :
Dum mea rusticitas, si non valet arte polita
Carminis, at certe valeat pietate probari.   15
Rupe sub hac eadem, quam proxima pinus obumbrat,
Haec eadem nobis frater meditatur Amyntas,
Quem vicina meis natalibus admovet aetas.
M. Iam puerum calamos et odorae vincula cerae
Iungere non cohibes, levibus quem saepe cicutis   20

14. *Nunc mea* D1. Barth. c. *Tum mea.* Burm. c. *arte politi.* *non* *si* D4.
15. *valet* aψ.
16. *sub hec* R2. Glaes. c. *sub haec eadem.*
17. *Hec* R1.2. Gud. c. *Hac eadem.* *meditatur* f1.vaI.π, and apparently D1.3.4. *meditatus* D2. rell. libri.
18. Barth. c. *vicena meis natalibus amovet aestas.* Heins. c. *bis dena meis natalibus admovet aestas* or *vix una meis natalibus amovet aestas.* Gronov. c. *vicina m. n. admonet aestas.* Burm. gives *vicena m. n. admovet aestas.*
19. *calamos odoratae* V. *odoratae* being probably introduced from a marginal gloss and *et* omitted in an attempt to make the line scan, despite the long second syllable.
20. *non* D1. All other MSS. give *nunc.* A MS. of Tit. gives *nunc cogis.* Tit. also mentions a reading *tunc cohibet.* Heins. c. *tun' coges.* Burm. approves *cohibes* or *prohibes.*

14. **Dum,** 'provided that.'
Mea rusticitas, 'my clownishness,' opposed to *cultus* in Ov. A. A. 3, 128.
15. **Pietate,** 'loyalty.'
17. **Eadem nobis** = *eadem nobiscum,* a Grecism found also in Ov. M. 13, 50: *Et nunc ille eadem nobis juratus in arma.*
Frater. In 1. Corydon's brother is Ornitus. Perhaps *frater* may be merely a term of intimacy, 'my brother shepherd.' See Hor. Ep. 1, 6, 54 : *frater, pater, adde : Ut cuique est aetas, ita quemque facetus adopta.* In 1. 4, however, the meaning is perhaps limited by the word *pater.*
Meditatur. The regular word for 'composing.' Cf. Virg. E.

1, 2 : *Silvestrem tenui Musam meditaris avena.* Hor. S. 1, 9, 2 : *Nescio quid meditans nugarum et totus in illis.*
18. The reading of the text seems the true one. It has been variously altered, on account of its supposed inconsistency with *fronte paterna* in line 21. Those words, however, denote the gravity and dignity of Corydon's expression, not his advanced age. Cf. Virg. A. 9, 275 : *te vero, mea quem spatiis propioribus aetas Insequitur.*
20. **Jungere non cohibes,** 'do you not prevent him joining,' &c. This reading, with a note of interrogation at the end of line 21, gives a suitable sense, and the in-

Ludere conantem vetuisti fronte paterna ?
Dicentem, Corydon, te non semel ista notavi :
Frange, puer, calamos, et inanes desere Musas ;
I, potius glandes rubicundaque collige corna,
Duc ad mulctra greges, et lac venale per urbem   25
Non tacitus porta.   Quid enim tibi fistula reddet
Quo tutere famem ? certe mea carmina nemo

21. *cantantem* P.   Tit. on VIII. 12 (which compare) mentions a
reading *voce paterna.*
22. *non te* VGD4.R1.2.rabo.
23. *et manes* R2.   *collige* for *desere* d1., probably from next line.
24. *I potius* D1.   *Et potius* vulg.   *Et procul* G.
25. *Duc multum greges ad et lac* D1.
27. *tutare* D3.   *tacere* D2.   *taceare* VGR1.r.   *tueare* d2.   Heins.
c. *solere.*   *nemo mea carmina nemo* D4.

finitive after *cohibere,* though rare,
may be justified by Cic. Tusc. 3,
25, 60 : *nam et necessitas ferendae
conditionis humanae quasi cum
deo pugnare cohibet admonetque
esse hominem,* where Kühner con-
siders *cohibet,* not *prohibet,* to be
the true reading.

If, following Wernsdorf and
the majority of the MSS. and edi-
tions, we read *nunc* instead of
non and place a full stop at the
end of line 21, *cohibes* will mean
'permit,' which signification, the
opposite of that in the classical
age, Wernsdorf says is found in
later writers. Cf. Du Cange's
Lexicon sub. voc.

In an Excursus on this passage
Wernsdorf conjectures *jungere
connives,* which, owing to a cor-
rupt pronunciation, he thinks was
written *cohibes,* and the *nunc,*
which is quite out of place, in-
serted to make up the syllable
apparently deficient.   He does
not, however, give any example of
conniveo with an infinitive.

23. Inanes, 'empty-handed,'

'needy,' 'poverty-stricken.' Cf.
Plaut. Most. 3, 1, 44 : *hic homo
est inanis,* 'without money.'

Tenuis is found in the same
sense, Cic. Inv. 1, 25, 35 : *servus
sit an liber, pecuniosus an tenuis.*
For the small remuneration of lite-
rary work cf. Juv. 7, 27, &c. :
*frange miser calamos, vigilataque
proelia dele,* &c.   Martial 9, 74,
9 sq. : *Frange leves calamos, et
scinde, Thalia, libellos Si dare
sutori calceus ista potest.*

26. Non tacitus. An allusion
to similar street cries is found in
Plin. 15, 19, 21, 83 : *Ex hoc genere
sunt, ut diximus, cottana et cari-
cae quaeque conscendenti navem
adversus Parthos omen fecere M.
Crasso, venales praedicantis voce,
cauneae.*

27. Tutere, 'ward off,' 'avert.'
Cf. Cic. B. C. 1, 52 : *ipse prae-
sentem inopiam quibus poterat
subsidiis tutabatur,* and VI. 70,
where the vulgate reading is *tu-
tabimur,* instead of *mutabimus.*
The usual meaning is 'to protect,'
'defend.'

Praeter ab his scopulis ventosa remurmurat Echo.
C. Haec ego, confiteor, dixi, Meliboee, sed olim :
Non eadem nobis sunt tempora, non deus idem. 30
Spes magis arridet : certe ne fraga rubosque
Colligerem, viridique famem solarer hibisco,
Tu facis, et tua nos alit indulgentia farre.
Tu nostras miseratus opes docilemque iuventam,
Hiberna prohibes ieiunia solvere fago. 35

28. *Praeterquam his* π.
30. *nunc* for *sunt* ψt.
32. *solaret* D1. *iam me solarer* Tit.
34. *Tu nostri* ψ. Barth. c. *tu nostri miseratus ope es. miseratus
op . . . . docilemque* D1.
35. *pellere* VGD.2.3.4.R.1.2.rd1.2.abo.

28. **Praeter** = *praeterquam,
nisi.* Similarly *quam* is omitted
after *plus* in Virg. G. 4, 207: *neque
enim plus septuma ducitur aestas.*
Ventosa . . . echo. Auson.
Epigr. 11, 3, calls echo *aëris et
linguae filia.*
Remurmurat, probably, as
Wernsdorf says, with a play on
remunerat : 'no one rewards my
verses save Echo, child of the wind,
with its responsive whispers.'
Munerare is found IV. 57.
29. **Sed olim,** ' but that was
long since.' Nous avons changé
tout cela.
Compare the well-known *Dic-
tum Lotharii I.* in Matth. Bor-
bonius : *Omnia mutantur, nos et
mutamur in illis ; Illa vices quas-
dam res habet, illa vices.*
These lines are usually quoted
with *tempora,* instead of *omnia.*
This passage of Calpurnius evi-
dently refers to the accession of
an emperor who patronised poetry,
while his predecessor neglected
it. See Introd., page 18.
Non deus idem, 'our god, i.e.
emperor, is changed.' Cf. Virg.
E. 1, 6.

31 sq. Cf. III. 82 sq., where
Mopsus is said to support life in
this miserable manner.
Rubos, ' bramble-bushes ' used
for the berries that grew on them,
called *mora,* ' blackberries.' See
Ov. M. 1, 105 : *in duris haerentia
mora rubetis.*
Hibisco. Commonly supposed
to be the marsh-mallow, but
Pliny, 20, 4, 14, 29, says it is like
a parsnip. In Virg. E. 2, 30,
some think a rod made of the
shrub *hibiscum* is meant, and ib.
10, 71, we find it was suitable for
making baskets.
33. **Farre.** From which the
best bread was made, and not from
hordeum. See note on III. 85.
34. **Nostras opes,** exiguas sci-
licet et inopiam potius. Werns-
dorf. Cf. Cic. Quint. 1, 2 : *tenues
opes.*
35. 'You prevent me from hav-
ing to satisfy my hunger with
beech-nuts in winter.' **Fagus**
used for beech-nuts as *rubos* above
for the berries of the blackberry
bush. Cf. Virg. G. 1, 159 : *Con-
cussaque famem in silvis solabere
quercu.*

H

Ecce nihil querulum per te, Meliboee, sonamus ;
Per te secura saturi recubamus in umbra,
Et fruimur silvis Amaryllidos, ultima nuper
Littora terrarum, nisi tu, Meliboee, fuisses,
Ultima visuri, trucibusque obnoxia Mauris   40
Pascua Geryonis, liquidis ubi cursibus ingens
Dicitur occiduas impellere Baetis arenas.

37. *Satyri* R1.   *satyri* VG4.r.
40. *visurus* d1.o. *visura* H. *trucibus* (*que* omitted) VD1.4.R1.2.rboψ.
Barth. c. *trucibus qua*. Haupt c. the whole line ran thus, *Visuri
trucibus tristes obnoxia Mauris.*
41. *Geryonis* D1.   *germanis* D3.R2.   *germani* VGD2.R1.rad1.2.
Germanus D4.
42. *Bexis* D1.   Lines 43–49 are omitted in D2.

36. 'Lo! it is owing to you,
Meliboeus, that I utter no note of
complaint.'

38. Silvis Amaryllidos, com-
monly explained 'the woods in
the neighbourhood of Rome,' and
thought by Wernsdorf to allude
to some position of honour or
emolument held by the poet at
Rome, Amaryllis being supposed
to represent Rome, in accordance
with the hypothesis of La Cerda
and others, who think that Ama-
ryllis and Galatea, in Virg. E. 1,
denote respectively Rome and
Mantua. The theory, however,
is improbable, and Virgil seems
merely to have adopted the names
used by Theocritus. It is better,
therefore, to follow Adelung, who
thinks that Amaryllis was a shep-
herdess of Corydon's acquaint-
ance.

38–40. Haupt points out two
objections to these lines : firstly,
we should expect this order of the
words *ultima nuper ultima terra-
rum . . . Littora visuri:* secondly,
an elision is seldom found in Cal-

purnius, save in the first foot, and
therefore *trucibusque* is doubtful.
Now the Neapolitan MS. omits
que, and Haupt therefore suggests
that lines 38 and 39 should stand
as in the vulgate, and that line 40
should be : *Visuri trucibus tristes
obnoxia Mauris.*

Obnoxia, &c., 'exposed to
the Moors,' on account of the
nearness of Spain to Africa. Cf.
Sall. Cat. 48 : *plerique Crasso ex
negotiis privatis obnoxii*, 'under
obligations to Crassus.'

41. Geryon is called *pastor
Iberus* by Martial 5, 65, 11. He
was a mythic king of Spain, with
three bodies. Hercules carried
off his oxen.

42. ' The Guadalquiver is said
to strike upon the western sands,'
i. e. flow into the western sea.
Cf. Lucan 5, 437 : *Cum glacie
retinente fretum non impulit
Ister.*

Dicitur. This word is appro-
priate in the lips of a countryman
who knew about distant coun-
tries only by report.

Scilicet extremo nunc vilis in orbe iacerem,
Ah dolor, et pecudes inter conductus Iberas
Irrita septena modularer sibila canna : 45
Nec quisquam nostras inter dumeta Camoenas
Respiceret : non ipse daret mihi forsitan aurem,
Ipse deus vacuam, longeque sonantia vota
Scilicet extremo non exaudiret in orbe.
Sed nisi forte tuas melior sonus avocat aures, 50
Et nostris aliena magis tibi carmina rident,
Vis, hodierna tua subigatur pagina lima ?

49. *exaudirer* R2. Burm. c. *nunc exaudiret.* Glaes. c. *ab orbe.*
50. *advocat* D1.Gabo. *avocat* VR1.r.
51. *Est nostris* b. *aliena magua tibi* D1. Mod. cites a reading
pagina ridet.
52. *Vix* R2.a. *hodierna* R1.2.raf1.va1.πd2. *aliena* d2.pβa2.sgf2.bo.
sbiagatur R2. *subigat vir* pa2.

43. Scilicet, 'doubtless.'
Vilis jacerem, 'I would lie
neglected and in no esteem.' Cf.
Ov. P. 1, 3, 49 : *Orbis in extremi
jaceo desertus arenis.*
44. Ah dolor. Cf. III. 59.
Conductus, 'as a hireling.'
45. Septena . . . canna = *sep-
tem cannis.* Cf. Ov. M. 2, 682 :
dispar septenis fistula cannis.
Sibila, of an unskilful perform-
ance on the pipe as in X. 10.
**46. Nostras inter dumeta
Camoenas,** ' my wood - land
strains.'
49. Scilicet extremo. On ac-
count of these words occurring
also in line 43, D2. has omitted
lines 43–49, either because the
repetition was considered to show
that the passage was spurious or
because the similar commence-
ments of lines 43 and 49 led the
copyist to overlook the interven-
ing lines.
Exaudiret. Used of hearing

from a distance or with diffi-
culty.
50. Melior sonus, 'sweeter
sounds.' Cf. Hor. Ep. 1, 2, 5:
nisi quid te detinet, audi.
51. Aliena . . . carmina, ' the
poems of others.'
Rident, 'are pleasing, attrac-
tive.' Cf. Hor. C. 2, 6, 14: *Ille
terrarum mihi praeter omnes
Angulus ridet. Arridere* is used
in the same sense.
52. 'Are you willing that the
page we compose to-day should
be corrected by your file ?' Cf.
Mart. 10, 2, 3 : *Nota leges quae-
dam, sed lima rasa recenti.* Ov.
P. 1, 5, 19 sq. : *Scilicet incipiam
lima mordacius uti, Et sub judi-
cium singula verba vocem ? Su-
bigo* is here used figuratively. It
is used of 'whetting' in the literal
sense in Virg. A. 7, 627 : *subigunt
in cote secures.* For **pagina** cf. 1.
20, and Culex 26 : *Triste Jovis
Coeique canit non pagina bellum.*

H 2

Nam tibi non tantum venturos discere nimbos,
Agricolis qualemque ferat sol aureus ortum,
Attribuere dei, sed dulcia carmina saepe   55
Concinis, et modo te Baccheis Musa corymbis
Munerat, et lauro modo pulcher obumbrat Apollo.
Quod si tu faveas trepido mihi, forsitan illos
Experiar calamos, here quos mihi doctus Iollas
Donavit, dixitque : Truces haec fistula tauros   60
Conciliat, nostroque sonat dulcissima Fauno.
Tityrus hanc habuit, cecinit qui primus in istis

53. *non tantum v. discere ventos* in margin *ventos* (sic) D1.   *non
solum v. noscere nimbos* vulg.   *futuros noscere* VR1.r.
54. Werns. reads *nimbos Agricolis*.   *agricolae* D4.
56, 57. *Concinis et medio plus pulcher obumbrat* PVGR1.r.
59. *ductus* G.   *et heri quos* D2.3.4.R2.   *here quos electus Iolas* P.
62. *quos primus* D1.

53 sq. These lines are an ad-
ditional proof that Seneca is re-
ferred to under the name of
Meliboeus.   See Introd. page
12.
54. 'And what kind of sunrise
a golden sunset promises the hus-
bandman.' Wernsdorf, however,
comparing Virg. G. 1, 438, ex-
plains *ortum* of the rising of
storms.
56, 57. Two kinds of poetry,
tragic and lyric, are described in
these lines.   The ivy clusters were
sacred to Bacchus as the laurel to
Apollo.   See Ov. Trist. 1, 7, 2 :
*Deme meis hederas, Bacchica
serta, comis.*
58. 'But if you favour my timid
efforts.'   **Trepido.**   *Pavidus* is
similarly used to express the
nervousness felt in performing
before an audience, e. g. Virg. A.
5, 575 : *Excipiunt plausu pavi-
dos.*
59. **Iollas.**   This name is found

also in Virg. E. 2, 57 : 3, 76.
Corydon excuses his attempt to
imitate Virgil by showing that he
was acting on the advice of his
learned friend.   The same device
is found in Virg. E. 2, 36 sq. :
*Est mihi disparibus septem com-
pacta cicutis Fistula, Damoetas
dono mihi quam dedit olim, Et
dixit moriens : Te nunc habet
ista secundum.*   Ib. 6, 69 : *hos
tibi dant calamos, en accipe,
Musae, Ascraeo quos ante seni,
&c.*
61. So Amphion piped his
herds home, Virg. E. 2, 23 :
*canto quae solitus, si quando ar-
menta vocabat, Amphion, &c.*
62. **Tityrus,** i. e. Virgil, who
introduces himself under this title
in his first and sixth Eclogues.
The name is found in Theocritus,
and is probably the Doric form of
Σάτυρος.
Istis montibus, 'those moun-
tains of yours.'

QUARTA. 101

Montibus Hyblaea modulabile carmen avena.

M. Magna petis, Corydon, si Tityrus esse laboras :
Ille fuit vates sacer, et qui posset avena   65
Praesonuisse chelym, blandae cui saepe canenti
Allusere ferae, cui substitit advena quercus,
Quem modo cantantem rutilo spargebat acantho
Nais, et implicitos comebat pectine crines.
C. Est fateor, Meliboee, deus, sed nec mihi Phoebus   70

63. *modulamine* R1. *mulamine* D1.
64. *Agna petis* R2. the *M* being lost owing to its standing also for
Meliboeus at the beginning of the line.
66. *Praesonuisse* D1.ψ. The other MSS. give *Personuisse. blandae*
Vd1.2. Burm. *blande* rell.
69. Several MSS. give *comas* for *crines*, perhaps on account of the
preceding *comebat.*
70. *Et fat.* VGR1.r. *sed nunc* VGD4.R1.ra. *sed non* bo. *sed si*
a2.sgf2. *sed nec* R2.pd1.2.f1.π. Martell. c. *Est fateor, Meliboee :
deus sed si.*

63. Hyblaea, &c., 'a song
attuned to the Hyblaean pipe,'
i. e. the pipe of the Sicilian poet
Theocritus, who is referred to in
Virg. E. 10, 51 : *pastoris Siculi
modulabor avena.*
64. Magna petis, 'you aim
high.'
65. Vates sacer. Θεῖος ἀοιδός.
Poets were supposed to be in-
spired, and to be under the pro-
tection of Apollo. Cf. Hor. C.
4, 9, 28 : *Carent quia vate sacro.*
Avena praesonuisse chelym,
'with the reed-pipe surpass the
music of the lyre.' *Chelys,
chelym, chely,* are the only cases
which occur. It properly means
a tortoise like the pure Latin
testudo.
Praesono means 'to sound be-
fore,' in Ov. Am. 3, 13, 11 :
*Hinc ubi praesonuit sollenni tibia
cantu It per velatas annua pompa
vias.*

66 sq. Blandae, &c., 'and as
he sang wild beasts often fawned,
and sported near him.' *Alludo*
is found with accusative in XI. 10.
67. Cf. II. 15-20.
Cui substitit, &c., 'and the
oak, strange visitor, came and
stood by him.'
68. 'Whom but now as he
sang a Naid decked with the
ruddy acanthus.' Cf. Virg. E.
5, 6 : *Aspice ut antrum Silvestris
raris sparsit labrusca racemis.*
69. Combing the hair is often
used to express fondling, making
much of, e.g. Ov. M. 13, 735 :
id. Her. 13, 31.
70. i. e. Tityrus is, I admit, a
divine poet, but perchance Phoe-
bus will not be unfavourable to
me either. Wernsdorf compares
Cic. Orat. 1, 23 : *te in dicendo
semper putavi deum.* Cf. the
passage of Seneca quoted in note
on VII. 84.

Forsitan abnuerit ; tu tantum commodus audi :
Scimus enim, quam te non aspernetur Apollo.
M. Incipe, nam faveo, sed prospice, ne tibi forte
Tinnula tam fragili respiret fistula buxo,
Quam resonare solet, si quando laudat Alexim.   75
Hos potius calamos, magis hos sectare canales,
Et preme, qui dignas cecinerunt consule silvas.
Incipe, ne dubita. Venit en et frater Amyntas :
Cantibus iste tuis alterno succinet ore.

71. *annuerit* VGD4.R1.2.ra.   Mod. and Barth. correct *abnuerit*.
72. VR1.rabod2. prefix *Mel. Dicimus en quia te* VGR1.r.   *scimus enim quia te* R2.pf1.2.d2.aβa2.bo.   *quam te non aspernetur* vπ rell. *aspernatur* PR1.rβabo.   *non spernatur* f1.a1.
73. *respice* D4.
74. *Tumila* D2.3.   *nam* R1.   *tam* corr. ead.m.
75. *quam* d2.f1.π.   *Qua* VGR1.rad2.   *quae* D4.pβa2.f2.bo.   *Quo* PR2.
76. *Hoc p. c. m. hoc* pf1.2.βa2.   *Hospicius magis hos calamos sectare* D1.
77. *Et preme qui* D1.   *Per me* apβd2.a2.f2.boπ Barth. Ulit. Wernsd. Beck.   *Pro me* PVGD4.R1.rf1.va1.ψ Burm.   Burm. c. *Pro re qui. Per me* would mean 'meo hortatu et patrocinio,' *pro me* 'meo loco,' as v. 11, which would not suit the present passage.
78. *nec dubita* d2.pf1.2βa2.   *en* is omitted in D1.   *en quoque* bo.
79. This and the two following lines are omitted in PR1.

72. Quam te, &c., 'how far Apollo (i. e. the emperor) is from despising you.'
73 sq. If you imitate Virgil, do not take as your model his undignified love-song the Alexis, but the loftier strains of the Pollio.
74. Tinnula, 'tinkling, jingling.'
Fragili . . . buxo, 'frail, slender, box-wood,' emitting therefore a thin, feeble tone. Perhaps we may compare Tac. A. 14, 20 : *fractos sonos,* 'languishing, effeminate sounds.' *Fragilis* means 'crackling' in Lucr. 6, 112 : *fragiles sonitus chartarum,* and Virg. E. 8, 82 : *fragiles incende*

bitumine lauros.
Respiret. So Moore in his Melody on Music says : *Why should feeling ever speak, When thou canst* breathe *her soul so well ?*
75. Virgil celebrates the loves of Corydon and Alexis in his second Eclogue.
76. Canales, 'reed-pipe,' a meaning found, apparently, only in this passage.
77. Qui dignas, &c. The expression is borrowed from Virg. E. 4, 3 : *Si canimus silvas, silvae sint consule dignae,* 'if my verse be pastoral, still let it be worthy of a consul.'

Dicite, ne mora sit, vicibusque reducite carmen: 80
Tuque prior, Corydon, tu proximus ibis, Amynta.
C. Ab Iove principium, si quis canit aethera, sumat,
Si quis Atlantiaci molitur pondus Olympi:
At mihi, qui nostras praesenti numine terras
Perpetuamque regit iuvenili robore pacem,   85
Laetus et Augusto felix arrideat ore.
A. Me quoque facundo comitatus Apolline Caesar

80. Barth. c. *Ducite.* Friesem. c. the same or *redicite* for *reducite.*
nec mora D4.R2.d2.pβa2.f2.
82. *canat* D1.
83. Burm. c. *Atlantiacum molitur pondus, Olympum. pondus mo-
litur* D1. *molitur pondus* vulg.
84. *At nunc qui* PVGD2.3.4. R1.2.rabo.
85. *vivendi robore* VGR1. *partem* PD2.3.
87. *me* f1.π. *te* PGD2.3.R1.2.rad2.pβa2.f2.bo.

**80. Vicibusque reducite car-
men,** 'and in turns resume the
song,' i. e. sing in amoebean
strains. The same idea is ex-
pressed by *alterno ore* in line 79.
A similar use of *reducere* is found
in line 138: *Di . . . hunc juve-
nem . . . reducite,* i. e. receive
him back to yourselves. So in
the present passage 'take back
the song to yourselves in turn.'
There is doubtless a reference to
the common expression *ducere
carmen* (Ov. Tr. 1, 11, 18, and
elsewhere) = compose verses.
'And repeatedly in turn compose
verses.'
82. Cf. Virg. E. 3, 60: *Ab
Jove principium, Musae; Jovis
omnia plena.* Theocr. 17, 1:
ἐκ Διὸς ἀρχώμεσθα.
83. Atlantiaci Olympi, 'the
heaven borne by Atlas.'
Molitur: sc. *carmine,* 'attempts
to describe.'
84. Praesenti numine. Cf.
Hor. C. 3, 5, 2 : *praesens divus,*

opposed to the unseen gods of
heaven. The expression also
implies propitious power.
85. Regit . . . pacem. Cf.
line 8.
**86. Augusto . . . arrideat
ore,** 'smile upon me with his
imperial lips.' *Augustus* is here
an adjective, of or belonging to
Augustus, the surname given to
Octavius Caesar after he attained
to undivided authority, and after
him given to all the Roman
emperors, equivalent to Majesty
or Imperial Majesty.
87. Wernsdorf compares Stat.
Silv. 1. 14: *modo dexter Apollo,
Quique venit juncto mihi semper
Apolline Caesar Adnuat.* Haupt
is right in saying that this parallel
does not prove that Calpurnius
imitated Statius, which would
make the date of Calpurnius at
least as late as 90 or 95 A.D., in-
stead of the time of Nero; but he
is surely wrong in saying that
there is merely a verbal not a real

Respiciat, montes neu dedignetur adire,
Quos et Phoebus amat, quos Iuppiter ipse tuetur :
In quibus augustos visuraque saepe triumphos　　　90
Laurus fructificat, vicinaque nascitur arbos.

88. *amores* for *adire* D4. Burm. c. *amoenos.*
90. *visuraque* f1.π. *visuros* D2. *visurus* PGR1.2.rabod2. *visuris*
D3.d2.pβa2. *visuri* f2. Haupt approves of Ulitius' conjecture *visu-*
rae, but hesitates to accept the verb *fructificant,* which Ulit. gives in
the next line, and suggests *en fruticant* instead.
91. *fructificăt* p. *fructiferat* PGD2.4.R1.2.r. Barth. and Ulit.
c. *visurae s. tr. L. fructiferant.* Burm. c. *visurae s. tr. L fructificant,*
vicinaque libri omn. Barth. also c. *divinaque* or *et civica* (i. e. quer-
cus) or *unitaque* (de palma conjuge). Swarth. c. *vitisequa.* Ulit. also
c. *Erycinaque* (i. e. myrtus), or from Virg. E. 2, 54 explains *vicinaque*
of the myrtle. This last explanation Barth. also gives.

similarity between the passages.
On the contrary the resemblance
is rather in the meaning than in
the phraseology. The words used
are by no means very similar, but
both poets seem to have had the
common object of invoking divine
and imperial inspiration, an idea
which may have well occurred
independently to each.
88. Montes. Cf. II. 17.
89. Quos ipse, &c., ' of which
Jupiter himself is tutelary deity.'
90, 91. ' On which (mountains)
both the laurel blooms, destined
often to see imperial triumphs,
and its companion tree (i. e. the
oak) springs up.'
The rustic urges the emperor
to visit his upland haunts, on the
ground that they are loved by
Jupiter and Apollo, and are the
home of the laurel and oak, trees
which are the emblem and badge
of imperial distinction and vic-
tory.
Wernsdorf seems right in ex-
plaining **vicina arbos** of the oak.
He quotes Dion Cassius to show
that by a decree of the Senate

laurels were planted before the
palace of the emperor, and chap-
lets of oak-leaves hung on the
building with the inscription *Ob*
Cives Servatos. Ovid, Trist. 3, 1,
35 sq., says in reference to the
Palatine : *An Jovis haec, dixi,*
domus est ? Quod ut esse putarem
Augurium menti querna corona
dabat. Cujus ut accepi dominum,
Non fallimur, inquam, Et mag-
ni verum est hanc Jovis esse
domum. Cur tamen apposita
velatur janua lauro, Cingit et
augustas arbor opaca fores ? . . .
Causa, superpositae scripto testata
coronae, Servatos cives indicat
hujus ope. Adjice servatis unum,
pater optime, civem, Qui procul
extremo pulsus in orbe jacet. Cf.
Id. Fast. 4, 953 : *State Palatinae*
laurus, praetextaque quercu Stet
domus. Id. M. 1, 560 sq., it is
said of the laurel, *Tu ducibus*
Latiis aderis, cum laeta trium-
phum Vox canet et longas visent
Capitolia pompas. Postibus Au-
gustis eadem fidissima custos
Ante fores stabis, mediamque
tuebere quercum. Haupt objects

C. Ipse polos etiam qui temperat igne geluque,
Iuppiter ipse parens, cui tu iam proximus ipse,
Caesar, abes, posito paulisper fulmine saepe
Cressia rura petit, viridique reclinis in antro   95
Carmina Dictaeis audit Curetica silvis.
A. Aspicis, ut virides audito Caesare silvae

93. Heins. c. *ille parens. tam proximus* a, which Glaes. thinks is perhaps right. *proximus esse* D1.
94. Ulit. c. *abes. habes* GR1.r. *abis* alii omn. *ab his* a. *Caesar his pilis per fulmine* D1. Heins. c. *cui tu iam pr. ipsi Caesar agis.* Burm. and Gud. c. *Caesar ades.* Gud. also says *habes* may = *habitas.* Dorvill. c. *prox, esse, Caesar, aves.* Glaes. c. *proximus isse, Caesar, aves* or *tam proximus ecce, Caesar, abes.*
95. Heins. and Barth. c. *reclinis. reclivis* R2.f1.βboπ. *reclivus* D2.d2.a2.f2. *reclusus* PVGR1.rp. Burm. c. *refusus.*
96. *currentia* PVGR1.r.

to *visuraque* and prefers *visurae,* of course changing *fructificat* to the plural. The position of *que,* however, in *visuraque* may be defended by Virg. A. 5, 233 sq. : *Ni, palmas ponto tendens utrasque, Cloanthus Fudissetquepreces, divosque in vota vocasset.*

There is more justice in his objection to *fructificat,* which means 'to bear fruit,' not 'to sprout up.' He suggests *en fruticant.*

Barthius makes *vicina arbos* = *myrtus* quoting Virg. E. 2, 54 : *Et vos, o lauri, carpam, et te proxima myrte.* Wernsdorf, however, observes *vicina* and *proxima* have not the same meaning.

The allusion to city life, in referring to the trees before the palace, is not alien to bucolic poetry ; see the reference to the Palatine in line 159 and throughout VII.

93 sq. Cui tu, &c., ' to whom you yourself, Caesar, are already nearest.' Cf. Plaut. Aul. 2, 3, 8 :

nunc nobis prope abest (al. *adest*) *exitium.*

Jam, i. e. even before death.

Posito paulisper fulmine. Cf. Hor. C. 2, 10, 18 sq., where Apollo indulges in similar relaxation : *Quondam cithara tacentem Suscitat Musam, neque semper arcum Tendit Apollo.*

95. Cressia rura. Jupiter is said to have been brought up in Crete, where the Curetes, the most ancient inhabitants of the island, paid worship to him (as the Corybantes, who at a later period were identified with them, celebrated the worship of Cybele) with noisy music and armed dances.

96. Dicte, now Sethia, was a mountain in the eastern part of Crete, in a cave of which Jupiter was concealed from Saturn.

97 sq. Reverential silence is often mentioned as nature's tribute on the approach of a deity, and the emperor is here said to receive similar homage.

Conticeant ? memini, quamvis urgente procella,
Sic nemus immotis subito requiescere ramis,
Et dixi : deus hinc, certe deus expulit Euros :   100
Nec mora ; Pharsalae solverunt sibila cannae.
C. Aspicis, ut teneros subitus vigor excitet agnos ?
Utque superfuso magis ubera lacte graventur,
Et nuper tonsis exundent vellera foetis ?
Hoc ego iam, memini, semel hac in valle notavi,   105

99. *scit nemus* abo. *Scit deus* VGR1.r. *in montis* D2.
101. *Pharsaliae* libr. omn. except VGR1.r which have *Pharsalis*
= *Pharsales.* Glaes. gives *Pharsalae* from conjecture. Haupt approves
of the conjecture of Heins. *Parrhasiae.* Burm. c. *Moenaliae. solve-
runt* R1.2.bo, and omn. libr. except d2.pβa2.f2., in which *sonuerunt* is
found. *sonuernin* s. Heins. c. *sonuerunt.*
104. *Ut nuper* o. *tonsus* D4.R2. *exundent* d1.2.f1.2.boπ. *exun-
det* D4.R2. *exudent* PVGD2.R1.rapβa2. *ubera* PGR1.rabo. *foe-
tus* D2. Tit. c. *setis.*
105. *nam memini* D2. Tit. c. *semel haud.* Burm. c. *ego non*
(*memini*) *semel.*

100. **Expulit Euros,** 'has
driven away, dispelled the east
wind.'
101. 'And forthwith the Phar-
salian reeds set free their piping
notes,' i.e. the pipes sound as by the
inspiration of the god. Thessaly,
in which Pharsalia is situated, is
said by Wernsdorf to have been
celebrated for its pasture lands,
whence the allusion here. **Phar-
salae** is a doubtful form sug-
gested by Glaeser instead of the
common reading Pharsāliae, which
violates the metre. Haupt ap-
proves of *Parrhasiae* conjectured
by Heinsius. The allusion would
then be to Pan, and would answer
to line 106 where Pales is intro-
duced. *Parrhasius* is an adj.,
from the town of Parrhasia in
Arcadia, Pan's haunt.
Solverunt sibila. Cf. Stat.
Theb. 11, 604 : *suspiria solvit.*
It is unnecessary to follow Haupt

in adopting Heinsius' correction
sonuerunt.
Haupt mentions, but with dis-
approval, a theory of Sarpius that
these lines contain an allusion to
Lucan's Pharsalia, and that Amyn-
tas is Lucan himself.
102. **Excitet,** ' revives.'
104. ' And how when the dams
have just been shorn their wavy
fleeces grow luxuriantly.' Some
read *exsudent*, because Varro 2, 2,
says that sheep should be shorn
when they begin to sweat. But
this, as Wernsdorf observes, is
inappropriate, as the shearing is
described as just past, and, more-
over, the meaning required is that
of abundance, luxuriance. Cf. Tac.
Or. 30 : *exundat et exuberat elo-
quentia.*
105 sq. Special prosperity of
their flocks was attributed by the
ancients to the immediate presence
of the gods.

Et, venisse Palen, pecoris dixisse magistros.
A. Scilicet omnis eum tellus, gens omnis adorat,
Diligiturque deis : quem sic taciturna verentur
Arbuta, cuius iners audito nomine tellus
Incaluit, floremque dedit, cui silva vocato   110
Densat odore comas, stupefacta regerminat arbos.
C. Illius ut primum senserunt numina terrae,
Coepit et uberior, sulcis fallentibus olim,

106. *poteras* d1.2. (in the latter *pecoris* in margin). *poteris* D3.R2.
pereris D2. *paene pecoris* D1. *dixise magistro* R2.
109. Barth. cites *numine tellus.*
111. *Densat honore* d1.2. Ulit. c. *odora.* Heins. c. *odora* or *honora.*
stupefactaque germinat D4.d1.2.abo. Heins. c. *tepefacta.*
112. *ut primo* D1. *ut primum* vulg.
113. *succis* VD4.R1.2. rad2.pf1.2.βa2.bo. *sulcis* Gvπ.

107. Scilicet omnis, &c.,
'aye, and all the earth, &c.'
108. Diligitur deis. Dat. of
agent after passive verb, instead
of *ab* and ablative.
Quem sic, &c., 'since the ar-
butus trees pay him silent homage,
as you perceive (sic).'
109. Arbuta. *Arbutum,* which
is properly the fruit of the arbute,
or strawberry tree, is here used
for the tree itself (*arbutus* f.), as
in Virg. G. 3, 300 : *jubeo fron-
dentia capris Arbuta sufficere,*
i. e. *frondes arbuti,* 'that you
give the goats a supply of arbute-
shoots.'
Iners . . . tellus, 'the slug-
gish, immovable earth.' Hor. C.
3, 4, 45, contrasts *terra iners* with
mare ventosum, 'the sea stirred
by every wind.' Cf. Ib. 1, 34, 9:
bruta tellus, 'the dull earth.'
110. Incaluit. From *inca-
lesco.*
Cui silva, &c. ' In whose
honour, when he is invoked, the

wood spreads its thick and fra-
grant foliage.' *Odora* agreeing
with *silva* would be preferable to
odore, but lacks authority. The
ablative may be defended by Virg.
A. 1, 519 : *templum clamore pete-
bant,* ' sought the temple amidst
shouting.'
111. Densat, 1st conj., for *den-
seo,* see 1. 9.
Stupefacta, &c , ' the awe-
struck tree sprouts forth again.'
This meaning of *stupefacta* is sup-
ported by vii. 40. Wernsdorf
explains ' withered,' ' parched,'
but gives no instance of similar
use. The trees, like all the rest
of creation, are awe-struck by the
emperor's presence, but notwith-
standing, feel the advantage of his
beneficent power. Similarly per-
sonal feeling is attributed to an
inanimate subject in Virg. A.
6, 33 : *Attonitae magna ora do-
mus,* ' spell-bound house.'
113. Sulcis, &c., 'though for-
merly the furrows used to disap-

108 *ECLOGA*

Luxuriare seges, tandemque legumina plenis
Vix resonant siliquis, nec praefocata malignum   115
Messis habet lolium, nec inertibus albet avenis.
A. Iam neque damnatos metuit iactare ligones
Fossor, et inuento, si fors dedit, utitur auro.
Nec timet, ut nuper, dum iugera versat arator,

114. *legumine* f2.
115. Heins. c. *Foeta sonant siliquis. prefocata* R1.r. *praevocata* vs.
perforata D4. *proferata* R2.
116. *inextibus* D3.
117. *clam natos* D4.R2. *detatos* a. Perhaps we should read *clam nactus.*
118. *Fessor* p. *fors* D4.R2. Barth. Burm. Ulit. Beck. *sors*
R1.rapβf1.2.a2.sboπ Ulit.
119. *verset* pβa2.f2. *vertit* a.

point my hopes.' Cf. Ov. A. A.
1, 450 : *Sic dominum sterilis saepe
fefellit ager.* Hor. Epod. 16, 45 :
*Germinat et nunquam fallentis
termes olivae.*
114. Uberior . . . luxuriare,
' grow in ranker abundance.'
Legumina, ' pulse, any legu-
minous plant,' especially the
' bean,' which is described Virg.
G. 1, 74 : *laetum siliqua quassante
legumen.*
115. Vix resonant, sc. because
the beans are large, and fill the
pods. In Virg. G. 1, 76, they are
called *silvam sonantem.*
Praefocata, ' choked.'
Malignum . . . lolium, 'churl-
ish,' ' unfruitful,' ' barren tares.'
The epithet is more correctly ap-
plied to barren ground, e.g. Virg.
G. 2, 179 : *collesque maligni.* The
opposite qualities are expressed
by *benignus,* e.g. Hor. Ep. 1,
16, 8 : *si rubicunda benigni Corna
vepres et pruna ferant,* 'brambles
turned fruitful.' Ov. Am. 1, 10,
56 : *benignus ager.* Cf. Virg. G.
1, 154 : *Infelix lolium et steriles
dominantur avenae.*

116. Nec inertibus, &c., ' nor
is white with unproductive oats.'
117 sq. For the allusion in this
passage, see Introd. page 6.
Damnatos, ' hateful,' ' wretch-
ed,' because the instrument of
toil, as in Propert. 5, 11, 15 : *dam-
natae noctes.* Cf. Hor. C. 3, 18, 15 :
*Gaudet invisam pepulisse fossor
Ter pede terram.*
Jactare ligones, ' to ply the
hoe vigorously.' Cf. Virg. G.
2, 355 : *duros jactare bidentes,* on
which passage Conington sug-
gests that *jactare* is employed,
because the *bidens* was used more
like a pickaxe than a hoe.
This passage seems to have
been suggested by Hor. S. 2, 6,
10 sq. : *O si urnam argenti fors
quae mihi monstret ! ut illi, The-
sauro invento qui mercenarius
agrum Illum ipsum mercatus
aravit, dives amico Hercule.*
118. Et invento, &c., ' and
uses the gold he finds, if chance
gives it to him.'.
119 sq. **Nec timet,** &c., ' nor
does the ploughman fear, as lately,
while he turns up his broad

Ne sonet offenso contraria vomere massa,   120
Iamque palam presso magis et magis instat aratro.
C. Ille dat, ut primas Cereri dare cultor aristas
Possit, et intacto Bromium perfundere vino,
Ut nudus ruptas saliat calcator in uvas,
Utque bono plaudat paganica turba magistro,   125

121. Heins. c. *prenso. et* D1. *ac* vulg. *arator* f1.v.
122. *ut flavae cereri* R2.
123. *profundere* P. *infundere* R2. *Bromium . . . fundere* D4.
124. *psalat* D1. *psallat* R1.ra. *psalsat* VG. *saliat* vulg. *inuvas* R2. Ulit. c. *psallat c. ad uvas.* Heins. c. *ruptas calcet vindemitor uvas.* Glaes. c. *ruptis psallat c. in uvis.* Wernsd. defends *saliat* from Virg. G. 2, 382 sq.: *Praemiaque ingeniis pagos et compita circum Thesidae posuere, atque inter pocula laeti Mollibus in pratis unctos saluere per utres.* This passage is further identified with the present by *pagos*, for which we have a parallel in line 125 *paganica turba*.
125. *Utque bono plaudat paganida turba magistro* D1. Burm. c. *paganica. Ut quoque turba bono plaudat signata* vulg. *signata* tπ. Barth. Ulit. Burm. *saginata* PVD4.R1.rapβa2.f1.2.boψ Werns. Beck. *saginato* d2. *sagmata* R2. Tit. c. *sagnata.* Mod. and Dempster c. *satiata* (whence through erroneous spelling *saciata* might come *saginata*) or *saturata.* Heins c. *Sicana,* or *pagana,* or *sic grata.*

acres, lest an ingot of gold should ring as it meets and strikes against the ploughshare, and now he openly presses on more and more eagerly with deep-driven plough.' In Juv. 4, 37 sq. there is a vivid description of the trouble in which, whoever found anything that could be claimed as the property of the Emperor, might be involved, during the time that the *delatores,* or informers, flourished.

122 sq, It is owing to the Emperor that the husbandman can pay due observance to the several deities.

123. Bromium. Βρόμιος, the noisy one, a title of Bacchus, on account of the tumultuous cele-

bration of his festivals. 'And honour Bromius with libations of (hitherto) unbroached wine.'

124. Nudus, i.e. in the tunic only, without the upper garment, as we sometimes use the word 'strip' of a man throwing off his coat to work with greater freedom. Cf. Virg. G. 1, 299: *nudus ara, sere nudus.* Hes. Works and Days 389: γυμνὸν σπείρειν, γυμνὸν δὲ βοωτεῖν.

125. Paganica turba. Cf. Goldsmith's Deserted Village: *And all the village train, from labour free, Led up their sports beneath the spreading tree.*

The *Compitalia* were suppressed in B. C. 68, but revived by Augus-

Qui facit egregios ad pervia compita ludos.

A. Ille meis pacem dat montibus : ecce per illum
Seu cantare iuvat, seu ter pede lenta ferire
Gramina, nullus obest : licet et cantare choreis,
Et cantus viridante licet mihi condere libro,   130
Turbida nec calamos iam surdant classica nostros.

126. *Dum facit* Barth.
127. A MS. of Tit. gives *motibus*.
128. *laeta* vulg.   *ter penta lenta ferire* Dɪ.   *lenta* VGRɪ.2.rafɪ.tψ.
129. *Gramina* aga2.sπ and Mod. c. *Carmina* Dɪ.Rɪ.2. rdɪ.2.pfɪ.βbo.
nullus obest licet et cantare coreis Dɪ.   *non nullas licet hic cantare
choreas* vulg.   *coreas* R2.   Burm. c. *non molles licet hic.*   Barth. c.
non nullas (= nullas non).
131. *jam surdat* Dɪ.   whence Glaes. c. *jam surdant.   exsurdant*
vulg.   *exundant* D4.R2.

tus (Suet. Aug. 31). They were
under the presidency of the *Ma-
gistri vici,* and it would depend
principally on the president (*ma-
gister*), whether they were cele-
brated with *éclat* (*egregios ludos*).
Were it not for the word *compita*
in line 126 it would be more natu-
ral to suppose that the festival re-
ferred to is the *Paganalia,* or
Ambarvalia.
127. **Per illum,** ' it is owing
to him.'
Ter pede, &c., ' tread the slug-
gish grass in triple measure,'
dance the *trois temps !* Cf. the
passage quoted from the Odes of
Horace on line 117 sq. The mu-
sical rhythm is similarly expressed,
whether in reference to dancing or
singing. See Hor. S. 1, 10, 42 sq. :
*Pollio regum Facta canit, pede ter
percusso.* It is difficult to defend
ferire Carmina in this connexion
(Hor. S. 2, 3, 274 : *feris . . .
verba* is not a parallel), although

that reading has the support of the
Neapolitan MS., and is adopted
by Wernsdorf and Adelung.
On this and the following line
Wernsdorf quotes Virg. A. 6, 64 :
*Pars pedibus plaudunt choreas et
carmina dicunt.*   Cf. Milton's
Comus : *Come, knit hands, and
beat the ground In a light fan-
tastic round.*
129. **Nullus obest,** 'no one
hinders.' For *nullus = nemo,* cf.
Quint. 8 prooem. 16 : *hoc nullus
nisi arte assequi potest.*
Cantare choreis, i. e. to sing
and dance.
130. 'And I may treasure up
my songs on the green bark,' i.e.
carve the words on a tree, as
Faunus did in 1. 20, 21.
131. 'Nor do braying trumpets
now drown the sound of our
pipes.'
Surdant, if that is the true
reading, seems to be found here
only.

C. Numine Caesareo securior ipse Lycaeas
Pan recolit silvas, et amoena Faunus in umbra
Securus recubat, placido quin fonte lavatur
Nais, et humanum non calcatura cruorem   135
Per iuga siccato velox pede currit Oreas.

A. Di, precor, hunc iuvenem, quem vos, neque fallet, ab ipso
Aethere misistis, post longa reducite vitae
Tempora, vel potius mortale resolvite pensum,
Et date perpetuo coelestia fila metallo :   140

---

132. Heins. c. *Lycaeas.* *Lycaeus* π Barth. Ulit. Beck. *Lievo* D1.
Lyaeo VGrpβf1.a2.f2.bo.
134. Haupt. c. *placido quin. placidoque in* vulg. Heins. c. *placito-que. levatur* d1.2.
136. Heins. c. *sicca cito.* Tit. c. *soccato. pede velox* D1.
137. Heins. c. *huc juvenem. neque falet* D1. *non fallor* a. *nisi fallor* vulg.
138. Gud. c. *ad longa.* Barth. cites *reducite secla.*
139. Heins. c. *revolvite. mortale solvite* D4.R2.
140. *purpureo* D3.

---

132. ' Under the divine protection of Cæsar, Pan himself with more confidence frequents again the groves of Mount Lycaeus.' Lycaeus was a lofty mountain in Arcadia. For *recolere,* in sense of 'revisit,' cf. Phaedr. 1, 18, 1 : *Nemo libenter recolit, qui laesit, locum.*

134. **Quin,** ' nay.' This is Haupt's emendation for *que.* Even the timid nymphs are free from fear. For this use of *quin* in reaching a climax, or ending an enumeration, cf. Hor. C. 1, 10, 13 : *Quin et Atridas . . . Priamus . . . fefellit.*

135. **Humanum,** &c., ' without the risk of treading on human blood.'

136. **Per juga,** ' over the mountain tops.'

Siccato . . . pede. Cf. II. 14 : *sicco Dryades pede.*

137. Hunc juvenem, &c. Cf. Virg. G. 1, 500 : *hunc saltem everso juvenem succurrere saeclo Ne prohibete.*

138. Post longa, &c., ' bring him back to heaven only after a long term of life.' Cf. Hor. C. 1, 2, 45 : *serus in caelum redeas.*

139. Mortale resolvite pensum, ' untwine his mortal thread,' i.e. make him immortal. *Pensum* is the wool weighed out to a slave to spin in a day, and is here used of the thread spun by the fates.

140. In this line **coelestia fila** continues the allusion to the thread of the fates, and **perpetuo metallo** refers to Hesiod's division of time, by which the successive ages are denoted by different metals, gold, silver, bronze, &c. *Perpetuo metallo,* therefore, means an age that knows no end, as contrasted with those of gold,

Sit deus, et nolit pensare Palatia coelo.

C. Tu commutata seu Iuppiter ipse figura,
Caesar, ades, seu quis superum sub imagine falsa
Mortalique lates (es enim deus) : hunc, precor, orbem,
Hos, precor, aeternus populos rege : sit tibi coeli   145
Vilis amor, coeptamque, pater, ne desere pacem.

141. *Scit* P.
142. Haupt c. *Tu commutata. Tu quoque mutata* Glaes. *Te quoque* R1.
144. *etenim deus hunc precor* D1. *et enim hunc precor* D4. *et enim hunc deprecor* pβa2.sgf2., from which readings Glaes. gives *es enim deus : hunc precor &c. et enim hunc rege deprecor* R2. *etenim hunc cole deprecor* D3. *aeternum hunc te precor* d1.2. *vivas et hunc* VGR1.rf1.a1. *vivas et tunc* abo. *vivas atque et hunc* vt. Tit. cites *vivas* or *venias atque hunc precor.*
145. *aeternos* (i. e. Romanos) D4.R2.pβf1.2.a2.
146. *coeptamque* R1.af1.2.a2.soπ. *captamque* d1.2. Gud. c. *coeptamque pati.* Ulit. c. *coeptamque. curam.* Heins. c. *spretamque* or *cassamque patri. desere pacem* D1. *desere terram* vulg.

silver, &c. ' Grant him a heavenly thread of existence, marked by an everlasting metal.' Cf. Sen. Ludus de Morte Claudii : *Mutatur vilis pretioso lana metallo, Aurea formoso descendunt saecula filo.*
141. ' Let him be a god (sc. here on earth), and not wish to make up for the loss of the Palatium by heaven,' i.e. exchange the Palatium for heaven. Cf. Lucan 1, 45 sq.: *te, cum statione peracta Astra petes serus, praelati regia coeli Excipiet.*
142. Tu commutata is Haupt's emendation for *tu quoque mutata,* on the ground that it is absurd to introduce reference to a second Cæsar at the end of the poem. But *tu quoque* does not necessarily imply a new person, as appears from v. 39. ' Whether, Cæsar, you are present among us, being really Jupiter himself, under a changed form, &c.'

143. Seu quis, &c., 'or whether being one of the gods you lie concealed under an assumed and mortal semblance.'
For *falsus* = assumed, cf. Ov. A. A. 1, 618 : *Fiet amor verus qui modo falsus erat.*
144. Es enim deus is Glaeser's emendation based on the Neapolitan MS. *et enim,* &c. Cf. Virg. A. 1, 328 : *o dea certe.*
146. Coeptamque . . . ne desere pacem, 'and do not abandon the era of peace which has been just inaugurated ': see line 127.
Pater. This title is often applied to the gods, and, therefore, here to the Emperor. Here only, however, does Calpurnius apply it to the Emperor, whom elsewhere he calls *juvenis.* It is a title of respect not necessarily implying age, and there is no good ground for arguing from its use

M. Rustica credebam nemorales carmina vobis
Concessisse deos, et obesis auribus apta :
Verum, quae paribus modo concinuistis avenis,
Tam liquidum, tam dulce sonant, ut non ego malim, 150

147. *memoralis* R1. *morales* R2. *nobis* d1.bo. *vobis* d2.
148. *Deas* D1. prim. man.
149. Haupt approves of *quae paribus*, which is found in PVGbo.
quae imparibus D4.d2.pβf1.a2.tf2.π Glaes. *quem paribus* D1. *quam
paribus* D2.r.
150. *sonant* d1.2.a Beck. Glaes. gives *canunt*, which he says is found
in most books. Burm. c. *cadunt.* See Notes 2 on 152 sq. Modius
reads *sonant*, and says *canunt* was introduced from the familiar (*illud
tritum*) *Fistula dulce canit volucrem dum decipit auceps.*

that Calpurnius wrote under
Carus. The passage is evidently
an imitation of Hor. C. 1, 2,
41 sq.: *Sive mutata juvenem
figura . . . in terris imiteris . . .
serus in coelum redeas . . . Hic
ames dici pater atque princeps.*
147. Rustica, 'rough, clown-
ish.'
Nemorales deos, 'the sylvan,
woodland deities.'
148. Obesis auribus, ' coarse,
unrefined ears.' *Obesus* has two
opposite meanings, ' eaten away,
lean,' and ' that has eaten itself
fat, plump.' From the latter
comes the figurative sense found
in this passage, and also in Hor.
Epod. 12, 3: *naris obesae.* The
opposite term is *acutus,* Hor. S.
1, 3, 29: *minus aptus acutis
Naribus.*
149 sq. ' But what you have
just now sung on well-matched
pipes (i. e. with equal skill) sounds
so clear and sweet that I would
not prefer to sip of the nectar
which the Pelignian swarms
gather' (sc. rather than to listen).
Quae paribus. This Haupt
adopts instead of the common
reading *quae imparibus,* because

Calpurnius avoids eliding long
syllables. The Neapolitan MS.
reads *quem paribus.* Cf. II. 3 :
*formosus uterque nec impar Voce
sonans.* In line 150 Haupt rejects
as unexampled *canunt,* which is
given in the vulgate, and substi-
tutes *sonant,* which most MSS.
give in line 151 instead of *solent*
given by Glaeser. In the latter
line he reads *legunt.* Cf. In it is to be ob-
served that *sonare* is a favourite
word with Calpurnius.
Lambere nectar. Cf. Theocr.
8, 83 : Κρέσσον μελπομένῳ τευ
ἀκουέμεν ἢ μέλι λείχειν. II. 20 :
nectareos apis intermittere flores.
In Plaut. Cas. 2, 8, 21, to express
supreme pleasure, *mel mihi videor
lingere.*
Peligna. Ascensius restores
this word instead of the unmean-
ing *Pelvina.* The Peligni were a
people of Central Italy, the mo-
dern Abruzzo Citeriore. Ovid
was born at Sulmo in this district,
to which there may perhaps be an
allusion, as Horace compares him-
self to a Matine bee (C. 4, 2, 27:
apis Matinae More). See Ov.
Am. 3, 15, 3 : *Quos ego composui,
Peligni ruris alumnus.*

I

Quod Peligna legunt examina, lambere nectar.
C. O mihi quam tereti decurrens carmine versus
Tum, Meliboee, sonet, si quando in montibus istis
Dicar habere Larem, si quando nostra videre
Pascua contingat ; vellit nam saepius aurem   155

151. *Quot* Dɪ. *Pelvina* Dɪ.2.GRɪ.ra. *sonant* PD2.3.4.Rɪ.2.rd2.
legunt adɪ.2.bo. Heins. c. *fovent.* Glaes. gives *solent.*
   152. *Olim quae tereti decurrent* Dɪ. Glaes. *O mihi quam tenero
decurrunt* vulg.
   153. *Tum* vulg. Glaes. c. *Dum. Tunc* Dɪ.2.4.GRɪ.2.rabo. Haupt,
however, says Dɪ. has *Nunc,* not *Tunc.* Some explain *sonent = sona-
bunt.* Mod. thinks there was a verb *sonëre. sonant* GD4.Rɪ.2.r.
in has considerable MS. authority, but is omitted in D2.4., and Haupt
rejects it on account of the elision, and because it is unnecessary.
   154. *Dicat* GRɪ.rd2.fɪ.aɪ. *Dicam* D4.
   155. *contingat* Dɪ. *contigerit* vulg.

152 sq. I have given in the text Haupt's conjectural reading. ' O how my verses that run in humble strain would then resound, Meliboeus, if ever,' &c. It is unnecessary, with Wernsdorf, to assume a confusion of futures of first and third conjugation in *sonet,* nor need we, with Modius, suppose that the form *sonëre,* found in Ennius, is here used.

In support of his reading, Haupt quotes Culex 34 sq., where he has introduced a similar emendation : *Mollis sed tenui decurrens carmine versus Viribus apta suis Phoebo duce ludere gaudet.*

For *teres* applied to poetical composition cf. the use of *tenuis* Hor. C. 1, 6, 9 : *conamur tenues grandia,* 'poets of humble power,' ' authors of trifling, amorous lays.' The same idea is expressed by *deductum* in the passage quoted from Virgil on line 155.

It is perhaps worth suggesting that in the vulgate a confusion may have occurred between line 153 and line 150, *sonent* (or *sonant*) and *canunt* being transposed. This would give *sonant* in line 150, the very word which Haupt conjectures in that place, and suggest *canet* in 153, thus obviating the difficulties which have been raised about the mood and tense of *sonent.* The unusual expression *versus canet* may perhaps be justified by Cic. Verr. 2, 3, 44, 105 : *quum in eis conviviis symphonia caneret.*

For the other readings of this difficult passage see Notes 1.

Although most MSS. give *in* before *montibus* Haupt is doubtless right in omitting the preposition, which is unnecessary to the sense. See Introd. page 15.

154. Corydon contrasts the good fortune of having a homestead of one's own with the hard lot of a hired labourer (see line 44). His poetry will assume a loftier strain when poverty no longer compels him to devote all his attention to the sheepfold.

155. Contingat, ' if I ever

Invida paupertas, et dixit: ovilia cura.
At tu, si qua tamen non aspernanda putabis,
Fer, Meliboee, deo mea carmina : nam tibi fas est
Sacra Palatini penetralia visere Phoebi.
Tu mihi talis eris, qualis qui dulce sonantem   160
Tityron e silvis dominam deduxit in urbem,
Ostenditque deos, et spreto, dixit, ovili,
Tityre, rura prius, sed post cantabimus arma.
A. Respiciat nostros utinam fortuna labores

156. Heins. c. *ovilia cura.* *vilia cura* R1.2.rad1.2.βf1.va1.boπ.
Barth. Ulit., and according to Haupt D1. Glaes., however, attributes
to D1. *vilia rura*, which is also found in pa2.f2.
157. *Et tu* PVGR1.rad2. *tamen* PVGD2.3.R1.rabo. *modo*
d2.pβf1.a2.tf2.π vulg. *Et cui siqua mihi* D4.R2.
160. *Tum mihi* D3.R2.d2.pβa2.gf2. *erit* D4. *qualis mihi* V.
161. *Tironiam silvis* R2. *Tyroniam silvis* D2.GR1.r. Burm. c.
Tyronem. a silvis D3.4.abo. Tit. c. *ad urbem.*
162. Heins. c. *deis*, which is approved by Wernsd. and adopted by
Beck. *dixit olivo* R1.r.
163. Heins. c. *cantabis et* or *cantabitis*.
164. *Despiciat* (corrected *Respiciat*) d2.

have the good fortune to see a
farm of my own.'
Vellit. Perfect. Cf. Virg. E.
6, 3, sq. : *Cum canerem reges et
proelia, Cynthius aurem Vellit, et
admonuit : Pastorem, Tityre, pin-
guis Pascere oportet ovis, deductum
dicere carmen. Vulsi* both in
simple and compounds is some-
times found in post-Augustan
writers, but *velli* is the usual form.
See Roby, i. p. 262.
156. Invida, 'unkindly.'
157. Tamen. Though my
verses are not such as I could
write under more favourable con-
ditions, 'yet' if you think any of
them possessed of merit, &c.
159. There is probably a double
reference to the emperor, who is

associated with Apollo in line 87,
and who lived on the Palatine,
and to the library in the temple
of Apollo on the Palatine : see
Hor. Ep. 1, 3, 17 : *Scripta, Pala-
tinus quaecunque recepit Apollo.*
160–163. With this passage
should be carefully compared
Martial's Epigram 8, 56, on liter-
ary patronage. Tityrus is of course
Virgil, his patron is Maecenas, and
arma refers to the Æneid, the
loftier style of which is attributed
by Martial to the influence of
court patronage. For **dominam
. . . urbem** cf. IX. 84, and Hor.
C. 4, 14, 44.
164. Respiciat. The word is
similarly used in Virg. E. 1, 27 :
libertas . . . respexit inertem.

Pulchrior, et meritae faveat deus ipse iuventae :   165
Nos tamen interea tenerum mactabimus haedum,
Et pariter subitae peragemus fercula coenae.
M. Nunc ad flumen oves deducite : .iam fremit aestas,
Iam sol contractas pedibus magis admovet umbras.

165. Gud. c. *emeritae. mentae faveat* R1. Heins. c. *deus iste.*
166. *Hos tamen* R2. *in terra* d1. *iactabimus* D1.
168. *Hunc ad* R2. Heins. c. *premit aestas.* Ulit. c. *aestus.*

165. Pulchrior, 'fairer,' 'more favourable.' Cf. Hor. C. 1, 36, 10: *pulchra dies,* ' the auspicious day.'
Meritae, ' deserving.' Cf. Virg. G. 2, 515 : *meritosque juvencos ;* and VIII. 61.
166 sq. Amyntas proposes to get ready the courses for a hastily-prepared supper, doubtless to be shared by Meliboeus. Virgil's first Eclogue ends with a like hospitable invitation.
168 sq. **Jam fremit,** &c., ' the raging heat of summer is now prevailing, and the sun is shortening the shadows, and bringing them nearer to our feet,' i.e. it is now midsummer, and, moreover, the noon-tide hour. **Fremit** is probably a simile from wild beasts. Cf. Claud. Stil. 2, 460: *non torvo fremat igne Leo* (sign of the zodiac).

It is unnecessary to substitute *aestus* for *aestas.* Meliboeus means that it is not only mid-day, but also midsummer heat.

ECLOGA QUINTA.

MYCON.

THIS Eclogue is to be classed with the Georgics of Virgil rather than with his Eclogues. It is to a great extent an imitation of the third Georgic, and contains a number of precepts, addressed by the aged Mycon to his pupil Canthus as to the management of his sheep and goats. Though the subject-matter is not very interesting, this Eclogue is not deficient in smoothness of versification, and it contains many felicitous descriptions of pastoral scenes, both in summer and winter.

Forte Mycon senior, Canthusque, Myconis alumnus,
Torrentem patula vitabant ilice solem,
Cum iuveni senior praecepta daturus alumno
Talia verba refert tremulis titubantia labris :
M. Quas errare vides inter dumeta capellas,　　　　5

In praesenti aegloga dantur praecepta pastoralia filio a patre, et est didascalia, unus enim pater tantum loquitur R1.rd2. Inscribed *Mycon* since Barth.

1. *orte micon* R2. *Morte* (corrected *forte*) b.a adds *Poeta.*
2. *vitabant illice* D1., whence Glaes. reads as in the text. *vitabant arbore*, vulg.

1. Myconis alumnus, 'foster-son of Mycon.' See line 9.
2. 'Were sheltering themselves from the burning sun under a spreading oak.' Cf. Sir P. Sidney's Arcadia, 10, 66, Lamon's Song: *While they did ward sunnebeames with shadie bay.*
4. Titubantia, ' faltering,' through the feebleness of age. Cf. Juv. 9, 198 : *Una senum facies, cum voce trementia membra.*

Canaque lascivo concidere gramina morsu,
Canthe puer, quos ecce greges a monte remotos
Cernis in aprico decerpere gramina campo,
Hos tibi do senior iuveni pater, ipse tuendos
Accipe, iam certe potes insudare labori,   10
Iam pro me gnavam potes exercere iuventam.
Aspicis, ut nobis aetas iam mille querelas
Afferat et baculum premat inclinata senectus ?
Sed qua lege regas et amantes lustra capellas,
Et melius pratis errantes mollibus agnas,   15

6. *Cana que* R2. *Vanaque* D1. This line and the next are transposed in D1.
7. *quas ecce gr. a m. reductos* ψ. Barth., from ψ, writes *Quas—reductas*, and in line 9 *has*, in line 24 *clausas*.
8. Burm. c. *pabula campo.*
10. *certo* R2. Burm. c. *iam per te.*
11. *iuvencam* P.
12. *ut nobis aetas iam mille* D1. *nobis iamdudum mille* vulg. Burm. c. *Adspice iam nobis ut dudum.*
14. *quem* D1., whence Glaes. c. *qua en lege.* This, however, is doubtful, owing to the elision. See Introd. page 15 sq. Burm. c. *saxa* for *lustra.*

6. Cana, 'glistering with morning dew.' Cf. Virg. G. 3, 325 : *dum mane novum, dum gramina canent.* Ov. F. 3, 880 : *Canuerint herbae rore recente quater.*

Lascivo. The adjective is often applied to goats, and is here transferred to their mode of feeding. Cf. Virg. E. 2, 64 : *Florentem cytisum sequitur lasciva capella.*

Concidere, 'cropping,' 'browsing.'

7. Greges, properly used of sheep, and here opposed to *capellae.* See line 29 : *campos ovibus, dumeta capellis . . . dabis.*

10 sq. ' You can now certainly toil and sweat, and exert your vigorous youth instead of me.'

12. Mille querelas. Cf. Hor.

A. P. 173 : *(senex) difficilis, querulus, laudator temporis acti.*

13. Baculum premat, 'leans upon a staff.' Cf. Stat. Theb. 4, 582 sq. : *Nec jam firmanti baculo, nec virgine fida Nititur.*

Inclinata, 'bent down,' 'stooping.' Cf. Apul. Met. 8, p. 166 : *senex gravatus annis totus in baculum pronus.*

14. Lustra, 'thickets,' as opposed to the open meadows. Cf. line 29, where *dumeta* is used, and Virg. A. 11, 570 : *in dumis interque horrentia lustra.*

15. Melius, &c., 'the lambs which had better stray in the soft meads,' sc. than in the mountain pastures. Cf. Liv. 1, 13, 3 : *melius peribimus quam sine alteris vestrum viduae aut orbae vivemus.*

Percipe. Vere novo, quum iam tinnire volucres
Incipient, nidosque reversa lutabit hirundo,
Protinus hiberno pecus omne movebis ovili.
Tunc etenim melior vernanti gramine silva
Pullat, et aestivas reparabilis inchoat umbras,　　20
Tunc florent silvae, viridisque renascitur annus,
Tunc Venus et calidi scintillat fervor amoris,
Lascivumque pecus salientes accipit hircos.
Sed non ante greges in pascua mitte reclusos,

17. *habitabit* PGD2.3.R1.rd1. Scriver. c. *locabit. lutabit* bo.
18. *movebit* GD3.
19. *etenim melior* D1. Instead of *melior* we find *tota* (*a* being length-
ened by arsis) in VGD4.R1.2.rad1.2.f1.va1.tψ. *toto* in pβa2.sf2.boπ.
Wernsdorf reads *toto*, but censures the double epithet of *gramine*, and
considers this to be one of the passages to which Calpurnius had not
given the final revision. All the books give *silva :* but Beck objects to
it on account of *silvae* in line 21, and adopts Hoeufftius' conjecture :
totus vernanti gramine saltus. Burm. c. *nobis vernanti germine.*
Heins. c. *Tunc etiam lato,* or *exorto,* or *toto vernatrix gramine,* or *ver-
nante toro, tunc gramina.*
20. *Bullat* D3. *Pullulat aestivas reparabilisque* d1. *inchoat undas*
P. Wernsd. c. *induit umbras.*
24. *mitte reclusos* D1. *mittito clausos* vulg. *clausas* vψ. Wake-
field c. *mittere clausos.* The reading of D1. is doubtless right, the vulg.

16. Percipe, 'learn.'
Tinnire, 'to twitter.'
17. Nidosque, &c., 'and the
returning swallow daubs its nest
with mud.' Cf. Ov. F. 1, 157:
(*hirundo*) *luteum celsa sub trabe
fingit opus.*
18. Of the same season Ovid
says, F. 1, 156 ; *ludit et in pratis
luxuriatque pecus.* Cf. Hor. C
1, 4, 3 : *ac neque jam stabulis
gaudet pecus.*
19 sq. ' For then the wood, with
sprouting grass, buds forth more
richly, and reviving, begins to form
the summer shade.'
20. Reparabilis is found in
same sense in Aus. Idyll. 18, 6 :

Phoenix reparabilis ales, i. e
coming to life again. Wernsdorf,
however, takes it actively, as in
Pers. 1, 102 : *reparabilis adsonat
echo.*
21. Florent silvae, an un-
pleasing tautology after *silva pul-
lat,* perhaps, according to Werns-
dorf, intended to represent the
verbosity of the old shepherd.
Renascitur. Cf. 1. 42.
22. Scintillat. Wernsdorf com-
pares σπινθῆρες ἐρώτων, Nonnus
Dionys.
24. Reclusos, 'turned loose,'
while at the approach of winter
they were housed again : see line
103. Cf. Virg. G. 3, 323: *In*

Quam fucrit placata Pales.   Tum cespite vivo·   25
Pone focum, Geniumque loci Faunumque Laresque
Salso farre voca : tepidos tunc hostia cultros
Imbuat; hac etiam, dum vivit, ovilia lustra.
Nec mora, tunc campos ovibus, dumeta capellis,
Orto sole dabis, simul hunc transcendere montem   30
Coeperit et primae spatium tepefecerit horae.
At si forte vaces, dum matutina relaxat
Frigora sol, tumidis spumantia mulctra papillis

mittito clausos being a mere conjecture of some one who thought *mitte*
and *reclusos* to be tautological, both expressing the letting of the flocks
out of the pens.   Translate ' Do not let the flocks out of the pens, and
turn them into the pasture until,' &c.   In spring the flocks which had
been penned up (*claudere*) at the close of the year were let out (*reclu-
dere*) and sent to pasture.   See line 103 : *cum pecudes extremus clau-
serit annus*.   In 11. 96 we have *reclude canalem*, ' let out the stream.'
The first syllable of *recludo* is common.   Virg. A. 7, 617 : *More iube-
batur tristesque recludere portas*.
   25. *fuerat* D1.   *fuerit* vulg.   *tu* PD2.3.R2.pβa2.sf2.g, which Glaes.
thinks is right.
   26. *geniumque foci* PVD2.3.GR1.rd2.   *Laresque* D1.   *Laremque* vulg.
   28. *hac et dum vivat* D1.   *ac ĕt* R2.   *ac etiam* PVGD3.R1.rad1.2.bo.
Dorvill. and Burm. c.   *hac etiam*.   *atque etiam* pβf1.2.a2.s vulg.   Burm.
c. *ante tamen, dum vivit*.
   30. This and the three following lines are omitted in R1.   *accedere*
PVD2.3.rapβa2.f2.d2.bo.   *accendere* G.   *attendere* R2.   Glaes. c. *es-
cendere*.
   31. *ut* D3.4.pf1.va1.tψ.   Heins. c. *perfecerit horae*.
   32. *vacet* G.   Lines 32–35 are omitted in D4.R2.
   33. Haupt approves of Barthius' conjecture *spumantia mulctra*, and
quotes in its support *spument trimultra* as the reading of D1.   Glaes.

*saltus utrumque gregem atque in
pascua mittes*.   On the reading,
see Notes 1.
   25. Placata Pales : apparently
a private sacrifice to the goddess
is meant, and not the Palilia cele-
brated in April.
   Cespite vivo, build an altar of
' fresh sods.'
   27. Tepidos, ' warm with
blood.'
   28. Hac, sc. *hostia*.
   29. See note on line 7.

   30. Orto sole.   This precept
was for spring : see line 16.   In
summer the flocks left the fold
before dawn : see line 52.
   Simul = *simul ac*.
   Hunc.   This word gives vi-
vidness to the passage, Mycon
pointing to the mountain as he
speaks.
   31. Primae spatium horae,
' the course of the first hour.'
   33 sq. **Tumidis,** &c., ' the milk
which will flow in the morning

Implebit, quod mane fluet, rursusque premetur
Mane, quod occiduae mulsura redegerit horae.   35
Parce tamen foetis, nec sint compendia tanti,
Destruat ut niveos venalis caseus agnos :
Nam tibi praecipuo foetura coletur amore.
Te quoque non pudeat, quum serus ovilia vises,
Si qua iacebit ovis partu resoluta recenti,   40
Hanc humeris portare tuis, natosque tepenti
Ferre sinu tremulos et nondum stare paratos.
Nec tu longinquas procul a praesepibus herbas,
Nec nimis amotae sectabere pabula silvae,

gives *spument trimulca* as the reading of D1. Glaes. reads *spument
tibi. capellis* VG.
34. *Implebis quod mane fluet* D1., whence Haupt c. *Implebit quod
mane fluet. quod massa* ψ. *quo messe* a. Glaes. reads *Implebis, quod
messe fluat.* Barth. c. *quo massa fluat.* Ulit. c. *Inde premes, quod
mane fluat,* or *Nocte premes, quod mane fluit.* Heins. c. *papillis Ampla*
(or *Imbre*) *tibi quo massa fluat.* Martell. c. *nocte* for *messe.* Wernsd.
c. *Implebis, quae pressa fluant.* Glaes. c. *Hinc plebi et quod mane feras.*
35. *coegerit* Barth.
37. *et* d1.2. *teneros* D4.R2.
38. *coletur* D1. *colatur* vulg.
39. *ne* for *non* va. *tendis* for *vises* D2.3. (in the margin of which
poscis) D4. *tendit* (*-is* corrected by same hand) R2.
41. *natoque parenti* d2.pβa2.sf2. *natosque parenti* Pf1.gtbo. *patenti*
D3.4.R2. *tepenti* GR1.raπ.
42. *paratas* D1. Burm. c. *peritos.*
43. *Ne* avt. *Hec tu* R2.
44. *amotae* R1.rad1.2.boπ. *admotae* Gpβa2.f1.2. *nec minus ad-
motae* D2.3.4. *Et minus amotae* P. *sectare ad pabula* GR1.r.

will fill up the pails foaming from
the swelling dugs; and again, what
the milking of the evening hour
brought in will be pressed (sc. to
make cheese) in the morning.'
Mulctra. Virg. E. 3, 30, makes
this word feminine. Hor. Epod.
16, 49 makes it neuter, as here.
35. Mulsura is found only in
this passage.
36. Nec sint, &c., 'nor let
economy (of the milk for cheese-
making) be of such consequence

that the cheese for the market
should ruin the snow-white lambs,'
viz. by depriving them of the
nourishment of the milk. The
same advice is given in Virg. G.
3, 176 sq.
39–42. Cf. Tib. 1, 1, 31 sq. : *Non
agnamve sinu pigeat, fetumve
capellae Desertum oblita matre
referre domum.*
43 sq. Cf. Virg. G. 1, 354 sq. :
*quid saepe videntes Agricolae pro-
pius stabulis armenta tenerent.*

Dum peragit vernum Iovis inconstantia tempus.   45
Veris enim dubitanda fides : modo fronte serena
Blandius arrisit, modo cum caligine nimbos
Intulit, et miseras torrentibus abstulit agnas.
At cum longa dies sitientes afferet aestus,
Nec fuerit variante deo mutabile coelum,   50
Iam silvis committe greges, iam longius herbas
Quaere, sed ante diem pecus exeat : humida dulces
Efficit aura cibos, quoties fugientibus Euris
Frigida nocturno tinguntur pascua rore,
Et matutinae lucent in gramine guttae.   55
At simul argutae nemus increpuere cicadae,

45. *peragunt* D1. *peragit* vulg.
46. *forte serena* pβ.
48. *tondentibus* GR1.raf1.va1.bo. *condentibus* V. Heins. c. *Impulit*
et mersas.
49. *Et cum* R2. *sitientibus* VGR1.rabo. *adferat* PD4.
53. *Effugit* G. Heins. c. *Sufficit. auris* D4.
54. *tanguntur* PD2.3.4.R2.d2.pa2.f2.
55. Heins. c. *matutino. in gramina* D4.b Barth. *in germine* D1.
56. *Ut simul* D3.R2.d2.pa2.f2. *argute* R2. *arbutae* GR1.r.
Ulit. c. *inrupere.*

45. 'While the changeable wea-
ther is finishing, seeing to an end,
the spring season.' If *peragunt*,
the reading of the Neapolitan
MS., be adopted, *inconstantia*
will be the plural of a neuter
noun, *inconstantium*, found here
only.
46. **Serena**, often used of clear,
bright weather, as in the motto for
a sundial, *Non numero horas nisi
serenas.*
47. **Blandius arrisit**, 'smiles
enticingly.' **Arrisit—intulit—
abstulit** correspond to Greek
gnomic aorists.
48. **Abstulit**, 'sweeps away.'
49. **Longa dies**, 'the long
days,' 'summer time.' Cf. Hom.

Od. 22, 301 : ὥρῃ ἐν εἰαρινῇ ὅτε
τ' ἤματα μακρὰ πέλονται.
50. **Variante deo.** Cf. line 45 :
Iovis inconstantia. 'And the sky
is no longer changeable with un-
certain weather.'
51. **Iam** sq., 'then, and not
till then, trust the flocks to the
woodland pastures,' which were
at a distance : see line 44.
Longius, 'at a greater dis-
tance.'
53. **Fugientibus Euris**, 'when
the wind falls.'
54. 'The cold meadows are
drenched with night dew.'
55. 'And the morning dew-
drops sparkle on the grass.'
56. 'But as soon as the chirp-

Ad fontem compelle greges, nec protinus herbas
Et campos permitte sequi : sine protegat illos
Interea veteres quae porrigit esculus umbras.
Verum ubi declivi iam nona tepescere sole   60
Incipiet, seraeque videbitur hora merendae,

57. *ne* a.

58. *Et campos* Di.PVGRi.rabo.   *Vel campos* vulg.   *si ne* f2.   *sive*
(corrected *sine*) di.   *sed protegat* Di.
59. Heins. c. *proiicit.*
60. *declivis* Di., leaving *sole* to be construed with *tepescere*, which is
awkward when *tepescere* means 'to cool,' as it does here, although
natural enough when it means 'to be heated,' as in Ov. M. 3, 412 :
Silvaque sole lacum passura tepescere nullo. Heins. c. *declini. declivo
iam nova* D3.   *nova iamque tepescere* D4.   *nova tamque tepescere*
R2.
61. *ferae. ora* G.   *serique videbitur hora premendi* Di., erroneously
lengthening the first syllable of *serum.* Glaes. c. *Incipietque, serique
videbitur hora premendi.*

ing tree-crickets make the grove
resound,' i. e. a couple of hours
before noon, and during the heat
of the day, as appears from Virg.
G. 3, 327 sq. : *Inde, ubi quarta
sitim coeli collegerit hora Et cantu
querulae rumpent arbusta cica-
dae;* and Id. E. 2, 13 : *Sole sub
ardenti resonant arbusta cicadis.*
For the causative use of *increpare*,
cf. Ov. M. 12, 51 sq. : *qualemve
sonum, cum Iuppiter atras Incre-
puit nubes, extrema tonitrua red-
dunt.*
57 sq. Nec protinus, &c.,
'nor permit them uninterruptedly
(i. e. without retiring for shelter
from the noon-tide heat) to follow
the grass and open fields ; allow
the oak, which spreads its aged
shade, to shelter them meantime,'
i. e. until evening : see next lines.
For this somewhat rare use of
protinus, cf. Virg. A. 9, 337 sq. :
felix, si protinus illum Aequasset

nocti ludum in lucemque tulisset.
60. Declivi, 'sloping towards
the west,' 'westering.' Cf. Plin.
8, 50, 76, 203 : *in occasum de-
clivi sole,* where, however, Sillig
follows the oldest MSS. in read-
ing *declini,* which Heinsius conjec-
tures to be the true reading here.
Milton, in *Comus,* uses the expres-
sion 'the slope sun.' `
Nona, sc. *hora.* For the el-
lipsis cf. Hor. Ep. 1, 7, 71 : *Post
nonam venies.*
Tepescere, 'to cool off, de-
crease in heat.' Cf. Mart. 2, 1,
13 : *Te conviva leget mixto quin-
cunce, sed ante Incipiat positus
quam tepuisse calix.* This verb
is sometimes used of the cooling
down of passion, e. g. VIII. 13 :
*Nunc album caput et Veneres
tepuere sub annis.* Its more usual
meaning is 'to grow warm.'
61. Serae hora merendae,
'the hour for a late luncheon.'

Rursus pasce greges et opacos desere lucos.
Nec prius aestivo pecus includatur ovili,
Quam levibus nidis somnos captare volucris
Cogitet, ac tremuli dent mulctra coagula lactis.　　65
Succida iam tereti constringito vellera iunco,
Cum iam tempus erit maternas demere lanas,
Hircorumque iubas et olentes caedere barbas.

62. *Rustice pasce* R2. *Rustice graeges pasce ut* D4.
63. *aetivos* D1.
64. *laevibus ac nidis* ψ. *sonos* D3. *somno* R2. *volucres* D1.R2.
Barth. punctuates after *volucris*.
65. Glaes. prints *Cogitet, et tremuli tremebunda coagula lactis,* re-
marking that the words are corrupt and probably made up from III.
69. *ac tremuli* VR1.r. *ad tremuli* bo. Ascens. gives from his own
conjecture *ad tremuli te ferto coagula.* The remarkable reading *tre-
mulo tremebundo fruniat ore* is found in D1. Whence Glaes. c.
volucres Cogitet, atque ales tremulo fritinniat ore, which is improbable
on account of the elision, and because the first syllable of *fritinnio* is
short, or *volucris Cogitet, ac tremulo tremebunda* (*gemebunda ?*) *fri-
tinniat ore.* With the vulg. (printed by Glaes.) we must supply *sunt*
or *fiunt.* Heins. c. *Cogitet, i, tremuli preme munda,* or *Cogitet, et
tremuli premere uda c. l.* Burm. c. *Cogitet, hinc tremuli preme munda.*
Wernsd. c. *Cogitet, ac tremuli dent mulctra c. l.*
66. *constringito* a. *cum stringes* d1.2. (in the latter *constringere* in
margin). *vinco* (i. e. either *vinclo* or *iunco*) R1.r. Heins. c. *succida
da.* Burm. c. *sucida quum t. c. u. i. Et iam. Iam* can hardly be right,
as it occurs in next line. Perhaps we should read *Si cupias t. con-
stringere v. i.* and put comma instead of period at end of line 68. ' If
you desire to bind up the fleeces when shearing time comes, yet first
separate the flock,' &c.
67. *Tum iam* d1.2. Burm. c. *maturas.* Glaes. thinks this and
preceding verse should be thus restored: *Succidua at tereti cum stringes
vellera iunco, Tum iam,* &c.
68. *Hircet* D1.

64. A description of eventide,
as in Sil. Ital. 2, 215 : *Sicut agit
levibus per sera crepuscula pennis
E pastu volucres ad nota cubilia
vesper.*

66. 'Now (i. e. at the same
time, at eventide) bind the greasy
fleeces with swathes of rushes, if

it be the season for shearing the
dams.'
Succida vellera are fresh
fleeces, as explained by Varro R.
R. 2, 11, 6 : *tonsurae tempus
inter aequinoctium vernum et sol-
stitium, cum sudare coeperint
oves, a quo sudore recens lana
tonsa succida est appellata.*

Ante tamen secerne pecus, gregibusque notatis
Consimiles include comas, ne longa minutis,   70
Mollia ne duris coeant, ne candida fuscis.
Sed tibi cum vacuas posito velamine costas
Denudabit ovis, circumspice, ne sit acuta
Forfice laesa cutis, tacitum ne pustula virus
Texerit occulto sub vulnere, quae nisi ferro   75
Rumpitur, ah miserum fragili rubigine corpus
Arrodet sanies, et putrida contrahet ossa.

69. *Ante tuum* a.

70. Barth. c. *coma.* Burm. c. *comis. nec longa* D2.3.

71. *Molli ne* Barth. *Media* D4.R2.

73. *Denudavit* D1. *Denudabit* vulg. Burm. c. *Denudarit.*

74. *Forcipe* D1. Glaes. says that Ascens. mentions *Forfice* and *Forpice* as other readings.

75. Heins. c. *sub vellere.*

76. *ah miserum* R1.rf1.va1.boπ. *en miserum* d1. *en* (corrected *ah*) d2. *in miserum* VD2.3.4.R2.pβa2.f2. Titius punctuates (*ah miserum*) *fragili.* Heins. c. *porrigine* or *prurigine.*

77. *Arrodet* D1. *Corrodet* vulg. Ulit. c. *scabies* cf. Gratius Faliscus, Cyneg. 408, 409 : *At si deformis lacerum dulcedine corpus Persequitur scabies, longi via pessima leti. putria contrahit* D3.

69 sq. Separate the sheep according to the quality of the wool, and make up the several kinds of wool in separate bundles.

72 sq. ' But when your sheep has stripped his sides and left them clear of wool, be on the watch lest the skin may have been injured by the sharp shears.' *Forfex* is fem., and is to be distinguished from *forceps,* ' pincers.'

74. Pustula, ' a blister.'

75. Cf. Virg. G. 3, 452 sq. : *Non tamen ulla magis praesens fortuna laborum est, Quam si quis ferro potuit rescindere summum Ulceris os.*

76. **Rumpitur,** 'is cut.' Cf. Ov. M. 12, 249: *Rumpere sacrifica molitur colla securi.* Ib. 15, 464 sq. : *vituli qui guttura ferro Rumpit.*

Fragili rubigine, 'tender ulcer.' *Fragile corpus* 'a frail, weak, body,' is found in Cic. Sen. 18, 65. The epithet which is more suitable to the body is here applied to the disease affecting the body.

77. **Arrodet,** 'will eat away.'

Putrida contrahet ossa, 'will shrivel up the bones into a crumbling mass.' Cf. Virg. G. 3, 484 : *omniaque in se Ossa minutatim morbo collapsa trahebat.*

Providus (hoc moneo) viventia sulphura tecum,
Et scillae caput, et virosa bitumina porta,
Ulceribus laturus opem ; nec Brutia desit   80
Dura tibi ; liquido picis unguine terga, memento,
Si sint rasa, linas : durae quoque pondera massae
Argenti coquito, lentumque bitumen aheno,

78. *haec* VGR1.rbo.   *moneo ut* D1.   *liventia* in a MS. of Titius
and af1.va1.t.
    79. Heins. c. *scillae capita. et virosa* D1.   *vitata* D4.   *vittata* D2.
et intacta D3.   *buctata* VGR1.ra.   *atque intacta* vulg.   Ascens. c.
buxata. Burm. c. *ructata.* Wolf c. *nitrata.* Haupt says D1. reads
portes.
    80. *Vulneribus* D1.   *ne Brutia* Barth.
    81. *Cura tibi* a.   Glaes. reads *et liquido simul ;* but Haupt quotes
D1. as his authority for *liquido picis,* omitting *et.   liquido picis ungere*
d2.pβa2.f2.bo.   *picis lingere* R2.   *pacis ingere* D2.   *unguere* PD4.
simul unguine GR1.raf1.va1.   *inguine* D1., according to Glaes.   Mod.
c. *picis unguine.*   Burm. c. *Dura* or *Pura tibi liquidoque hinc unguine*
or *hinc liquido simul.*
    82. *Si tibi rasa* d1.2.   *rara* R2.   *Si sunt rara linas durae quoque
pondera massae* D1.   *Si sunt rasa linas villi quoque pondera melle*
vulg.   *vini quoque pondera melle* VD4.R2.   *vini quoque pondera molle
Argentum* P.   *vini quoque pondere molle Argentum* GR1.r.   Ulit c.
vini quoque pondera in olla Argenti c. l. b. ahena or *in uno* [*in illo*]
Arg. c. sqq. Heins. c. *pondera amellis Argenti incoquito.*   Modius
reads *Si sint rasa, linas, vivi quoque pondera melle Argenti coquito.*
    83. Haupt c. *Chalcanthi* for *Argent.*.

78. Providus, i. e. to be pre-
pared for the event of injuring the
skin while shearing.
    Viventia sulphura, Cf. Virg.
G. 3, 449 : *viva sulphura,* native
sulphur as opposed to *factitium :*
see Conington's Virgil l. c.
    79. Scillae caput, ' head of a
sea-leek.'
    Virosa, ' strong-smelling.'
    80. Brutia sc. *pix.* According
to Pliny the best quality of pitch
was prepared in the country of
the Bruttii.
    81. Haupt, differing from
Glaeser, says this is the reading

of the Neapolitan MS., and it
makes the omission of *pix* with
Bruttia more intelligible. The
common reading is *et liquido
simul.*
    83. Haupt objects to **argenti**
as being a metal not plentiful
among shepherds, and as being
useless for marking purposes. He
conjectures *chalcanthi. Chalcan-
thum,* ' copperas-water ' is in
pure Latin *atramentum sutor-
ium,* a blacking used in colouring
leather.
    Lentumque bitumen aheno,
' and sticky pitch in a caldron.'

Impressurus ovi tua nomina, nam tibi lites
Auferet ingentes lectus possessor in armo.　　　　85
Nunc etiam, dum siccus ager, dum fervida tellus,
Dum rimosa palus et multo torrida limo
Aestuat, et fragiles nimium sol pulverat herbas,
Lurida conveniet succendere galbana septis,
Et tua cervino lustrare mapalia fumo.　　　　　90
Obfuit ille malis odor anguibus ; ipse videbis

85. *Auferet* R1.Grπ. *Afferet* ad2.pβf1.a2.f2.bo. *in armo* D1.2.3.4.
Barth. says it is doubtful whether *arvo* or *arno* is the reading of ψ. *in
arvo* d2.pβa2.f2.boπ. *ovili* PVGR1.rf1.va1.t.
　86. *Nunc etiam* D1.f1.va1. *Tunc etiam* vulg. *dum succus* D1. *cum
siccus* abo. *quom siccus* VGR1.r.
　87. Tit. c. *emulso torrida*, which might be supported by Catull. 68.
110: *Siccare emulsa pingue palude solum. turbida* cd. Titii. *lino* v.
　88. *nimium* D1.2.PVGR1.ra. *nimius* vulg. *minius* R2. Heins.
c. *vulnerat*.
　89. *tectis* D3.
　90. Heins. c. *et sua*.
　91. *Obfuit ille* D1. *Obfuit iste* vulg. *Obfuerit malus iste odor*
VGR1.r. *malis dolor* R2. Burm. c. *Obvius iste*.

84. Impressurus, &c., ' when
you are about to stamp your name
on a sheep.' Cf. Virg. G. 3, 158:
*Continuoque notas et nomina gen-
tis inurunt.*
　Lites, &c , ' will save you from
many a dispute.'
　85. Lectus, &c., ' the name of
the owner on the shoulder,' lit.
the owner read.
　87. Rimosa palus : Cf. Virg.
G. 3, 432 : *Postquam exusta
palus, terraeque ardore dehis-
cunt.*
　88. Wernsdorf says this line is
an instance of the carelessness of
Calpurnius. He meant to say
fragiles pulverat glebas but for the
metre substituted *herbas* (covers
the grass with dust), and so the
epithet *fragiles* becomes unsuit-
able. It is, however, possible that

the meaning is ' reduces the very
grass to dust,' in which case the
epithet is appropriate enough.
　89. Lurida galbana, ' yellow-
ish galbanum,' a kind of gum-
resin, of strong odour, and bitter,
acrid taste. Cf. Virg. G. 3, 415,
where also its use is recommended
for driving away serpents.
　90. Cervino . . . fumo, i. e.
cervini cornus fumo.
　91. Malis, ' poisonous.' Cf.
Virg. A. 2, 471 : *coluber mala
gramina pastus.*
　The force of **ipse** is, you need
not depend merely on my word,
you will see for yourself the threat-
ening serpents sink back. *Tol-
lentemque minas* is said (Virg.
G. 3, 421) of a serpent raising
itself in a threatening manner,
hence the appropriateness of *cadere*

Serpentum cecidisse minas ; non stringere dentes
Ulla potest uncos, sed inani debilis ore
Marcet, et obtuso iacet exarmata veneno.
Nunc age vicinae, circumspice, tempora brumae   95
Qua ratione geras. Aperit cum vinea sepes,
Et portat lectas securus circitor uvas,
Incipe falce nemus vivasque recidere frondes.
Nunc opus est teneras summatim stringere virgas,

> **94.** *Manet* P.
> **95.** *Nunc age* D1.GR1.rabod2.   *Tunc age* vulg.
> **96.** Burm. c. *Quae.* Heins. c. *feras.*
> **97.** *portas* R2.   *circitor* D1.   *vinitor* vulg.
> **98.** *iuvasque* R2.   Heins. c. *nimiasque.*
> **99.** *Nunc opus* D1.   *Tunc opus* vulg.

to express its sinking back to the ground.

92. Stringere dentes . . . uncos, 'show their barbed teeth.' Cf. Ov. Am. 1, 6, 14 : *Non timeo strictas* (i. e. bared) *in mea fata manus.* The expression is an adaptation of *stringere gladium* 'to draw a sword.' Cf. Bentley's reading in Hor. C. 1, 6, 18: *strictis unguibus.*

93. Inani, 'powerless' to bite. Cf. Virg. A. 4, 449: *lacrimae . . . inanes,* 'tears powerless to produce any effect,' 'unavailing tears.'

94. Exarmata. This word is used of serpents deprived of their power of injuring in Sil. Ital. 1, 401 : *nec non serpentes diro exarmare veneno Doctus.*

95. Vicinae . . . brumae, 'approaching winter.'

Circumspice. Cf. line 73.

96. Aperit cum vinea sepes, 'when the vineyard opens its rows for gathering.'

97. 'And the watchman, free from anxiety, carries home the gathered grapes.' When the grapes he had been set to watch were safely housed, the watchman would be relieved from his anxious task. *Vinitor,* the vine-dresser, is the common reading. The Neapolitan MS. gives *circitor,* which is also found in the Priapeia 16, 1 sq. : *Quid mecum tibi, circitor moleste ? Ad me quid prohibes venire furem?* In military language it meant 'patrols.'

If *vinitor* be read, *securus* probably means free from anxiety about the weather and the health of the crops.

98. 'Begin to prune the wood, and to cut off the fresh leaves,' sc. to serve as winter fodder for the cattle. The man who did this was called *frondator :* see Virg. E. 1, 56.

99. 'It is now you should gather the tender twigs on the top.' The tender twigs grow on the top and should be lopped off while fresh, and not left to wither and be blown off by the wind, when they would be useless.

Nunc hiemi servare comas, dum permanet humor,   100
Dum viret, et tremulas non excutit Africus umbras.
Has tibi conveniet tepidis foenilibus olim
Promere, cum pecudes extremus clauserit annus.
Hac tibi nitendum est : labor hic in tempore noster,
Gnavaque sedulitas redit et pastoria virtus.   105
Nec pigeat ramos siccis miscere recentes,

100. *Nunc hiems servare* D1., whence Glaes. c. the reading of the
text. *Tum debes servare* vulg.
102. *Has tibi cum veniet* D1. *Ast tibi* VD4.R1.rbo. *Ast ubi*
PR2.d2.pβfι.2.a2. *tepidas* π Barth. Ulit. *tepidis* vulg. *senilibus* D3.
103. *Ponere* D4.R2.
104. *Sic tibi nitendum est : labor hoc in tempore noster* vulg., which
Glaes. prints, although he says it can hardly be correct : he himself
conjectures *Hac tibi nitendum : labor hinc*, which Haupt approves of,
save that he would follow D1. in reading *hic* for *hinc*. *Hoc tibi nec-*
tendum labor hic D1. *Hic* ψ. *Dic* d1.2. *in tempora* D4. Modius
reads *Dic tibi, nitendum est, labor hoc in tempore noster.*
105. *redit et pastoralia* D1. *venit et* vulg.
106. *Ne pigeat* D1.R1.d1.2.

101. Tremulas . . . umbras.
Cf. Pope's Summer Pastoral :
Where dancing sunbeams on the
waters play'd, And verdant al-
ders form'd a ' quivering shade.'
102. Foenilibus, ' hay-loft,'
only used in plural. Cf. Virg.
G. 3, 320: *nec tota claudes foenilia*
bruma.
For **olim** referring to future
time, cf. Virg. A. 1, 203 : *forsan*
et haec olim meminisse juvabit.
103. The cattle are housed in
winter and let out again in spring :
see line 24.
104. ' In this way you must
busy yourself, such is our work at
the proper time.' Cf. Liv. 33, 5, 2 :
ni pedites equitesque in tempore
subvenisset.
105. I. e. the necessity comes
round incessantly for untiring in-
dustry on the part of the shepherd.

106-109. ' Nor be reluctant to
mingle fresh branches with the
dry ones, and to supply new sap,
lest nipping winter with its rain-
clouds come on you, and with
severe frost and congealed snow
forbid you to bend down the
trees of the wood and bind to-
gether the leaves.'
I have adopted Haupt's emen-
dation, *vetet* for *velis*, but think
his suggestions *dum* for *ne*, and
incursare for *incurvare* unneces-
sary.
Siccis, sc. *ramis.*
Torrida. The active sense ' bit-
ing,' ' nipping,' is rare. The mean-
ing is usually either ' pinched,'
' nipped,' with cold, or far more
commonly, ' parched,' ' dried up '
with heat. Perhaps the passive
meaning might be retained here,
' frost-bitten winter.'

K

Et succos adhibere novos, ne torrida nimbis
Instet hiems, nimioque gelu nivibusque coactis
Incurvare vetet nemus et constringere frondes.
Tu tamen aut leves hederas aut molle salictum   110
Valle premes media : sitis est pensanda tuorum,
Canthe, gregum viridante cibo : nihil aridus illis,
Ingenti positus quamvis strue, prosit acervus,
Virgea si desunt liquido turgentia succo,
Et quibus est aliquid plenae vitale medullae.   115
Praecipue gelidum stipula cum fronde caduca
Sterne solum, ne forte rigor penetrabile corpus

---

107. Heins. c. *sulcos ;* cf. IV. 113. Martell. c. *licet horrida,* and in
109 *velit nemus.* Ulit. c. *ne, ut torrida nimbis Instat hiems* (i. e.
quando hiems est, ne incurvare velis). Burm c. *ne, turbida nimbis
Cum stet hiems—Incurvare velis.* Haupt c. *dum* for *ne.*
    108. Glaes. adopts *coactus* from P. *coactis* vulg.
    109. *velis* omn. libr. Ulit. and Burm. adopt *velit* from Martelli's
conjecture. *vimen* for *nemus* VGR1.rf1.vd2. Tit. and Heins. c.
vimen et stringere. Haupt c. *Incursare vetet.*
    110. *Tum tamen* f2.
    111. *premens* P. *premes media* D1. *gelida* vulg.
    114. *desunt* D1. *desint* vulg.
    116. *stipulae cum fronde* D1., whence Glaes. gives *stipula cum.
stipulis et fronde* vulg.
    117. *Sintne solum* D1. *Sterne polum ne forte riget* R2.

---

111. **Premes,** 'lop.' Cf. Hor.
C. I, 31, 9: *Premant Calena falce
quibus dedit Fortuna vitem.* If
frost and snow prevented him
from cutting other trees he might
lop the smooth-leaved evergreen
ivy and soft willow.
    Pensanda, 'should be allayed.'
See note on III. 83.
    112. **Viridante cibo,** 'green
fodder.'
    114 sq. **Virgea** probably agrees
with *pabula,* which is easily sup-
plied from the foregoing *cibus.*
'If fodder of sprouts be wanting
which is swollen with sap and
full of life and vigour.'

Medulla is the 'marrow' of
bones, the 'pith' of plants, so
that *plenae medullae* (genitive of
quality) 'full pithed' is a natural
expression for richness and vigour.
    116. 'Above all strew the cold
ground with straw and fallen
leaves.' This precept is given by
Virg. G. 3, 297 sq.
    Fronde caduca. Cf. Virg. G.
1, 368.
    117. **Rigor,** 'a chill.'
    Penetrabile, 'easily pierced'
with the cold. The active sense,
'piercing,' 'penetrating,' is more
common.

Urat, et interno vastet pecuaria morbo.
Plura quidem meminisse velim, nam plura supersunt :
Sed iam sera dies cadit, et iam sole fugato   120
Frigidus aestivas impellit Noctifer horas.

118. *et extremo vastet praecordia* D4. *externo vastet* R2. *penetralia*
PVD3.R1.2.rad1.2., which probably arose from *penetrabile* in the pre-
ceding line. G actually gives *penetrabile* in this line.
119. *meminisse velim* D1. *monuisse velim* vulg.

118. **Urat**, 'nip.' It is re-
markable that the same verb is
used to describe the effect of heat
and cold. Compare the use of
torridus, line 107, and Livy 21,
32, 7 : *pecora jumentaque torrida
frigore.*
Pecuaria, neut. pl. 'herds of

cattle.' We also find *pecuaria*
fem. sing.
121. **Impellit** is used like
pelleret in VIII. 47, 'hastens on
the summer hours.'
Noctifer is equivalent to
Hesperus, which occurs in IX.
90.

ECLOGA SEXTA.

ASTILUS, LYCIDAS, MNASYLLUS.

THIS Eclogue is appropriately entitled Litigium. It is on the whole the least successful of the poems of Calpurnius.

Astilus and Lycidas quarrel over a decision given by the former in a contest between Nyctilus and Alcon. It is proposed to settle the dispute by a trial of poetic skill between Astilus and Lycidas; but as they seem about to lose their temper, Mnasyllus, whom they have chosen arbiter, breaks off the contest.

A. Serus ades, Lycida : modo Nyctilus et puer Alcon
Certavere sub his alterno carmine ramis,

In hac Aegloga interlocutores Hastilus et Lycidas pastores Emuli et dissidentes R1.ra. The following varieties occur in the spelling of the proper names :—*Astilus, Hastilus, Astylus, Mnasyllus, Manasilus, Mnasilus.* This Eclogue is inscribed *Litigium* in f1.π, &c., until Wernsd.

1. *Ectus* VGr. *Tectus* R1. *Laetus* d1.2. *Aetus* D4.R2. *Letus* D2.3. Burm. c. *Lentus* from VII. 1, where there is also a remarkable variety in the readings. It is possible that *Aetus* and *Letus* may have come from *Ectus* by joining to it respectively the initial letters A = *Astilus* and L = *Lycidas.* Conversely in VII. 1, the reading *Entus* seems to have arisen from separating the initial L of *Lentus* to represent *Lycotas.*

1. **Serus**, 'too late.' Cf. Quint. 12, 1, 31 : *neque enim rectae voluntati serum est tempus ullum,* 'it is never too late to mend.'
2. **Alterno carmine** = *amoebaeo carmine* 'responsive, amoebean song.' In Ov. F. 2, 121 : *Dum canimus sacras alterno carmine Nonas, alterno carmine* means elegiac verse, interchanging between hexameter and pentameter.

Iudice me, sed non sine pignore. Nyctilus haedos
Iuncta matre dedit : catulum dedit ille leaenae,
Iuravitque genus : sed sustulit omnia victor.   5
L. Nyctilon ut cantu rudis exsuperaverit Alcon,
Astile, credibile est, si vincat acanthida cornix,
Vocalem superet si dirus aedona bubo.

3. *aedes* R2.

4. *Laconum Juravitque* cd. Titii. Heins. c. *Laconem* or *Lacaenae.*
Some punctuate *ille, leaenae Juravitque.*

6. *et* VGR1.rbo. Glaes. c. *Nyctilon en cantu.* *exuperaverat* bo.
Glaes. cites *exuperaverit* from some old books.

7. *Ast ille* R2. *si vincat* D1.d1.2. *ut vincat* vulg. The vulg. puts
a note of interrogation after *credibile est.* Heins. c. *sic,* as also in the
following line, for *si.* Kannegieter c. *ita vincat.*

8. *si* vulg. Heins. c. *sic.* *si turpis* D3. *turpior* VGD2.4.R1.2.rd2.,
which reading was doubtless owing to a belief that *aedona* was a tri-
syllable.

3. Judice, &c., 'with me as
umpire, and not without a stake.'
On the contrary, in II. 22, Thyrsis
says : *me judice pignora . . .
irrita sint moneo.*
4. Juncta matre, 'along with
its mother.'
Catulum leaenae, 'a pup of .
the lion breed,' perhaps, as we
say, 'a wolf-hound,' or more
likely following the tradition men-
tioned by Pliny 8, 40, 61, 147,
that dogs are begotten of tigers,
wolves, &c. Probably, however,
Heins. is right in conjecturing
Laconem for *leaenae.* Spartan
dogs, like Newfoundland with us,
were famed for strength and vigi-
lance. Cf. Hor. Epod. 6, 5 :
*qualis Molossus aut fulvus Lacon,
Amica vis pastoribus.*
5. Juravitque genus, 'and
affirmed its breed on oath.'
Sed sustulit, &c., 'but the

conqueror carried off all.' These
words express the rustic's wonder
at the value of the stakes.
7. Acanthida. The *acanthis* f.
(pure Latin, *carduelis*), 'the
thistle-finch,' or 'gold-finch,' is a
small bird of dark green colour.
Wernsdorf quotes the following
note on this passage from Eras-
mus : ' Acanthis enim vocalis est
avis, et in primis canora. Cornix
obstrepera quidem, sed minime
canora.'
8. Aedona. *Aedon* f. 'the
nightingale,' pure Latin *luscinia.*
Cf. IX. 61.
Bubo m., except Virg. A. 4, 462
where it is f. : 'the horned owl.'
Greek βύας. A bird of evil omen,
whence called *dirus.* Cf. Theocr.
5, 136 : οὐ θεμιτόν, Λάκων, ποτ'
ἀηδόνα κίσσας ἐρίσδεν, οὐδ' ἔποπας
κύκνοισι. Virg. E. 8, 56 : *certent
et cycnis ululae.*

A. Non potiar Petale, qua nunc ego maceror una,
Si magis aut docili calamorum Nyctilus arte,   10
Aut cantu magis est, quam vultu, proximus illi.
L. Iam non decipior ; te iudice pallidus alter
Venit, et hirsuta spinosior histrice barba ;
Candidus alter erat, levique decentior ovo,
Et ridens oculis crinemque simillimus auro,   15
Qui posset dici, si non cantaret, Apollo.
A. O Lycida, si quis tibi carminis usus inesset,

9. *Non pociar* D1.   Ascens. c. *Ne potiar.*   *Te potiar* R1.rd1.boπ
vulg.   *Te patiar* pβf1.2.va1.2.t.   *Petale* aπ.   *Crotale* VGR1.rf1.2.bo.
Crocale D1.2.4.d1.2.pts.   *torqueor una* abo.

10. *Simagis* R2.   *Si magna aut* D1.

12. *Iam non* D1.   *Iam nunc* vulg.   *panetas* VGR1.r.   Wernsd. c.
panicus (*Panos forma*).   Heins. c. *squalidus.*

13. Heins. c. *hirsutam sp. hystr. barbam.*

14. *levique* D1.R1.2.ra.   *lenique* pa2.f2.   *aevo* D3.d1.

15. *viridans* GR1.rad2.

17. *inesset* D1.   *adesset* vulg.

9. Non potiar Petale, 'may
I never win Petale.' *Non* for *ne*
is found only in poetry and post-
Aug. prose. Ov. A. A. 3, 129:
non sint sine lege capilli. If *Te
patiar* be read, the meaning is,
'may I continue to find you un-
kind.'
10 sq. 'If Nyctilus has any
more claim to rank anywhere near
to him (Alcon) either from his skill
in playing the pipes, or from his
singing, than he has from his
personal appearance.'
Docili calamorum arte. Cf.
II. 28 : *dociles avenas.*
12. Pallidus, 'pale.' In line
14 **candidus,** 'fair.'
13. Histrice, 'porcupine.'
Compare Hamlet, Act 1, scene 5.

*And each particular hair to stand
on end,* Like *quills upon the
fretful porcupine.* We have a
description of the *Histrix* or *Hys-
trix* in Claudian Idyll. 2.
15. 'With laughing eyes and
golden hair.'
16. You might call him Apollo,
unless you heard him sing, when
you would perceive that he fell
short of the god in *that* respect.
This is of course ironical. It is
what *Astilus* would have thought
(*te judice*).
17. Si quis, &c., 'if you had
any skill in song.' For the use
of **inesset** cf. Ov. F. 2, 224 :
*Quosque vident sternunt ; nec
metus alter inest.*

Tu quoque laudatum posses Alcona probare.
L. Vis igitur, quoniam nec nobis, improbe, par es,
Ipse tuos iudex calamos committere nostris ?   20
Vis conferre manus ? veniat licet arbiter Alcon.
A. Vincere tu quemquam ? vel te certamine quisquam
Dignetur, qui vix stillantes, aride, voces
Rumpis et expellis male singultantia verba ?
L. Fingas plura licet : nec enim potes, improbe, vera   25

18. *Alterna probare* Dı. Haupt c. *nosses* for *posses.* See Notes 2.
19. *pars est* R2.
20. *calamis* V. *nostros* Dı., whence Glaes. c. *Ipse tuis i.c.c. nostros.*
21. *manum* D2.3.4.R2.d2.pβa2.f2. *veni licet* R2. *veniat vel* fı.vaı.π
Barth. *vel veniat* VGRı.r. Ulit. c. *veniat velit.* Heins. c. *veniat vel
hic* or *veniatque vel. haud nunc erit arbiter Alcon* a.
22. *Vinces tu* Dı. Glaes. c. *Vincen.*
23. *qui vis* Dı. *quid vis* D4.R2. Heins. c. *titubantes* or *strigantes :*
the latter word, however, would violate the metre, as the first syllable
is short, see Virg. Cat. 8, 19 : (*laeva, sive dextera*) *Strigare mula,
sive utraeque coeperant. aride* Rı.ra. Wernsd. says all the other
books have *arida.* Heins. c. *fauces.*
24. *Rumpit et expellit* D3.
25. *improba verba* R2. *verbo* VGRı.ra. These readings are pro-
bably due to *verba* at the end of the preceding line. Tit. and Barth. c.
vera, of which Wernsd. and Glaes. approve.

18. Posses. Haupt (Hermes
vol. 6, page 390) thinks the true
reading to be *nosses* not *posses.*
The latter word, he says, would
be weak and unmeaning. The
poets often join *novi* with the
infinitive of another verb, e.g.
IX. 64 : Virg. A. 8, 316 : Ov.
Ep. 6, 53.
19. Nec = *ne quidem,* as in
Mart. 6, 77, 1 : *Cum sis tam
pauper, quam nec miserabilis Irus.*
' Since you are not a match even
for me.' It might, however, be
translated : ' since you are not a
match for me either.'
20. 'Judge though you were,
will you match your reed pipe
against mine ? '

Ipse judex, referring to the
words of Astilus in line 3.
Nostris, sc. *calamis.*
21. Veniat, &c., i. e. Alcon
himself may be the umpire if you
like.
22. Vincere tu quemquam,
sc. *potes :* see line 25. Cf. Virg.
E. 3, 25 : *cantando tu illum.* We
would expect *Vincere te,* &c. ; or
vinces of Dı. may be right.
**23. Vix stillantes . . . voces
Rumpis,** 'with difficulty jerk
out notes drop by drop.'
Aride, ' dry voiced' : see note
on III. 59.
24. Expellis, &c., ' you blurt
out miserably broken expressions.'
25. Fingas is emphatic. ' You

Exprobrare mihi, sicut tibi multa Lycotas.
Sed quid opus vana consumere tempora lite?
Ecce venit Mnasyllus : erit, nisi forte recusas,
Arbiter inflatis non credulus, improbe, verbis.
A. Malueram, fateor, vel praedamnatus abire,   30
Quam tibi certanti partem committere vocis.
Ne tamen hoc impune feras : en aspicis illum,
Candida qui medius cubat inter lilia cervum?
Quamvis hunc Petale mea diligat, accipe victor.

29. *inflatis non credulus* D1., which Heins. c. as well as *inflatis non cedimus*. *Arbiter. Insta nunc non* vulg., which Wernsd. retains and explains ' press on (to get a proof in deeds) since you are so reluctant to believe words.' Burm. c. *non credimus*.
30. *praedam nactus* vulg. Barth. c. *praedem*. Burm. c. *nec praedam* or *nec praeda mactus*. Heins. c. *praemia pactus*. Gud. c. *praeda tactus*, explaining *praeda* as equivalent to *munus* from line 48. *nactus abires* d1.2. Tross. Observ. critt. ch. 4, p. 17, conjectures *praedamnatus. natus abire* D1.
31. Heins. c. *palmam*.
32. *Ne t.h.i. feras* D1. *Nec t.h.i. feres* vulg.
33. *melius* GR1.D2.r.

may tell as many lies as you like, for you cannot bring true reproaches against me.'
26. Sicut tibi multa Lycotas, sc. *vera exprobravit.*
27. Vana lite, 'fruitless wrangling.'
29. ' A judge who puts no trust in pompous language.'
30. Vel, ' even.'
Praedamnatus, ' condemned beforehand,' i. e. before being heard. Cf. Suet. Aug. 56: *ne destituere ac praedamnare amicum existimaretur.* The vulgate reads *praedam nactus*, which, in order to suit the context, must be explained, ' I had rather even when I had found a booty go off without taking it.' This, however, is quite opposed to the natural sense of the words, viz. : ' to go

off with booty,' (as in Ov. M. 3, 606, 607 : *Utque putat, praedam deserto nactus in agro, Virginea puerum ducit per littora forma*) and the reading of the Neapolitan MS. *natus* for *nactus* supports *praedamnatus*, which is adopted by Glaeser.
31. ' Than match a single note of my voice against you as my competitor.'
32. Ne tamen, &c., ' however, that you may not escape unpunished for this presumption.' Cf. Cic. Fam. 13, 77, 3 : *cum multos libros surripuisset nec se impune laturum putaret, aufugit.*
33 sq. For the description of the stag see note on line 38, and Virg. Æ. 7, 483 sq.
34. Victor, 'if victorious.'

Scit frenos et ferre iugum, sequiturque vocantem　　35
Credulus, et mensae non improba porrigit ora.
Aspicis, ut fruticat late caput, utque sub ipsis
Cornibus et tereti pendent redimicula collo ?
Aspicis, ut niveo frons irretita capistro
Lucet, et a dorso, quae totam circuit alvum,　　　40
Alternat vitreas lateralis cingula bullas ?
Cornua subtiles ramosaque tempora molles

---

35. *frenos et* PD1.2.3.4.GR1.2.rad2. *frenos, scit* vulg.
37. *fruticat* R1. *fruticet* PVD2.4.R2.d2.pβa2.f2. *fruticem late
capit* D1. Heins. c. *sub hirtis.*
38. *et tereti pendent* D1. *tereti lucent* vulg. This and following line
are wanting in GR1.r.
40. *Lucet etiam a dorso* D1.
42. Titius found *sutiles* (which gives a suitable meaning but violates
the metre) in a very old copy. Heins. c. *Cornua sutilibus molles
ramosa corollis.* Burm. thinks *subtiles* is a corruption of the name of
some other flower besides the rose.

---

36. Credulus, ' with confi-
dence.'
Mensae, &c., 'stretches out its
mouth gently, not offensively, to
the table.'
37. Ut fruticat, &c., ' how
its head branched with wide
antlers.'
38. Redimicula, ' necklet.'
Cf. Ovid's description of the
sacred stag, M. 10, 110 sq. :
*Ingens cervus erat ; lateque paten-
tibus altas Ipse suo capiti prae-
bebat cornibus umbras : Cornua
fulgebant auro, demissaque in
armos Pendebant tereti gemmata
monilia collo. Bulla super fron-
tem parvis argentea loris Vincta
movebatur : parilesque ex aere
nitebant Auribus in geminis
circum cava tempora baccae.
Isque metu vacuus, naturalique
pavore Deposito,* &c.
39. Ut Niveo, &c., ' how its

forehead glitters, bound with a
snow-white head-band.'
40 sq. Et a dorso, &c., ' and
from his back, the side girth,
which runs right round his belly,
suspends glass amulets on this
side and that.' Cf. Ov. Rem.
Am. 236 : *Ut nova velocem cingula
laedat equum ?*
Cingulum n. is used of a belt
worn by human beings, *cingula* f.
of animals, according to Servius.
This distinction, however, is not
always observed.
42 sq. If the text be correct it
must mean, ' roses twine in a
slender wreath (**subtiles**) round
his horns and softly (**molles**)
round his branching temples.'
There is, however, doubtless
something wrong. *Sutiles,* in
violation of the metre, is quoted
by Titius from an old copy as a
variant for *subtiles,* and Burmann

Implicuere rosae, rutiloque monilia torque
Extrema cervice natant, ubi pendulus apri
Dens sedet, et nivea distinguit pectora luna.   45
Hunc ego, qualemcunque vides, Mnasylle, paciscor
Pendere, dum sciat hic se non sine pignore vinci.
L. Terreri, Mnasylle, suo me munere credit :
Aspice, quam timeam. Genus est, ut scitis, equarum
Non vulgare mihi, quarum de sanguine ponam   50

44. *Externa cervice natant, vel pend.* D1. Ulit. c. *nitent.* All MSS. except D1. read *notant.*
46. *Hunc sicut cumque vides Mnasille paciscor* D1. *vides in valle, paciscor* vulg.
47. *Perdere* PD1.
49. *quem* D1. Heins. c. *et scitis.*
50. *vulgare* D1. *iugale* vulg., which should be scanned *iŭgălĕ.* Barth. c. *Non iunctum ante.* Ulit. c. *Coniugiale.* Burm. c. *Non venale.* Gebhard. c. *non subigale.*

suggests that the name of some flower may be concealed under this corruption.

43. Rutilo torque qualify **monilia,** 'a collar with red chain,' i. e. a collar or necklet of gold. Lucan 9, 364, uses *rutilum metallum* for 'gold.' Cf. Theocr. 11, 40 sq. : τρέφω δέ τοι ἕνδεκα νεβρὼς πάσας μαννοφόρως. Virg. A. 7, 278 : *Aurea pectoribus demissa monilia pendent.*

44 sq. Natant 'swing to and fro from the bottom of his neck.' Cf. Ov. A. A. 1, 516 : *nec vagus in laxa pes tibi pelle natet.*

Ubi pendulus, &c., 'where the pendent tusk of a boar sits well, and marks the stag's breast with a snowy crescent.'

Sedet is used of attire, as we say a dress *sits well.* See Quint. 11, 3, 140 : *pars togae ita sedet melius.*

45. Cf. Anth. P. 6, 246 : κόσμος ὀδοντοφόρος. Stat. Theb. 9, 688 sq. : *nemorisque notae sub pectore primo Jactantur niveo lunata monilia dente.*

46 sq. 'This stag, just as you see him, Mnasyllus, I agree to pay, provided that (i. e. in order that) this fellow (i. e. Lycidas) may know that he is not defeated without a stake.'

Qualemcunque, i. e. handsome and valuable as you see him to be. Cf. the dispute about the relative value of the stakes in Theocr. 5, 25 sq.

48. 'He imagines, Mnasyllus, that I am frightened by his stake.' The value of the stake Astilus was willing to offer would show how confident he was of victory. *Munere* is equivalent to *pignore* in the preceding line.

49. Genus, 'a breed.' It is to be noticed that Virgil and Theocritus do not represent shepherds as possessing horses.

50. Non vulgare, 'not commonplace.' This is the reading of the Neapolitan MS. The Vul-

Velocem Petason, qui gramina matre relicta
Nunc primum teneris libavit dentibus. Illi
Terga sedent, micat acre caput, sine pondere cervix,
Pes levis, adductum latus, excelsissima frons est,
Et tornata brevi substringitur ungula cornu,   55
Ungula, qua viridi sic exsultavit in arvo,
Tangeret ut fragiles, sed non curvaret, aristas:
Hunc dare, si vincar, silvestria numina iuro.

51. *Veloci* VGR1.rabo. *Pegasum* d1.2., which violates the metre. *gramine* R1. *gramen* D4.R2.
53. This verse (which is wanting in P) is usually placed after 54, but Glaeser arranges as in the text following bo. Ulit. c. *micat aure, caput s. p. curvum* or *cernuum.* Heins. c. *sine pondere pernix* or *venter.*
54. This line is omitted in VGD4.R1.2.ra. *excelsissima frons est* bo. *excelsissima cervix* vulg., repeating *cervix* from preceding line.
55. *Ut tornata* ψ. *Et coronata* d1.2, in violation of metre. *curvata* D4.R2. *collo* P.
56. *quam* D1. *quae* vulg. *qua* pβa2.f2. *auro* G.
57. *non sed* ψ. Barth. c. *non et. si non* D1. This and following line are wanting in VGR1.r.
58. *Nunc* D2. *Hunc dari se vincar* D4. *Huic dari sinnicor* R2. *si vincas* d1.2.a.

gate *non jugale* (scan *iŭgălĕ*) means 'that has never borne the yoke,' and might be considered a counterblast to what Astilus says of his stag in line 35 : *scit ferre jugum.* .

Ponam, ' I will stake.' Cf. Virg. E. 3, 36 : *pocula ponam Fagina.*

51. Petason. This name of a horse is said to be from πέτομαι, or the collateral form πέταμαι. It does not occur elsewhere, and not unnaturally gave rise to the variant *Pegasus,* which, however, violates the metre. The common noun *petasus* = πέτασος is, of course, connected with πετάννυμι. Verus is said to have had a horse called *Volucer,* and Caligula one called *Incitatus.*

53. Sedent, 'is deep set.'

Micat acre caput, 'his spirited head tosses,' ' he tosses his head proudly.'

Sine pondere cervix, 'his neck is light, graceful, not clumsy.' Cf. Virg. G. 3, 79 : *illi ardua cervix.*

54. Adductum latus, ' his flank is narrow.' Cf. Virg. G. 3, 80 : *brevis alvus.*

55. 'And his shapely foot is bound below with a short horny hoof.'

57. A familiar mode of describing great speed. Cf. the description of Camilla in Virg. A. 7, 808 : *Illa vel intactae segetis per summa volaret Gramina, nec teneras cursu laesisset aristas.*

58. Silvestria, &c., ' I swear by the woodland deities.'

M. Et vacat, et vestros cantus audire iuvabit.
Iudice me sane contendite, si libet : istic   60
Protinus, ecce, torum fecere sub ilice Musae.
A. Sed ne vicini nobis sonus obstrepat amnis,
Gramina linquamus ripamque volubilis undae.
Namque sub exeso raucum mihi pumice lymphae
Respondent, et obest arguti glarea rivi.   65
L. Si placet, antra magis vicinaque saxa petamus,
Saxa, quibus viridis stillanti vellere muscus
Dependet, scopulisque cavum sinuantibus arcum
Imminet exesa veluti testudine concha.
M. Venimus, et tacito sonitum mutabimus antro,   70

60. Burm. c. *sani. contendere* d1.2. *contemnite* R2. Heins. c.
ista.
65. *galearia* D1. *gl. ruris* d1.n.
68. Heins. c. *scrupisque. stipulisque c. stravantibus* R2.
69. Heins. c. *exesae v. t. conchae.*
70. Burm. c. *mutabimus. mutavimus* D1. *ructabimus* VGrad2.
ructantibus R1. *tutabimur* vulg. *turbabimur* D2.4. Heins. c. *hic
tacito s. vitabimus antro.*

59. Vacat, ' I have leisure and
will be happy to hear your songs.'
60. Sane contendite, si libet,
' contend then if you wish.' *Sane*
is often used with imperatives in
colloquial language like the Eng-
lish ' then, pray then, if you will.'
Istic Protinus, &c., ' there
forthwith, without more ado, be-
hold the Muses have made a
(grassy) couch for us under the
oak.' The bucolic poets often
represent the Muses as serving
them. Cf. Virg. E. 3, 85 :
*Pierides vitulam lectori pascite
vestro.*
62. Nobis . . . obstrepat, ' din
our ears.'
63. Volubilis, ' flowing.' Cf.
Hor. Ep. 1, 2, 43 : *Labitur* (sc.
amnis) *et labetur in omne volubilis
aevum.*

64 sq. ' For under the worn,
porous rock the waters re-echo
to me hoarsely ; and the gravel
of the babbling brook annoys me.'
Observe the alliteration in *arguti
glarea rivi.*
67. Stillanti vellere muscus,
' moss with dripping fleece,' a
happy simile in the lips·of a shep-
herd who had often seen the drip-
ping sheep on the bank after
washing.
68 sq. Scopulisque, &c., ' and
a shell roof, like a hollow tortoise
shell (lit. a tortoise shell, as it were,
having been hollowed out), over-
hangs the rocks which form a hol-
low and winding arch.'
70. ' We have arrived, and will
exchange the din for the silent
cave.'

Seu residere libet, dabit, ecce, sedilia tophus,
Ponere seu cubitum, melior viret herba tapetis.
Nunc mihi seposita reddantur carmina lite,
Nam vicibus teneros malim cantetis amores :
Astile, tu Petalen, Lycida, tu Phyllida lauda.　75
L. Tu modo nos illis iam nunc, Mnasylle, precamur,
Auribus excipias, quibus hunc et Acanthida nuper
Diceris in silva iudex audisse Thalea.

71. *tophis* Dɪ.
72. *vir et herba* R2.　*videt herba* G.　*tapetis* fɪ.vaɪ.p.　*lapillis*
PVD2.3.4.GRɪ.2.rdɪ.2.apβa2.f2.bo.　Ulit. c. *mediis v. h. lapillis.*
76. *Nos ipsi* GD4.R2.dɪ.2.pβa2.f2.abo.　Glaes. c. *nos illis ipsis,*
Mnasylle, precamur.
77. *accipias* Dɪ.　*excipias* vulg.
78. *Thalia* VGa.　*Thalaea* t.　Tit. c. *Theloni.*　Heins. c. *Galesa.*
See Notes 2.

72. **Ponere cubitum,** 'to re-
cline.' Cf. Hor. S. 2, 4, 39 : *Lan-
guidus in cubitum jam se conviva
reponet.* Id. C. 1, 27, 8 : *cubito
remanete presso.*
Melior, &c., 'the green grass
is better than couch-covers.'
Tapete, is, n. makes the pl.
tapetia or *tapeta.* We also find
an acc. sing. *tapeta,* nom. pl. *ta-
petae,* acc. pl. *tapetas,* abl. pl.
tapetis and *tapetibus.*
It was customary to cover the
couches with such rugs. See Ov.
M. 13, 638 : *positisque tapetibus
altis.*
73. 'Now give up wrangling,
and rehearse your songs to me.'
For *reddere,* 'to render' a song,
cf. Hor. C. 4, 6, 43 : *ego dis ami-
cum . . . Reddidi carmen.*
74. 'For I would rather hear
you sing alternately of tender
love,' sc. than hear you quarrel-
ing.
76-78. The context shows that
these words contain some allu-

sion offensive to Astilus ; but
more than this we do not know.
Wernsdorf suggests that Acan-
this is a witch, quoting Propert.
4, 5, 61, where a witch of that
name is mentioned ; that *Thalea*
is connected with the *thalli* or
mystic boughs mentioned in the
Ciris, 376 ; and that the allusion
is to some magic rites in which
Astilus took part. He also sug-
gests that *Thalea* may be equiva-
lent to *Sicilian,* from the nymph
Thalia mentioned by Macrobius,
and in his Addenda proposes to
explain the passage of a wood
sacred to this nymph, in which
persons accused of theft were tried.
Adelung, with more probability,
thinks that Acanthis was a shep-
herd who had defeated Astilus
on some occasion when Mnasyllus
was judge. Wernsdorf and Ascen-
sius think *Thalia* is equivalent to
viridante, connecting it with the
Greek θάλεια.
Perhaps some light may be de-

A. Non equidem possum, cum provocet iste, tacere.
Rumpor enim merito : nihil hic, nisi iurgia, quaerit.   80
Audiat aut dicat, quoniam cupit ; hoc mihi certe
Dulce satis fuerit, Lycidam spectare trementem,
Dum te stante palam sua crimina pallidus audit.
L. Me, puto, vicinus Stimicon, me proximus Aegon

80. *Rumpe enim* D4.R2. *enim et merito* d1.2.
81. *ut dicat* D3.4.R2. Tit. cites *et dicat.* Barth. c. *ut dicit.* Heins.
c. *Audeat : audiri quoniam cupit. capit* P. *quoniam libet* Tit.
83. *me stante* G. Barth. cites a reading *testante,* and c. *testem ante.*
Ulit. c. *testata palam.* Heins. c. *te teste palam.* Burm. c. *te astante.*
Guid. cites *crimina* from some old MSS. So also Tit.af1.va1.πd2.
carmina VD3.4.R1.2.rd2.bopβa2.f2.

rived from the opening lines of
Virgil's sixth eclogue : *Prima
Syracosio dignata est ludere versu
Nostra nec erubuit silvas habitare
Thalia,* in which Thalia is the
patroness of bucolic poetry. ' The
wood of Thalia ' would thus mean
' the wood in which contests in
bucolic poetry are wont to take
place,' and would sufficiently ex-
plain the nature of the transaction
between Astilus and Acanthis,
which, according to the usual ex-
planations, is not indicated in the
text. It may be noticed that,
according to Servius, *Thalea,* not
Thalia, is the true reading in Vir-
gil. For the proper name Thalia
used as an adjective, compare the
analogous use of *Sychaeus* in
Virg. A. 4, 552 : *cinis Sychaeus,*
' ashes of Sychaeus.'
I am indebted to Mr. Purser
for a further suggestion on this
difficult passage. He takes *Thalia*
as nom. case and explains ' a very
Thalia (i. e. Muse of bucolic
poetry) in your skill as judge.'
80. Rumpor enim merito,
sc. *irâ,* ' I am ready to burst
with anger, and that with good

reason.' This meaning of *rumpi*
is found in Cic. Q. F. 3, 1, 9,
where it is explained by *stoma-
chari : ut his malis reïpublicae
licentiaque audacium, qua ante
rumpebar, nunc ne movear qui-
dem. Nihil est enim perditius his
hominibus, his temporibus. Ita-
que ex republica quoniam nihil
jam voluptatis capi potest ; cur
stomacher, nescio.* Cf. Virg. E.
7, 26 : *invidia rumpantur ut ilia
Codro.*
Rumpi is generally used of great
effort in running or speaking, and
should be so taken in Hor. S. 1, 3,
136, where Lewis and Short erro-
neously explain it of anger.
Nihil nisi, &c., ' he is only
seeking a quarrel.'
81. Audiat, &c., ' let him
either hear or speak since he will
have it so,' i. e. I am willing that
either he or I should commence.
83. Te stante, i.e. in your pre-
sence, you being witness.
Pallidus. Cf. Hor. Ep. 1, 1,
61 : *nulla pallescere culpa.*
84. Puto, ' I suppose it was at
me Stimicon, &c., laughed.' This
and the following lines are ironical,

Hos inter frutices tacite risere volentem   85
Oscula cum tenero simulare virilia Mopso.
A. Fortior o utinam nondum Mnasyllus adesset :
Efficerem, ne te quisquam tibi turpior esset.
M. Quid furitis ? quo vos insania tendere iussit ?
Si vicibus certare placet—sed non ego vobis   90
Arbiter : hoc alius possit discernere iudex.
Et venit, ecce, Mycon, venit et vicinus Iollas :
Litibus hi vestris poterunt imponere finem.

85. *tacite fixere* P.
87. *non dum* VR2.d2.b.   Beck writes from his own conjecture *non
nunc.*   Burm. c. *modo nunc Mn. abesset,* or *modo non Mn. adesset.*
88. *nec te* ψ.   *necte* D1.d1.f1.va1.   *te* is omitted in VGR1.   *ne
etiam quisquam turpior* D4.R2., whence Glaes. c. *ne te iam quisquam
turpior.*
89. *facitis* VGR1.rabo.   *quae vos* vulg.   Guid. and Ulit. c. *quo
vos,* which is the reading of D1., and is supported by Virg. A. 5, 670 :
Quis furor iste novus ? quo nunc, quo tenditis, inquit ?
90. Barth. c. *sic non ego.*
92. Heins. c. *en vicinus.*   *Iollas* R1.ra.   *yollas* R2.
93. *hi nostris* P.   *in vestris* R2.

Lycidas feigning to accuse him-
self of what Astilus had really
done. Cf. Virg. E. 3. 10.
86. Wernsdorf has the follow-
ing note : ' *Simulare virilia,* cum
tamen essent Venerea, ait Titius ;
sed Burmannus : cum essent
puerilia, nec viri partes perage-
rent.'
88. Astilus threatens to dis-
figure Lycidas with his fists. Cf.
Stat. Theb. 4, 106 ; *Herculea
turpatus gymnade vultus.*

89. Quo, &c., ' to what ex-
tremities does your passion bid
you go ? '
90. Si vicibus, &c. Aposio-
pesis. Mnasyllus was about to
mention the conditions on which
he would allow them to contend,
but suddenly breaks off, and re-
fuses to act as judge.
Wernsdorf reads *sic* for *si,* and
puts a note of interrogation after
placet, comparing Virg. A. 1, 253 :
sic nos in sceptra reponis ?

ECLOGA SEPTIMA.

LYCOTAS, CORYDON.

THIS Eclogue is specially interesting, on account of the information it gives about the Roman amphitheatre. Corydon, on his return from the city, describes to his friend Lycotas the amphitheatre itself, and the wonderful exhibitions of which it was the scene.

Templum is the inappropriate title which this Eclogue bears. *Amphitheatrum* would be more suitable, and it has been suggested that *templum* may be a mistake for *theatrum*, which is found in the Editio Tigurina.

As to the emperor referred to, see Introduction, page 2 sq., and also the Appendix.

L. Lentus ab urbe venis, Corydon; vicesima certe
Nox fuit, ut nostrae cupiunt te cernere silvae,

In hac ecloga (*egloga septima* a) tractantur (*tractatur* r) *magnificentia urbis et ludorum Imperatoris* VR1.ra. *Interlocutores Lycotas et Corydon amici* R1.ra, save that R1. omits *amici*. Both inscriptions are added at the foot of the page in d2. *Ecloga* VII. *et ultima Calphurnii*. *Lycotas et Corydon* b. *Lycoras* pd1.2. (in the latter corrected to *-tas*). The inscription *Templum* is found in f1.π and the other editt. until Wernsdorf. According to Burm. t has *Theatrum* added in the margin. Pithoeus c. *Amphitheatrum*, and this is found in the margin of the editio Duacensis, 1632.
   1. *Queltus ab* D4. *Entus* Vrd2. See Notes I on VI. I.
   2. Heins. c. *Nox ruit. te visere* V.

1. **Lentus ab urbe venis,** 'you are slow in returning from town.'
   Vicesima nox. Cf. I. 77.

The Romans counted the beginning of the day from midnight.
   2. **Ut,** 'since.' For the past twenty nights our woods have

Ut tua moerentes exspectant iubila tauri.

C. O piger et duro non mollior axe, Lycota,
Qui veteres fagos, nova quam spectacula, mavis   5
Cernere, quae patula iuvenis deus edit arena.

L. Mirabar, quae tanta foret tibi causa morandi,
Cur tua cessaret taciturnis fistula silvis,
Et solus Stimicon caneret pallente corymbo;

---

3. *Ut tua* D1. *Et tua* vulg.   *sibila* D3.4.R2., which Heins. also c.
and Burm. and Beck approve.
4. *o duro* R2.pβf1.2.a2.d2.   *non mollior* D1.   *iam durior* vulg.
axe D1.4.R2.d2.pβa2.f2.   *asse* P.   *esse* G.   *osse* R1.raboπ Barth. Ulit.
Heins. c. *aere.*
6. *munus Deus* d1.2.   *ardet ar.* PGD2.3.4.R1.2.ra (*edere* being
understood. See Beck).   *edit* V.   Ulit. c. *audet.*
7. *tanta foret tibi causa* D1.VGR1.rabo.   *causa foret tibi tanta*
R2.pf1.d2. vulg.
9. *Nec solum* D1.   *Stymicon* VR1.rd2.a2.   *fallente* PVGR1.r.
falente D2. Heins. c. *palante. corymbos* D4. Wernsd. c. *pallente
cicuta* or *canali.*

---

been wishing to see you. For *ut
= ex quo tempore* cf. Cic. Att.
1, 15, 2 : *ut Brundusio profectus
es, nullae mihi abs te sunt red-
ditae litterae.* With *cupiunt cer-
nere* and *expectant iubila* in the
next line cf. Moschus 3, 61 sq. :
καὶ νῦν λασαμένα (sc. Γαλάτεια)
τῷ κύματος ἐν ψαμάθοισιν ἵζετ’
ἐρημαίαισι, βοὰν δ’ ἔτι σεῖο δο-
κεύει.
3. Jubila. See note on 1. 30.
4. Duro . . . axe. Axles were
made of oak or other hard wood.
5. Veteres fagos, borrowed
from Virg. E. 3, 12, and opposed
to *nova spectacula.*
6. Juvenis deus, ‘the youth-
ful deity,’ i. e. Nero.
8. Cessaret, ‘was idle, was
hushed.’ Cf. Hor. C. 3, 19, 18 sq.:
*Insanire iuvat: cur Berecyntiae
Cessant flamina tibiae? Cur pen-
det tacita fistula cum lyra?* Ov.

F. 1, 699: *Sarcula cessabant,* ‘the
hoes lay idle, unemployed.’ 11. 18:
omnia cessabant.
9. ‘And Stimicon, all alone,
sang decked with pale ivy clus-
ters.’ Cf. Virg. E. 7, 25 : *Pas-
tores, hedera crescentem ornate
poetam.*
Pallente corymbo. Ablative
of description or quality.
For *pallens,* applied to *corym-
bus,* cf. Virg. E. 3, 39 : *vitis
Diffusos hedera vestit pallente
corymbos,* where Conington ob-
serves that the words *hedera pal-
lente* are probably not to be taken
with *vestit,* but as the material
ablative with *corymbos,* and that
the ivy referred to is that kind the
leaves of which are marked with
white, or rather with light yellow.
The reading *cicuta,* or *canali,* ‘a
reed-pipe,’ is inconsistent with
the epithet *pallente.*

L

Quem sine te moesti tenero donavimus haedo.　　　10
Nam dum lentus abes, lustravit ovilia Thyrsis,
Iussit et arguta iuvenes certare cicuta.
C. Scilicet invictus Stimicon et praemia dives
Auferat, accepto non solum gaudeat haedo,
Verum tota ferat, quae lustrat ovilia Thyrsis :　　　15
Non tamen aequabit mea gaudia, nec mihi, si quis
Omnia Lucanae donet pecuaria silvae,
Grata magis fuerint, quam quae spectamus in urbe.

10. *quem si te ne moesti tereno* D4.
11. *Thyrsus* GR1.r.　Lines 11–14 are omitted in D4.
12. *juvenis* R1.rabo.
13. *Scilicet* is the universal reading except in D3., where from a
second hand is found *Sit licet,* which was conjectured by Guid. and
Barth., approved of by Burm., and adopted by Beck. *prelia* G.
Heins. c. *invitis St. ut praemia divis Auferat acc. nec solum,* or *silvis*
instead of *dives,* the rest of the passage being left unaltered.　Glaeser
thinks *et* of vulg. can hardly be right, and proposes to substitute *ut* or
haec (whence might have come *hec, ec, et*).
15. *tuta* PGR1.rad2.
17. *Lutatae* D2.
18. *fu it q̃; que exspectamus* R2.　Heins. c. *spectavimus urbe.*
Glaes. c. *spectantur in.*

11. **Dum lentus abes,** 'while
you loitered away from home.'
Cf. Ov. Rem. Am. 243 : *Nec satis
esse puta discedere, lentus abesto.*
　Lustravit.　This, doubtless,
refers to the Palilia, or feast of
Pales, celebrated on the 21st of
April, which was the great shep-
herd-festival, and was often the
occasion of musical contests.　See
lines 20–22.
　12. **Arguta,** 'shrill.'
　13 sq.　'Aye, let Stimicon, un-
conquered and wealthy, carry off
the prize ; let him not only rejoice
in the kid which he has received,
but let him carry off the whole
fold which Thyrsis purifies.'

Scilicet.　Cf. Virg. G. 1, 493 :
scilicet et tempus veniet, 'aye, and
the time will come.'
　Et.　Glaeser and Heinsius are
hardly right in objecting to this
word.　It connects *invictus* and
dives.　Unconquered in poetic
contests, and, therefore, enriched
by the prizes he has won.
　Dives is proleptic = dives fu-
turus.
　17. Lucania was celebrated for
its pastures.
　18. **Quam quae spectamus
in urbe,** 'than the city sights.'
There is no necessity to change
the reading.　The present tense
is quite natural.　Corydon, fresh

L. Dic age dic, Corydon, nec nostras invidus aures
Despice : non aliter certe mihi dulce loquere,   20
Quam cantare soles, quoties ad sacra vocantur
Aut fecunda Pales aut pastoralis Apollo.
C. Vidimus in coelum trabibus spectacula textis
Surgere, Tarpeium prope despectantia culmen,
Immensosque gradus, et clivos lene iacentes.   25

19. *nec vostras inv. ares β. invidimus auris* b. *auris* R1.rao.
20. *liquore* D4.R2.
21. *Quod certare* PV. *cantare* D1. *certare* vulg. *soles* aπ and
Mod. c. *solet* D1.2.PVGR1.r. *solent* D4. R2.pβf1.2.a1.2.stbo. *vo-
cantur* D1.4.pβf1.2.a1.2.stbo. *vocatur*R1.raπ vulg. Glaes. c. *vocabat.*
22. *facunda* PD2. *secunda* p.
24. *Surgeret* f1. Mod. cites *probe despect.*
25. *Immensoque* D2. Haupt cites *Emensique* as emendation of
Schrader. *clivos* βf1.va1.tbo. *divos* R1.2.rapa2.f2. *dives paene
lacentes* d1.n. *dives poene latentes* and in margin *clivos leve iacentis*
d2. *lente iacentis* R1. Heins. c. *ceu clivos.* Burm. c. *ut clivos.*

from the city, says : ' All the herds
of the Lucanian woodlands could
not give me more pleasure than
the sights we see in town.'
19. **Nec nostras**, &c., ' be not
so churlish as to despise my at-
tentive ears.'
20. **Non aliter**, &c., ' you will
certainly utter to me sweet strains,
just as you are wont to sing,
&c.'
22. **Pastoralis Apollo.** Apollo
is said to have tended the flocks
of Admetus in Thessaly, to which
circumstance Euripides alludes
in a beautiful chorus, *Alcestis*
569 sq. Homer makes but few
allusions to the pastoral character
of this god. Cf. IX. 55.
23. **In coelum.** For this ex-
aggerated expression cf. the words
of Ammianus Marcellinus 16, 10,
14 : *Amphitheatri molem solida-
tam lapidis Tiburtini compage,
ad cujus summitatem aegre visio
humana conscendit.*

Spectacula, 'seats.' *Specta-
culum*, properly the show, spec-
tacle, hence the place whence
it is viewed, just as θέα means
both a sight and a seat in the
theatre. **Gradus** below means
' tiers.' In Tac. A. 14, 13, we
find *spectaculorum gradus.*
24. **Tarpeium**, &c., 'almost
looking down on, overtopping,
the Capitoline.' The Tarpeian
Rock was on the Capitoline. On
this passage see the Appendix.
25. **Immensos.** Haupt men-
tions with approval Schrader's
emendation *Emensi.*
Clivos lene jacentes, 'gently-
sloping inclines,' which connected
the seats, and led to the corridors.
Cf. Lucr. 4, 518: *cubantia tecta*,
' sloping,' ' inclining.'
Lenis is used of a ' gentle '
slope in Livy 5, 24: *lenis ab tergo
clivus erat.* *Lene* occurs as an
adverb only in verse ; the prose
form is *leniter.*

Venimus ad sedes, ubi pulla sordida veste
Inter femineas spectabat turba cathedras.
Nam quaecumque patent sub aperto libera coelo,
Aut eques aut nivei loca densavere tribuni.
Qualiter haec patulum concedit vallis in orbem,   30
Et sinuata latus, resupinis undique silvis,
Inter continuos curvatur concava montes:
Sic ibi planitiem curvae sinus ambit arenae,
Et geminis medium se molibus alligat ovum.
Quid tibi nunc referam, quae vix suffecimus ipsi   35

28. *petent* pβ (Guid. corrected to *patent*). *petant* ψ.
29. *Aut equos* R1.r. Heins. c. *densa habuere trib.*
30. *concedit* D1., which Burm. c. *contendit vallis* vulg.
31. *lacus* nd2.
32. This and the two following lines are omitted in PVGD4.R1.2. rad1.2.n.
33. *Sic ibi* D1.2.3., which Barth. and Heins. c. *Sic tibi* vulg.
35. *non suff.* D4. *q̃ nũc suffec.* R2.

26. Pulla, 'dingy.' Cf. line 81:
pullaque paupertas. The third
maenianum, or story, was reserved
for the *pullati*, or common people.
Above this was the gallery, which
contained seats for the women.
Pinder.
27, 28. These regulations as to
the seats seem to have been due
to Augustus. See Suet. 44: *sanxit
ne quis pullatorum media cavea
sederet. Feminis ne gladiatores
quidem . . . nisi ex superiore loco
spectare concessit.*
29. Nivei, 'white-robed,' op-
posed to *pullati.*
Densavere, 'thronged.'
30. Qualiter, 'just as.' Cf.
Ov. Am. 1, 7, 58 : *Qualiter ab-
jecta de nive manat aqua.*
Haec patulum, &c., 'this
valley opens into a wide cir-
cuit.'
31. 'And with winding sides

and woods sloping back in every
direction' from the plain.
32. 'With curved form winds
among the unbroken range of
hills.' Notice the alliteration.
33. 'So there the sweep of the
amphitheatre (**sinus curvae are-
nae**) surrounds, runs round the
plain.' The vulgate *sic tibi* means
'just so, you see,' *tibi* being ethi-
cal dative.
34. 'And an oval binds itself
in the middle with two corre-
sponding piles of building,' ex-
plained by Pinder to mean that
the amphitheatre presents the
appearance of two theatres turned
round on pivots so as to face each
other. See Appendix. Cf. Stat.
Silv. 3, 5, 91 : *Et geminam mo-
lem nudi tectique theatri.*
35. Suffecimus, 'were able,'
with an inf. as in Virg. A. 5, 21 sq.:
nec tendere tantum sufficimus.

Per partes spectare suas ? sic undique fulgor
Percussit : stabam defixus et ore patenti,
Cunctaque mirabar, necdum bona singula noram.
Tum mihi, tum senior lateri qui forte sinistro
Iunctus erat, Quid te stupefactum, rustice, dixit,   40
Ad tantas miraris opes ? qui, nescius auri,
Sordida tecta, casas, et sola mapalia nosti.

36. *it undique* GR1.r. *it* V with *ut* written above. *is me undi-
que* a.
38. Heins. c. *necdum bene,* which Beck adopts. Burm. c. *nec enim
nova singula.*
39. *Tum mihi tum* D1.2.3.a, which Beck adopts. *Tum mihi dum*
f1.2.va1.bo***π*** Barth. Ulit. Burm. *Tum mihi cum* D4. Burm. c. *Quum
mihi, qui senior lateri tum forte.*
40. *quid me* PVGD3.4.R1.2.ra. *qui me* D1. Ulit. c. *quid tu.*
42. This line is awkwardly expressed, and can hardly be the true
reading. Burmann's suggestion, *tesqua* for *tecta,* fails to make the line
satisfactory, and cannot adduce in its support any variation in the
MSS., which seem to be unanimous in reading *tecta.*

The editio Ascensiana gives *vides,* instead of *casas,* and this is
probably the true reading, for it restores the balance of the line, it
gives a suitable meaning, and it explains both the vulgate *casas* and
the variant *dabas,* which is found in VGR1.r. Translate : ' You
whose eyes are accustomed to shabby houses, and who are acquainted
only with huts.' This is very similar to the reproach in line 5 sq. : *Qui*

36. Per partes, ' partly, par-
tially.' Cf. Plin. Ep. 2, 5, 10 :
*quaedam ex iis talia erunt ut per
partes emendari possint.* Col. 1,
4, 5 : *quod etsi per partes nonnun-
quam damnosum est, in summa
tamen fit compendiosum.* This
explanation suits the passage, and
is adopted by Adelung, but is ren-
dered doubtful by *suas.* Perhaps
we should translate : 'things which
I myself could hardly see in their
several details.'
Fulgor, ' glitter.'
37. Percussit, ' struck, dazzled.'
Defixus, &c., ' rooted to the
spot and open-mouthed.'
38. Necdum, &c., ' nor had I

yet learned all the attractions.'
Wernsdorf explains **bona** 'quid in
singulis boni esset.' Heinsius pro-
poses to read *bene.*
**39 sq. Senior lateri ... junc-
tus.** Cf. Ov. F. 4, 377 : *at mihi
quidam Spectanti senior, contigu-
usque loco.* Ib. 5, 21 : *Et latus Oce-
ano quisquam deus advena junxit.*
41. Ad tantas, to be taken
with *stupefactum = you* need not
wonder that you are amazed at
this great magnificence; even I
am, who have grown old in the
city. Pinder.
42. Sordida tecta are in appo-
sition to *casas.* See Notes, 1.
Cf. 11. 60.

En ego tam tremulus, tam vertice canus, et ista
Factus in urbe senex, stupeo tamen omnia : certe
Vilia sunt nobis, quaecumque prioribus annis   45
Vidimus, et sordet, quidquid spectavimus olim.
Balteus en gemmis, en illita porticus auro
Certatim radiant ; nec non, ubi finis arenae
Proxima marmoreo praebet spectacula muro,

veteres fagos nova quam spectacula mavis Cernere. *Casas* was probably
a marginal explanation of the not very common *mapalia*, substituted
for *vides*, the only word in the line of the same metrical value, by the
mistake of a copyist. The similarity of A and V, and perhaps I being
written close to D, would lead to the omission of the first syllable of
vides. Dabas would then be a natural conjecture for *des*, which satis-
fies neither construction nor metre.

  43. *iam trem.* D1.a.   *tam trem.* vulg.   *et vert.* D1.2.4.PVGR1.2.ra.
tam vertice vulg.   Friesem. c. *iam vertice c. et ipsa. ac ista* D4.   *iam
tremulus et* Glaes.

  44. Before Burm. punctuated after *tamen.*

  48. *non tibi* D1.

  49. *marmorea praebet* D1.   *peragit* vulg.   *peragat* D4.R2.

43. Tremulus, 'palsied with
age.' Cf. line 73, *tremebunda se-
nectus.*

  44. Stupeo . . . omnia, 'am
amazed at everything': for active
sense governing an accusative cf.
Virg. A. 2, 31 : *Pars stupet in-
nuptae donum exitiale Minervae.*

  46. Sordet, 'seems shabby.'
Pinder says **vidimus** refers to
any sight whatever; **spectavi-
mus** to theatrical spectacles in
particular.

  47. Balteus, 'the belt,' or sur-
rounding wall, between the tiers
of seats in the amphitheatre,
usually called *praecinctio,* Gr. διά-
ζωμα.

  Porticus, 'the arcade, or
covered gallery,' at the top of the
building, where the women and
poorer classes sat.

  48. Certatim radiant, 'vie in
brilliancy.'

48 sq. **Nec non,** &c., 'and like-
wise, where the end of the arena
presents the seats nearest to the
marble wall(i.e. the *podium*),choice
ivory is inlaid on connected bars,
and unites into a cylinder, which,
turning smoothly on well-rounded
axle, by its sudden revolution de-
ceived the claws planted upon it,
and threw off the wild beasts.'

  **Ubi finis arenae . . . prae-
bet spectacula** describes the
spot where the arena ended and
the tiers of seats began, which
was marked by a marble wall,
with a revolving cylinder in front,
to prevent the possibility of the
beasts clambering up to the spec-
tators. The common reading, in-
stead of *praebet,* is *peragit,* from
which a similar meaning may be
elicited.

  Spectacula are doubtless the
seats, as in line 23 : here they are

Sternitur adiunctis ebur admirabile truncis,   50
Et coit in rotulum, tereti qui lubricus axe
Impositos subita vertigine falleret ungues,
Excuteretque feras.   Auro quoque torta refulgent
Retia, quae totis in arenam dentibus exstant,
Dentibus aequatis; et erat, mihi crede, Lycota,   55
Si qua fides, nostro dens longior omnis aratro.
Ordine quid referam ? vidi genus omne ferarum,

50. Glaes. c. *Cernitur.* Heins. c. *advectis.*
51. *colit* (corrected *cohit*) V. *colit* GR1.r. *cogit* D1. *in rotulum*
Gr. *rotulam* D1.aboπ Barth. Ulit. *qui* D1. *qua* vulg. *axem*
D2.R2.d2.apf1.βa2.f2.bo. *assem* GR1.r. Barth. c. *pluteum : teres
hic quo l. axis.* Lips. cites *rotulam teretem* or *ruplum. ruplus =
στροφεὺς γαλεάγρας.* For *qui* or *qua* Burm. reads *quo* (= *ut*). On
the variant *axem*, see Notes 2.
52. This line and the two following are wanting in PGR1.2.rad1.2.cn.
angues D1.
53. *tota refulg.* bo.
55. *Dentibus aequatis in harenam dentibus exstant* D2. (from the
preceding verse). Ulit. c. *auratis. erit* D4.R2. *creda* D1.
57. *referat* V. *referam vel genus esse* D1., whence Glaeser c. *refe-
ram, veluti genus ecce ferarum.*

the lowest tier, there the highest.
Wernsdorf, however, thinks the
word is here used of the thing ex-
hibited, viz. the wild beasts.
51. Rotulum. This form, not
rotulam, is doubtless correct. It
seems to explain the variant *axem*,
for *axe*, which would be given by
some copyist who, not knowing
that a fem. noun might have a
masc. diminutive, took *rotulum*
for an adjective, and required a
substantive for it to agree with.
The oft-repeated rule, that dimi-
nutives agree in gender with their
originals, must be discarded.
For example, we have *rana, ra-
nunculus; unguis ungula ; cu-
nae, cunabula; acus,* f. *aculeus;
fiscus, fiscina.*
54. Pinder has the following

note :—**Retia,** ' the nets which
project into the arena, hung on
solid elephants' tusks, all of equal
size and length.' These nets of
gold wire (**auro torta**), for the
purpose of keeping the wild beasts
at a distance, were suspended from
huge ivory poles, fastened into the
murus marmoreus of line 49.
**55 sq. Mihi crede . . . si qua
fides,** ' take my word for it, if
you have any trust in me.'
56. Dens longior, &c.   A
natural simile, as the share-beam
was called *dentale.* Professor
Ridgeway acutely observes, that
this, as well as the other meta-
phors put in Corydon's mouth, are
in keeping with the surroundings
of a rustic, e.g. *axis,* line 4, and
ovum, line 34.

Hic niveos lepores, et non sine cornibus apros,
Hic raram silvis etiam, quibus editur, Alcen.
Vidimus et tauros, quibus aut cervice levata 60
Deformis scapulis torus eminet, aut quibus hirtae
Iactantur per colla iubae, quibus aspera mento
Barba iacet, tremulisque rigent palearia setis.

58. *cornibus aprum* D4.R2. Heins. c. *uros.*
59. *Hic raram silvis* D1. *Hoc ticanam* R2. *Nocticanam* D4.d2.
Manticoram pβa2.f2.π vulg. Barth. c. *Manticoram silvis cinctam
quibus.* Ulit. c. *Et canam silv.* or *Manticoram et silvis etiam, quibus.*
Heins. c. *Manticoram, silvis etiam q. ed. Alce, Vidimus.*
  61. *scopulis* PD4.R2.
  62. *Iactatur* D3.
  63. *riget* V. *palearia saeptis* R2.

58. **Niveos lepores,** a rare sort
of hares, which Pliny, 8, 55, 81,
217, mentions as found on the
Alps; or perhaps ' Arctic hares.'
For the ' horned boars,' Pinder
cites Ælian, 17, 10 : Λέγει δὲ
Δίνων ἐν Αἰθιοπίᾳ γίνεσθαι ὓς τρί-
κερως.
  59. ' Here I saw the elk, which
is rare even in its native forests.'
  Alces, is, fem. These creatures
are described by Caesar in his
Gallic War, 6, 26, where he says
they had no joints in their legs,
and were obliged to sleep leaning
against a tree. The natives of the
Hercynian forest, therefore, used
to saw the trees half-through, so
that they readily gave way, and left
the elk an easy prey, as he could
not rise from the ground.
  The vulgate reads *Manticho-
ram* instead of *Hic raram.* ' I
saw the mantichora and the elk,
with his native forests'; i. e. the
trees of their native forests were
imported along with these foreign
animals, and planted in the
arena.

  The *mantichora,* μαντιχώρας, or
more properly μαρτιχώρας, is the
Persian *mard-khora,* ' man-eater,'
a fabulous Indian beast mentioned
by Ctesias, and said to be a com-
pound of a lion, a porcupine, and
a scorpion, with a man's head.
Some think it was the tiger.
  60. **Cervice levata.** They
seem to have no necks. Distin-
guish *lēvo* and *lĕvo.*
  61. The Syrian bulls, or Carici,
are described by Pliny, 8, 45, 70,
179 : *Syriacis non sunt palearia,
sed gibber in dorso. Carici quoque
in parte Asiae foedi visu, tubere
super armos a cervicibus emi-
nente.*
  Deformis . . . torus, 'an un-
sightly hump.'
  62. Per colla jubae. The
bisontes jubati of Pliny, 8, 15.
Professor Ridgeway thinks that
the humped (*torus*) bulls are
' buffaloes,' and the shaggy ones
(*hirtae jubae*) the ' urus.'
  63. Tremulisque, &c., ' and
their dewlaps are stiff, and covered
with waving bristles.'

Non solum nobis silvestria cernere monstra
Contigit: aequoreos ego cum certantibus ursis   65
Spectavi vitulos, et equorum nomine dictum,
Sed deforme pecus, quod in illo nascitur amni,
Qui sata riparum vernantibus irrigat undis.
Ah trepidi quoties nos discedentis arenae
Vidimus in partes, ruptaque voragine terrae   70

64. *Nec solum* D4.R2.d2.pβa2.f2.
65. *aequoreis* D1. *vidi cum* R2. With this line G ends.
66. *dictum* D1., which Heins. and Ulit. c. *dignum* vulg.
67. Ascens. and Barth. c. *Et deforme. quod Nillo* D1. *quod Nilo pascitur* R1.rabo. *qui Nilo nascitur amni* VD4. *quid illo pascitur* R2. Ascens. c. *quid Nilo nascitur.*
68. *vernantibus* D1., which Heins. c. or *refluentibus. venientibus* vulg.
69. *sol discedentis* D1., whence Haupt c. *sola. descendentis* vulg. Barth. c. *noctem cedentis arenae.* Glaes. c. *Ah trepidus q. sol discedentis arenae Vim vidit sparsam.*
70. *Viderimus partes* D4.R2. *in partis* R1.rab. *in pratis* o. Burm. c. *vidimus absorptas* or *immersas.* Haupt c. *Vidimus inverti.* Ulit. c. *ruptaeque.* Burm. c. *raptasque.*

65. Aequoreos . . . vitulos, 'sea-calves, seals': cf. Juv. 3, 238: *vituli marini.*
  Certantibus, i. e. accustomed to be pitted against the sea-calves, or simply put for *certantes cum ursis.* Pinder.
  Professor Ridgeway remarks that this passage implies a knowledge of the far north by the Romans of the time, as the bears referred to are doubtless Polar, the brown or black bear not preying on seals.
  66. Equorum nomine dictum, 'the hippopotamus.'
  67. Deforme pecus, 'unsightly beasts.'
  68. The rustic does not know the name of the Nile, but describes it by its well-known irrigation of

the fields. For an explanation of the rising of the Nile, see Heliodorus, Aethiopica, 2, 28.
  The vulgate *venientibus* means 'rising.'
  69 sq. Wernsdorf explains: how often did I look with fear into the spot where the sand descended, &c. He also says *descendens* may = *declivis, profunda*, namely, to a spectator looking down from above. Pinder thinks *in partes* should be taken with what follows—saw the beasts spring forth to their places in the deep arena. Haupt, from the reading of the Neapolitan MS. *sol,* instead of *nos,* conjectures *sŏla,* and reads *inverti* for *in partes.* See Introduction, page 7.

Emersisse feras ; et ab isdem saepe cavernis ·
Aurea cum croceo creverunt arbuta nimbo.

L. O felix Corydon, quem non tremebunda senectus
Impedit, o felix, quod in haec tibi saecula primos,
Indulgente deo, demittere contigit annos.   75
Nunc tibi si propius venerandum cernere numen
Sors dedit, et praesens vultumque habitumque notasti,
Dic age dic, Corydon, quae sit mihi forma deorum.
C. O utinam nobis non rustica vestis inesset !

71. *foras* ad1.2. (in the last corrected *feras*). *in hisdem s. cavernis*
D1. *et in iisdem* VR1.ra. *et aeisdem sepe* R2. From these readings
Glaes. c. *et ab isdem s. cavernis. et eisdem saepe latebris* vulg.
72. *croco* R2. *subito* D1. *arbusta* D1. *nymbo* R2. *nimbro* D1.
and also a MS. of Bartholinus, who thence c. *nimbo. libro* vulg.
74. *Impetit* R1.raπ. Tit. c. *Impulit.* Tit. and Burm. c. *primo.*
75. Glaeser says all his books give *dimittere.* Barth. c. *demittere,*
which has been the accepted reading since Burm. *quod nihil tibi* D1.
contigit agnos D4.R2.
77. *praeferens* D1. *referens* D4.R2.pβa2.sgf2.tad2. Heins. c. *Fors.*
Haupt thinks the elision should be removed by reading *habitum vul-
tumque,* or the plural, *vultus habitusque.*
78. *mihi* D1.2.VR1.rad2. *modo* vulg. Burm. c. *dic, Corydon,
mihi, quae sit forma,* or *quae sit nova forma.*
79. *vestis messet* d2. Haupt c. *obesset.*

71. In contrast to the wild
beasts a beautiful garden springs
up in the arena, while saffron
water falls in spray over the spec-
tators. Martial, de Spectaculis 21,
compares such an exhibition to
the garden of the Hesperides.
74 sq. **O felix,** &c., ' How
happy, in that by the kindness of
heaven it was your lot to cast your
early years in this age.'
76. Numen, i. e. the emperor.
77. Habitum, 'personal ap-
pearance, air, bearing.' Cf. Virg.
A. 1, 315 : *Virginis os habitum-
que gerens,* on which passage see'
Henry's *Æneidea.*
78. Forma deorum. Haupt

observes, the use of the plural
does not prove that the reference
is to two persons, viz. Carinus
and Numerianus, as has been
maintained by some commenta-
tors. The meaning is merely—
describe to me the emperor's
dress, &c., that I may know
what is the appearance of the
gods. This view is confirmed by
the following lines, in which one
individual alone is described.
79. O utinam. For the hiatus
cf. Hor. C. 1, 1, 2 : *O et praesi-
dium et dulce decus meum.*
Inesset, ' had not been on me':
cf. Ov. F. 4, 658 : *nec digitis an-
nulus ullus inest.* Haupt (Hermes,

Vidissem propius mea numina : sed mihi sordes, 80
Pullaque paupertas, et adunco fibula morsu
Obfuerunt ; utcunque tamen conspeximus ipsum
Longius, ac, nisi me visus decepit, in uno
Et Martis vultus et Apollinis esse putavi.

80. *Vidisset* ab.
81. *Nudaque* Vrabo. *et obunco* D4.R2. Ulit. c. *adeso.* Burm. c. *aheno.*
82. *Obfuerunt* R1.2.raπ. *obfuerint* PD2.4. *obfuerant* d2.pf1.2.βa2.sbo Barth. *utrunque* R1.rd1.2. (in the latter *utcunque* is added). *utrumque* D2.
83. *at nisi* pa2.sgf2. *et nisi* βf1.va1. Barth. *ac mihi me* D4.R2. *visus decepit et uno* D1. *decepit visus* vulg. Glaes. c. *visus deceperit, una.*
84. *Martis visus* R2. *putatur* VD1.2.4.R1.2.rabo. *putare* P. *putavi* vulg. Mod. c. *esse notavi.* Haupt c. *notatur.* The verb *notare* occurs in line 77 and IV. 105. Haupt's conjecture, as well as the reading *putatur*, is liable to the objection that it leaves the lengthening of the last syllable of *vultus* unaccounted for. Although I retain the vulg. *putavi*, yet I think that if *putavi* or *notavi* had been in the original, it is hard to account for the change to the more difficult *putatur*, which has such considerable MS. authority. If, however, the original was *putantur*, agreeing with *vultus*, nom. pl., the change to *putatur* would be very slight, and might arise from confusion with the preceding line, where the singular verb *decepit* is connected with *visus*. That such a confusion was possible appears from the fact that R2. actually reads *visus*, instead of *vultus*, in this line. It may be added that if *vultus* be plural here it would accord with Haupt's conjecture on line 77.

vol. 8, page 180) says *inesse* cannot be so used of dress, and that *obesset* is the true reading, notwithstanding the recurrence of that verb in line 82.
82. Obfuerunt, ' hindered me ': sc. from getting a nearer view.
Utcunque, ' somehow or another,' ' after a fashion': cf. Juv.

10, 271 : *exitus ille utcumque hominis.*
84. Nero is similarly described by Seneca Ludus de Morte Claudii 4 : *Ne demite, Parcae, Phoebus ait : vincat mortalis tempora vitae Ille mihi similis voltu similisque decore, Nec cantu nec voce minor.*

ECLOGA OCTAVA.

(NEMESIANI I.)

TIMETAS, TITYRUS.

THIS Eclogue, the first of the four attributed to Nemesianus, bears the
hybrid title Epiphunus. The proper form of the word, as Wernsdorf
says, is ἐπικήδειον or ἐπιτάφιον. It is modelled closely on Virgil's fifth
Eclogue entitled Daphnis, and also on the first and seventh Idyls of
Theocritus.

Timetas asks Tityrus to give a specimen of his poetic skill. The
latter excuses himself on the ground of his age, and in turn calls upon
Timetas, who forthwith rehearses a song he had written down in the
shepherds' familiar note-book, viz., the bark of a tree.

The subject of the song is a panegyric on Meliboeus (on whom see
Introduction, page 12 sq. and page 40), which seems to furnish the
strongest internal evidence we have for attributing the last four Eclogues
to Calpurnius. It is strange this evidence has been overlooked by those
who maintain the unity of authorship of the eleven Eclogues.

TIM. Dum fiscella tibi fluviali, Tityre, iunco
Texitur, et raucis resonant tua rura cicadis,
Incipe, si quod habes gracili sub arundine carmen
Compositum. Nam te calamos inflare labello
Pan docuit, versuque bonus tibi favit Apollo. 5
Incipe, dum salices haedi, dum gramina vaccae

*Cantantur laudes Meliboei vita functi : Amyntas et Tityrus
amici V. In hac Egloga* (a adds *octava*) *tractantur laudes Meliboei
vita defuncti. Interloquutores Amyntas et Tityrus amici* R1.ra. *Ty-
metas et Tityrus* (*Amyntas* added in the margin) *Interloquutores
Aegloga octava* d2.

From the time of Ugoletus until Wernsdorf's edition appeared, this
eclogue was commonly called the first of Aurelius Nemesianus. *Aurelii
Nemesiani Poetae Carthaginensis Aegloga prima incipit. Interlocutores
Timetas et Tityrus* pβ(2. *Aurelii Nemesiani Poetae Carthaginiensis
Egloga prima* f1. *Nemesiani poetae Chartaginensis Eclogae. Prima
Ecloga. Timetas et Tytirus* b. *Nemesiani Carthaginensis Prima Ecloga.
Timetas. Tytirus* o. *Tymetas et Tytyrus* Barth. Eclogues VIII. to
XI. are placed before the others in the editions up to a2., and after it
are similarly placed in b o t and the Frankfurt edition. The inscription
Epiphunus is found in f1.va1.π and the other editions up to Wernsd.,
who c. 'Επιτάφιος. Burm. c. *Epifunus.*

1. *Um* R2., with which compare the loss of the initial letter in V. 1;
IV. 1 ; VII. 1 ; and also I. 1, where af1.d2. give *ondum* for *nondum.
Cum* R1. *sistella* P. Barth. c. *cistella.*

2. *in mutua rura* D1. *immitua* PD2. *imitatur rura* Vr. *imitan-
tur rura* R1.a. Barth. c. *invitant rura.* Heins. c. *resonant sua rura.*
Glaeser c. *initantur rura. tua regna* cd. Titii. Haupt c. *raucis
rumpuntur rura,* comparing Virg. G. 3, 328 : *Et cantu querulae rum-
punt arbusta cicadae.*

5. *versusque* R2.abo.

1. Cf. Virg. E. 10, 71 : *Dum
sedet et gracili fiscellam texit
hibisco,* and III. 68.

2. Raucis, 'hoarse,' 'harsh-
toned,' 'chirping' : cf. V. 56 :
argutae cicadae. Virg. E. 2, 12
sq. : *At mecum raucis, tua dum
vestigia lustro, Sole sub ardenti
resonant arbusta cicadis.* For the
tree-crickets, as the accompani-
ment of summer, see Ov. A. A. 1,
271 : *Vere prius taceant volucres,*

aestate cicadae. Juv. 9, 68 : *Quid
dicam scapulis puerorum Aquilone
Decembri Et pedibus ? Durate
atque exspectate cicadas ?*

3. Gracili sub arundine, 'to
the slender reed-pipe.' Cf. Copa
2 : *Crispum sub crotalo docta
movere latus.*

5. Pan docuit. Cf. Virg. E.
2, 32 : *Pan primus calamos cera
conjungere plures Instituit.*

Detondent, viridique greges permittere campo
Dum ros et primi suadet clementia solis.
TIT. Hos annos canamque comam, vicine Timeta,
Tu iuvenis carusque deis in carmina cogis ?   10
Diximus, et calamis versus cantavimus olim,
Dum secura hilares aetas ludebat amores.
Nunc album caput, et veneres tepuere sub annis :
Iam mea ruricolae dependet fistula Fauno.

7. *Detonderet virilique* Dı. *Detrudent* VRı.r. *De tondent* R2.
greges PVDı.2.3.4.Rı.2.radı.2.bo Burm. *gregem* pβfı.2.a2.π Barth.
Ulit. *promittere* VRı.ra.
8. *Dum ros* Dı.fı.aı.bo. *Et ros* vulg. *dementia* R2.
9. *canamque comam vicine Timetĕ* Dı. *canamque meam, mihi care,
senectam* vulg. *meam hic care* Rı. *annos cantabo meam mihi* R2.
tibi care o. Haupt reads *Thymoeta* for *Timeta.*
10. *deos* R2.pdı.2. (in the latter corrected *-is*). *mihi carmina*
VRı.r.
11. *Diximus* PVDı.Rı. Guid. ex aliqq. exemplaribus, cdd. Titii,
rafı.aı.d2. Ulit. *Viximus* R2.pβd2.a2.f2.boπ Burm., Wernsd., Beck.
et calamis et versu Dı. *et calamis versu* PVRı.r. *calamo versu
cant.* ψ. Barth. c. *et calamo et versu,* which Burm. approves. Heins.
c. *calamis versus mandavimus.*
12. Heins. c. *hilaros. ludabat* Dı. *laudabat* D4.R2.
13. *ac veneres* Rı.2.rabo. *veres* P. *tepuere* fı.2.pβboπ which Ulit.
and Burm. approve. *stupuere* PD2.3.4.Rı.2.radı.2.c. Perhaps we
should read *periere.* This would accord better with *veneres,* which
usually means 'personal charms' not 'passion': not only is Tityrus'
hair white, but in other respects also his bloom is passed. The *s* of
veneres may have given rise to the unmeaning *speriere* whence the
corrections *stupuere* and *tepuere.* The latter form with *s* dropped
seems to lack MS. authority.
14. *Nam mea* Dı.2.3. *phauno* R2.

7. Detondent, 'crop.' Cf. v.
29 sq.
8. Primus sol, 'the morning
sun': *medius* (Phaedrus 3, 19),
'the noontide,' *supremus* (Hor.
Ep. 1, 5, 3), 'the evening.'
10. In carmina cogis, 'con-
strain to song.' Cf. Ov. Ib. 208:
cogi in lacrimas, 'constrained to
tears.' Hor. Ep. 1, 1, 3 : *quaeris
. . . antiquo me includere ludo.*

12. Ludebat amores, 'sang
sportive strains of love.' Cf.
Hor. C. 1, 32, 1 sq. : *si quid
vacui sub umbra Lusimus tecum.*
13. Veneres tepuere, 'pas-
sion has cooled down.' Cf. note
on v. 60.
Sub annis, 'under the weight
of years.'
14. Dependet fistula. It was
usual for those who ceased to

Te nunc rura sonant: nuper nam carmine victor   15
Risisti calamos et dissona flamina Mopsi,
Iudice me. Mecum senior Meliboeus utrumque
Audierat, laudesque tuas sublime ferebat;
Quem nunc, emeritae permensum tempora vitae,
Secreti pars orbis habet, mundusque piorum.   20
Quare age, si qua tibi Meliboei gratia vivit,
Dicat honoratos praedulcis tibia manes.
TIM. Et parere decet iussis, et grata iubentur.
Namque fuit dignus senior, quem carmine Phoebus,

15. P prefixes *Tim.* *Et nunc* VR1.2.rd1.2.af1.βtbo. *sonent* ψ.
nuper iam pβf1.va1.t. *carmina* D1.PR2.d1.pβf1.va1.t. *victos* D1.4.R2.
nam carmina victor vulg. *iam dum victor* ψ. *carmine victor* Wernsd.,
Beck., Adelung.
16. *flumina* d2.π. *diss.* *carmina* PVR1.rad2. *flamina mopso*
D4.R2.
20. *priorum* pβ. *modusque priorum* P.
21. r prefixes *Am.* to this line, *Tit.*, to line 23, and *Am.* to line 30.
So also R1., save that it prefixes *Am.* to line 29 not 30.
22. *Dicit.* d2. Glaes. *perdulcis* R1.
23. *Tim.* (corrected *Tyt.*) d2. *Am.* is added by a. *Tim.* is omitted
by pβf1.bo. *iussis (et* omitted) *grata* D1.

practise an art to devote the in-
struments of their craft to a god.
Cf. Hor. C. 3, 26, 4 : *barbiton
hic paries habebit.*
15. Te nunc, &c., ' with your
praises the country now resounds.'
Cf. line 26 and Ov. M. 10, 205 :
te carmina nostra sonabunt.
16. Virgil's Mopsus, on the
contrary, was a skilful poet.
19. Emeritae, &c., ' having
completed the period of life's
campaign,' ' whose warfare was
accomplished,' alluding to the
expression *emerita militia* (Suet.
Cal. 44). Cf. Sen. Ep. 93 : *om-
nibus vitae humanae stipendiis
functum.*
20. Secreti pars orbis. Cf.
Hor. Epod. 16, 63 : *Juppiter illa
piae secrevit litora genti.* The

allusion is to Elysium, which
Homer places on the west of
the earth. Virgil makes it part
of the lower regions and the resi-
dence of the shades of the Blessed.
The Elysium of Hesiod and Pindar
is in the Isles of the Blessed
(μακάρων νῆσοι), which they place
in the ocean.
22. The mention of the **tibia**
is appropriate, as it was used at
funerals. Cf. Ov. Trist. 5, 1,
48 : *tibia funeribus convenit ista
meis.*
23. ' It is both a duty to obey
your orders and your orders are
agreeable.'
24 sq. ' For the old man was
worthy to have Phoebus in his
verses, Pan with his pipes, and
Linus or Orpheus, the son of

Pan calamis, fidibus Linus aut Oeagrius Orpheus   25
Concinerent, totque acta viri laudesque sonarent.

Sed quia tu nostrae laudem deposcis avenae,
Accipe, quae super haec cerasus, quam cernis ad amnem,
Continet, inciso servans mea carmina libro.

TIT. Dic age; sed nobis ne vento garrula pinus   30
Obstrepat, has ulmos potius fagosve petamus.

TIM. Hic cantare libet, virides nam subiicit herbas

---

25. *fidibus siclis aut oeagr. O.* D1. *fidibus* R1.ra., whence Glaes.
has restored as in the text. *fidibusque Linus, modulatibus Orpheus*
vulg. *fidibusque limis modulantibus* R2. *modulantibus* f1.va1.t.
modulabitis R1. (with the mark + in the margin).
  26. *Contineret* V. *Concinerent totque acta* D1. *atque acta* vulg.
  27. *nostrae laudem deposcis* D1. *musam deposcis* vulg.
  28. PVD2.3.4.R1.2.rd1.2.nabo omit this line, and in the next read
quercus instead of *servans.* Heins. c. *super hoc.* Gud. c. *super hunc
quem cernis.* Beck and Klausen strangely print *vides ad amnem.*
  29. *Concinet* D4.R2.
  30. R1.r. prefix *Am.* abod2. prefix *Tyt. vento ne gracula* P. Burm.
c. *sed foliis cantu* or *cantum ne garrula.*
  31. *Obstrepet* D2. *fagosque* VR1.rabo.
  32. *subicit* D1. *subigit* PVR1.rψ. *sufficit* a. *suggerit* R2.d2.b
vulg. *Tim.* is omitted in R1.rad2.pf1.bo.

Œagrus, with the lyre, join in
celebrating him.'
  Concinerent. Cf. Hor. C. 4,
2, 33: *Concines majore poeta
plectro Caesarem.* Pan, Linus,
and Orpheus are also mentioned
together by Virgil E. 4, 55.
  27 sq. Cf. Virg. E. 5, 13 sq.:
*Immo haec, in viridi nuper quae
cortice fagi Carmina descripsi
et modulans alterna notavi, Ex-
periar.*
  Avenae. *Avena* properly 'oats'
is often used of a shepherd's pipe.
Cf. Milton's Lycidas: *Tempered to
the oaten flute,* and *But now my
oat proceeds.*
  28. Ad amnem, ' by the
river.'
  29. Inciso, &c., 'recording my

verses by the carving on its
bark.'
  30. Vento garrula, 'rustling
with the wind.'
  Nobis obstrepat. Cf. VI. 62,
Virg. E. 8, 22: *Maenalus ar-
gutumque nemus pinosque lo-
quentes Semper habet.*
  31. Cf. Virg. E. 5, 5: *Sive sub
incertas Zephyris motantibus um-
bras, Sive antro potius succedimus.*
  32. Hic, &c. Cf. Theocr. 5,
60: αὐτόθε μοι ποτέρισδε καὶ αὐτόθε
βωκολιάσδευ.
  Virides, &c. Cf. VI. 72:
melior viret herba tapetis.
  Subjicit, &c., 'the soft fields
spread beneath us a carpet of
green grass.'

Mollis ager, lateque tacet nemus omne; quieti,
Aspice, ut ecce procul decerpant gramina tauri.
Omniparens aether, et rerum causa, liquores,   35
Corporis et genetrix, tellus, vitalis et aer,
Accipite hos cantus, atque haec nostro Meliboeo
Mittite, si sentire datur post fata quietis.
Nam si sublimes animae coelestia templa
Sidereasque colunt sedes, mundoque fruuntur,   40

33. *laete tacet* D1. *genus omne* D4.R2. Burm. c. *pecus omne.*
34. *decerpunt* a. *deflectant flamina Cauri* cd. Titii.
35. d2. prefixes *Tim.* (corrected *Tyti.*) VR1.rd1.nb prefix *Tit.*
o prefixes *Tim.* a prefixes *Am. Omnipotens* D4.R2.
36. *tellus vitalis, et aer* R1.r Ulit., Burm.
37. *Accipe hos* D2.4.R2. *hos cantus* D1. *calamos* vulg.
38. *Miti ne sindatur post* P. *Miti ne sivi sentire datur* p. *post facta*
pβf1.a1. *quietem* D3.
39. *Iam si* Ulit. *templo* a.

**33, 34. Quieti . . . decerpant
gramina,** 'are quietly browsing.'
35 sq. He invokes the four ele-
ments : fire, water, earth, and
air.
  'O ether, parent of all ; and
moisture, first cause of things ;
and earth, mother of body ; and
life-giving air.'
  Aether was the upper pure air,
as opposed to *aer,* the lower at-
mospheric air. It seems to have
been accredited with a fiery na-
ture: see Cic. N. D. 2, 15 : (*astra*)
*oriuntur in ardore caelesti, qui
aether vel caelum nominatur.*
Virgil, G. 2, 325 applies to *aether*
the title *pater omnipotens.*
  For the active sense of **vitalis**
cf. Cic. N. D. 2, 45 : (*aer*) *vitalem
et salutarem spiritum praebet
animantibus.*
  38. Sentire, ' to have feeling,'
used absolutely as in Lucr. 3, 350 :
si quis corpus sentire refutat.
  Post fata, ' after death,' as in

Quint. 12, 11, 7 : *sentiet vivus
eam, quae post fata praestari
magis solet, venerationem.*
  Quietis, ' the dead,' lit. those
who are at rest. Cf. Rev. 14,
13 : *Blessed are the dead . . . for
they rest from their labours.*
  39. Sublimes animae. Cf.
Virg. A. 6, 720, where, how-
ever, the expression is used of
returning to earth from the lower
world.
  Coelestia templa, 'the regions
of the heavens.' The expression
is found in Lucr. 5, 1203 : *Nam
quum suspicimus magni coelestia
mundi Templa super.*
  40. Mundo, 'heaven,' 'the sky,'
as in Gratius Faliscus, 295 : *Dum
tepida indulget terris clementia
mundi.* Wernsdorf compares
Manilius, 1, 756 : *fortes animae
dignataque nomina coelo, . . .
Aethereos vivunt annos mundoque
fruuntur,* and Sen. Oed. 45 : *Tris-
tisque mundus nubilo pallet novo.*

Tu nostros adverte modos, quos ipse benigno
Pectore fovisti, quos tu, Meliboee, probasti.
Longa tibi, cunctisque diu spectata senectus,
Felicesque anni, nostrique novissimus aevi
Circulus innocuae clauserunt tempora vitae.   45
Nec minus hinc nobis gemitus lacrimaeque fuere,
Quam si florentes mors invida pelleret annos.
Nec tenuit tales communis causa querelas :

41. *Heu nostros* a. *In nostros* cd1.2. (in the latter corrected *Tu*).
Burm. c. *Tu nostris adv. modis.*
42. *vovisti* a. *novisti* D2.
44. *que* after *Felices* omitted in R2.ab. *animi* D4.rpβ. *faelices āi*
R1. *novissimus anni* D4.R2.
46. *vobis* cd1.2. (in the last corrected *n*). *lacrymae gemitusque*
Barth.
47. *Qua si* D1. *carperet annos* D2. Heins. c. *tolleret.* Burm. c.
perderet or *rumperet.* Glaes. c. *velleret.*
48. *Naec* β. *Haec* pa2.f2. Martell. and Heins. c. *Nec renuit.*
talis R1.rabo. *comunes* R2. Glaes. c. *talis communes.*

Adelung thinks *mundo* means
the earth, and explains : if though
they dwell in heavenly abodes
they yet take an interest in what
goes on upon earth.
41. Tu nostros, &c., ' give
ear to my strains.' For *advertere*
= *animum advertere;* cf. Tac. A.
13, 54 : *advertere quosdam cultu
externo in sedibus senatorum.*
Benigno, 'kindly.'
43 sq. ' You had a prolonged
old age, long esteemed by all,
and happy years, and the last
cycle in our age (i. e. in the life of
us men) brought to a close the
period of your inoffensive life.'
Circulus. Wernsdorf thinks
there is an allusion to the division
of life into *climacteres* (gradations)
or critical epochs marked by the
years 7, 14, 21, 28, &c.
For *circulus*, used of time, Lewis

and Short quote Sen. Ep. 12, 6 :
*mensis artiore praecingitur cir-
culo.*
Clauserunt. Cf. Hor. C. 2,
4, 23 : *Cujus octavum trepidavit
aetas Claudere lustrum.*
46 sq. We grieved as much as
if you had been carried off in the
flower of your age.
47. Invida, 'churlish.'
Pelleret, ' were hastening on.'
Wernsdorf compares v. 121 :
aestivas impellit Noctifer horas.
48. I. e. All were affected by
his death and burst into the fol-
lowing lament, *Heu,* &c. This
is better than Wernsdorf's ex-
planation of *communis causa* as
boni publici ratio. Some think
communis causa = death, the lot
of all. For *nec tenuit,* 'did not
restrain,' cf. Hor. A. P. 5 : *risum
teneatis, amici?*

Heu, Meliboee, iaces mortali frigore segnis
Lege hominum, coelo dignus, canente senecta,   50
Concilioque deûm. Plenum tibi ponderis aequi
Pectus erat. Tu ruricolum discernere lites
Assueras, varias patiens mulcendo querelas.
Sub te iuris amor, sub te reverentia iusti
Floruit, ambiguos signavit terminus agros.   55

49. *mortali* D1. *letali* vulg.
50. *dignus crnente* d2. *cernente sen.* d1. *cruente* nc.
51. *Consilioque* d1.2. *Consilioque deus* VR1.ra.
53. *Assuer asuaris : paciens* R2. All Glaeser's books give *Assueras.*
Assuetus d1. Barth. *varias patieris mulcedo* b. *pariens* P. Ulit. c.
patiens mulcensque. Wakefield c. *patiens mulcere.* Burm. c. *sapiens mulcere.*
54. *Subte ruris* R1. *viris* D1. Martell. and Heins. c. *iuris.*
ruris vulg. *venerantia iusti* d1.2.n.

49. Mortali frigore means the chill of death, such as mankind are liable to. ' Mortal,' in the sense it bears, in such a phrase as ' a mortal wound,' is never expressed by *mortalis* but by *mortifer.* For *frigus* = the chill of death cf. Virg. A. 12, 951 : *Ast illi solvuntur frigore membra, Vitaque cum gemitu fugit indignata sub umbras.*
Segnis, ' disabled.'
50 sq. ' By the law to which men are subject, although you are worthy of heaven, of a hoary old age, and of the council of the gods.'
51. Plenum tibi, &c., ' your breast was full of well-balanced, just, constancy.' For *pondus,* used of weight of character, i. e. firmness, constancy, compare Stat. Theb. 1, 289 : *nostri reverentia ponderis.* Id. Silv. 2, 3, 65 : *hilarisque, tamen cum pondere, virtus.* Prop. 2, 25, 22 : *Credule, nulla diu femina pondus habet.*

53. Varias, &c. Beck explains :—patiens (ferens, patienter audiens) querelas ita ut mulceas (lenias, componas eas), poetice pro, patiendo mulcens. ' Listening patiently to and soothing complaints.' For *pati* ' put up with,' cf. Hor. S. 1, 3, 141 : *Inque vicem illorum patiar delicta libenter.*
Mulcendŏ. For the short syllable, compare Juv. 3, 232 : *Plurimus hic aeger moritur vigilando ; sed illum,* and IX. 80.
54. Sub te, ' under you,' ' in your time.'
Reverentia justi, 'respect for justice.'
55. Ambiguos, &c., ' a boundary line marked out fields of doubtful ownership, fields that were under dispute.'
Signavit. Cf. Virg. G. 1, 126 : *Ne signare quidem aut partiri limite campum Fas erat.*

M 2

Blanda tibi vultus gravitas, et mite serena
Fronte supercilium, sed pectus mitius ore.
Tu calamos aptare labris, et iungere cera
Hortatus duras docuisti fallere curas.
Nec segnem passus nobis marcere iuventam,   60
Saepe dabas meritae non vilia praemia Musae.
Saepe etiam senior, ne nos cantare pigeret,
Laetus Phoebea dixisti carmen avena.
Felix o Meliboee, vale : tibi frondis odorae

---

56. *oscula ibi* D4. *oscula ibi vultus gr. et mitte* R2. Burm. c.
Mascula erat vultus. vultis gravitas D1.2.3. *sultus* d2. *vultu gra-
vitas* R1.rabod2., which Beck adopts on account of *fronte*. Martell.
c. and Beck adopts *severa*.
58. *optare labris* a. *et iungere* f1.va1.π. *coniungere* PVD2.3.
R1.2.rd2.apβa2.f2.bo.
59. *Hortatus* D1.atv; also conjectured by Ulit. *Horatus* f1.a1.
Oratus R1.2.rd1.2.apβa2.f2.π Barth. *Ornatus* bo. Heins. c. *Noras*
or *Gratus tu crudas.* *dura docuisti* R2. Burm. c. *diras* or *dubias.*
flectere V.
60. Beck reads *nobis passus* without authority of any MS. or edition.
61. *Sedabas meritae* PD1.4. *Sedabas meriti* R1.r. *sedabis merite*
R2. *Pendebas meritae* a.
62. *et iam* R2.
63. *Phorbea* VR1.r. Burm. c. *Laetius Orphea dix. duxisti* cdd.
Titii ψ Barth. Heins. c. *Praevius Hyblaea duxisti.*

---

56 sq. 'You had a courteous
dignity of countenance and mild
brow, with unruffled forehead, aye,
and a heart milder than your
face.'
57. Sed, is often thus used in
a climax. 'Tender was the ex-
pression of your unruffled brow,
but still more tender was your
heart.'
58 sq. 'By advising me to at-
tempt poetry you taught me how
to beguile pinching cares.'
Aptare . . . iungere. These
infinitives depend on *hortatus* in
the next line.
59. Docuisti fallere, 'taught
how to beguile.' Cf. Ov. Trist.

5, 7, 39 : *Detineo studiis ani-
mum, falloque dolores, Experior
curis et dare verba meis.*
60. Segnem . . . marcere, 'to
languish in idleness.'
61. 'You often gave to the de-
serving Muse rewards of no little
value.' **Meritae.** Cf. iv. 165.
62 sq. You often sang yourself
to encourage my performance.
64. Felix. Applied to the dead,
like the Greek μακαρίτης.
Vale. The expression used in
bidding farewell to the dead.
Frondis odorae Munera, 'gifts
of fragrant foliage,' as we place
wreaths of immortelles on the
tomb.

Munera dat, lauros carpens, ruralis Apollo :   65
Dant Fauni, quod quisque valet, de vite racemos,
De campo culmos, omnique ex arbore fruges,
Dat grandaeva Pales spumantia cymbia lacte,
Mella ferunt Nymphae, pictas dat Flora coronas.
Manibus hic supremus honos. Dant carmina Musae,   70
Carmina dant Musae, nos te modulamur avena,
Silvestris te nunc platanus, Meliboee, susurrat,
Te pinus ; reboat te, quidquid carminis Echo

66. *Dat faunus q. q. volet* di.2. (in the latter corrected *valet*).
lavet D4. Heins. c. *valent.*
67. *De messe culm.* Di.fi.vai.tψ. Burm. c. *De messo* (i. e. *de frumento messo*).
69. *Mala ferunt* Ri.rna. *pietas dat flore* Ri.r. *dant flore* aψ.
festas dat Flora P.
71. Di. omits *te*. Burm. c. *nos quae.*
72. *Silvestris te nunc* Di. *nunc te* vulg. *nunc et* vt.
73. *Te picris* (in Addend.) *Te picrus* (in Comm.) D4. *Te primis*
pβ (Guid. corrects *pinus*). *roborat* P. *Tunc quidquid* Di. *fert
quicquid* D3. *Te pienis reboat: fert quicquid carmine eccho* R2.

68. Grandaeva. This epithet is doubtless applied to Pales, as having been worshipped from very ancient times.

Spumantia, &c. Cf. Virg. A. 3, 66 : *Inferimus tepido spumantia cymbia lacte.*

69. Pictas . . . coronas, 'variegated chaplets.' Cf. the rites observed by Aeneas at the tomb of Anchises, Virg. A. 5, 77 sq. : *Hic duo rite mero libans carchesia Baccho Fundit humi, duo lacte novo, duo sanguine sacro ; Purpureosque jacit flores, ac talia fatur.*

70. Mānibus. Distinguish mănibus. The deified souls of the departed were called *manes*, (*mānus* = *bonus* whence *immanis* properly 'uncanny,') as benevolent spirits ; opposed to *larvae* and *lemures*, malevolent spirits.

Supremus honos, ' the last tribute,' i. e. the funeral ceremonies. Cf. Virg. A. 11, 59 sq. : *Haec ubi deflevit, tolli miserabile corpus Imperat et toto lectos ex agmine mittit Mille viros, qui supremum comitentur honorem.*

Dant carmina Musae. Cf. the recurring burden in Theocr. I : ἄρχετε βωκολικᾶς, Μῶσαι φίλαι, ἄρχετ᾽ ἀοιδᾶς.

72. Te . . . susurrat. For *susurro* with accus. cf. Mart. 3, 63, 5 : *Cantica qui Nili, qui Gaditana susurrat.*

73. Reboat, &c., ' every echo of the woods resounds your name.' *Quidquid* is acc., *Echo* nom., *silvae* dat. I have given the reading of Burmann, which is adopted by Klausen, and can appeal to *Respondet* of Di. in its support. For the other readings see Notes, 1. Cf. Virg. E. 1, 38 sq. : *Tityrus hinc aberat. Ipsae*

Respondet silvae ; te nostra armenta loquuntur.
Namque prius siccis phocae pascentur in arvis, 75
Hirsutusque freto vivet leo, dulcia mella
Sudabunt taxi, confusis legibus anni
Messem tristis hiems, aestas tractabit olivas,

Barth. punctuates *te, quicquid carminis, Echo* (sc. *reboat*) or
susurrat Te pinus : reboat te, quicquid carminis Echo : Respondent,
&c., which latter punctuation Wernsd. follows. Gebhard c. *te quid*
quit or *cit carminis Echo, Respondent*. Ulit. c. *te quidquid carminis*
exit. Burm. c. *reboat te, quicquid carminis Echo Respondet silvae*.
Glaes. reads *reboat te, quidquid carminis Echo Respondent silvae*.
74. *Respondet* D1., adopted by Beck. *Respondent* Glaes. and
Wernsd., which the latter defends from Virg. E. 10, 8 : *respondent*
omnia silvae. *loquuntur* Mf1.va1.π. *sequuntur* D1.2.3.rd2.apa2.f2.bo.
Haupt c. *arbusta* for *armenta* comparing Virg. E. 5, 64 : *Ipsa sonant*
arbusta. Ib. 1, 40 : (*te*) *ipsa haec arbusta vocabant*.
75. *nam prius in siccis* Guid. in lemm. *focae nasentur* R2. Tit.
found somewhere *pascentur*, which also occurs in ψ, and is adopted
since Burm. Cf. Virg. E. 1. 59: *pascentur in aethere cervi*. The other
editions read *nascentur. in armis* P.
76. *Vestitusque leo* pβa2.f2.d1.2. (in the last *Hirsutusque* is added).
Restitusque R2. *Vestibus* D1. Guid. and Tit. quote *Hirsutus* from
some MSS. Heins. c. *Insuetusque freto*.
78. This line is put after the following in VR1.2.rd1.abo. *tractavit*
D1. Burm. c. *iactabit*. Haupt c. *praestabit*.

te, Tityre, pinus, Ipsi te fontes,
ipsa haec arbusta vocabant. Ib.
6, 9 sq. : *Non injussa cano. Si*
quis tamen haec quoque, si quis
Captus amore leget, te nostrae,
Vare, myricae, Te nemus omne
canet.
74. Te loquuntur, 'speak of
you,' 'have you upon their lips.'
For construction cf. Cic. Milo 23,
63 : *multi etiam Catilinam atque*
illa portenta loquebantur. For
the sentiment cf. Virg. E. 5, 27
sq. : *Daphni, tuum Poenos etiam*
ingemuisse leones Interitum
montesque feri silvaeque loquun-
tur. Ib. 10, 8 : *Non canimus*
surdis ; respondent omnia silvae.
Theocr. 1, 71 sq. : τῆνον μὰν θῶες,
τῆνον λύκοι ὠρύσαντο, τῆνον χὠκ

δρυμοῖο λέων ἔκλαυσε θανόντα. For
Haupt's reading, *arbusta*, see
Notes 1.
75 sq. This 'affirmatio ἀπὸ τοῦ
ἀδυνάτου,' as Wernsdorf calls it, is
common in the poets, e. g. Virg.
E. 1, 59 sq.
76. The epithet *hirsutus* is ap-
plied to a lion also in Ov. M. 14,
207.
77. Taxi. Virgil says the yew
was prejudicial to bees : see G. 4,
47 : *neu propius tectis* (i. e. the
hives) *taxum sine*.
78. 'Gloomy winter will pre-
side over harvest, and summer
rear olives.' Cicero Fin. 5, 14,
uses *tractare* of the culture of the
vine ; so perhaps Haupt's conjec-
ture, *praestabit*, is unnecessary.

Ante dabit flores autumnus, ver dabit uvas,
Quam taceat, Meliboee, tuas mea fistula laudes.   80
TIT. Perge, puer, coeptumque tibi ne desere carmen.
Nam sic dulce sonas, ut te placatus Apollo
Provehat, et felix dominam perducat in urbem.
Namque hic in silvis praesens tibi fama benignum
Stravit iter, rumpens livoris nubila pennis.   85
Sed iam sol demittit equos de culmine mundi,
Flumineos suadens gregibus praebere liquores.

---

79. *nec dabit* PR1.rd2.   *Ante diem floris aurumnus ver dabat* a.
81. R1.rd2. prefix *Am.* *coeptumque tibi ne* D1., which Beck adopts.
ceptumque tibi neu b.   *coetumque tibi ne* a.   *coeptum tibi iam ne* vulg.
neu VR1.r.   *nec* D4.R2.   *coeptum tibi neuque des* f1.a1.
82. *Nam si* f1.va1.t.
83. *in urbem* D1.   *ad urbem* vulg.
84. Heins. c. *Iamque hic.* *hic silvis* libr. omn.   Hoeufft. c. and
Beck adopts *huc e silvis.*
85. *livorum iubila* cd1.2. (in the last corrected *livoris*).   *pennis* D1.
plena vulg.   *plene* PD2.   Barth. c. *rumpes liv. nub. plene.*
86. d2. has *Tyti.* in the margin.   *dimittit* PVD2.3.R1.2.ra.
87. *Fulmineos* pβ (Guid. corrects *flum.*).   *Fluminibus* V.

---

81. Coeptumque, &c., 'do
not give up the culture of poetry
which you have commenced.'
82. Dulce sonas. For adver-
bial use of *dulce* cf. Hor. C. 1, 22,
23 : *dulce ridentem Lalagen ama-
bo Dulce loquentem.*
Placatus, 'favourable,' εὐμε-
νής.
83. Felix, 'auspicious.' **Domi-
nam.** We find *dominae Romae*
in Hor. C. 4, 14, 44, and *dominae
urbis* in Martial 12, 21, 9.
**84. Praesens tibi fama be-
nignum Stravit iter.** These
words are also found in Stat.
Theb. 12, 812.   See Introd. page
19.
85. Livoris nubila, ' clouds
of malice.' Cf. Virg. A. 10, 809 :
nubem belli, where, however, the
idea may be somewhat different,
as in Hom. Il. 17, 243 : πολέμοιο
νέφος.
86. De culmine mundi, 'from
its meridian height.' For *mundi*
cf. line 40.
87. Cf. Virg. G. 3, 335 : *Tum
tenuis dare rursus aquas, et pas-
cere rursus Solis ad occasum.*

ECLOGA NONA.

(Nemesiani II.)

IDAS, ALCON.

In this Eclogue Idas and Alcon, two shepherd boys, lament the loss of their mistress, Donace, from whom the poem is named. Donace's parents have found it necessary to shut her up at home, and the boys reproach her for not appearing. This poem of Nemesianus is modelled on II. and III. of Calpurnius, but is much inferior in taste and execution. See Introduction, page 17.

The number of lines assigned to each of the singers is equal, as in Virgil's fifth and eighth Eclogues.

Formosam Donacen Idas puer et puer Alcon
Ardebant, rudibusque annis incensus uterque

In hac egloga (a adds IX.) *cantantur amores pueriles inter amicos pastores Idan, qui et Hastacus, et Alconem. In qua etiam Poeta ipse loquitur* (a adds *primus*) R1.rad2. All the older books have *Astacus et Alcon ;* but Wernsd., Tit., Martell., and Ulit. show that this is probably an error originating in the similar beginning of II. Pith. was first to give *Idas*. f1.va1.π. Barth. inscribe *Donace*. *Nemesiani Ecloga* II., vulg., before Wernsd.
  1. *Poeta* is added by R1.rd2.apbo. *Idas puer et* D1. *puer Idas* vulg. *Astacus* PD2.apbo.
  2. *intensus* d1.2.f1.va1.cβbo. *infensus* edit. Aurel.

1. Cf. II. 1, and Virg. E. 2, 1 : *Formosum pastor Corydon ardebat Alexim.*
2. **Ardebant,** 'burned with love for,' as in the passage of

Virgil quoted in last note, and Hor. C. 4, 19, 3. We find a similar use of *pereo* and *depereo*.
  Rudibusque annis, 'youthful, early years,' as in Quint. 1,

In Donaces Venerem furiosa mente ruebant.
Hanc, cum vicini flores in callibus horti
Carperet, et molli gremium compleret acantho,   5
Invasere simul, Venerisque immitis uterque
Tunc primum dulci carpebant gaudia furto.
Hinc amor et pueris iam non puerilia vota,
Quis anni ter quinque hiemes, et cura iuventae.
Sed postquam Donacen duri clausere parentes,   10
Quod non tam tenui filo de voce sonaret,

3. *furiosa* D1. *firmata* d1.2. (in the latter is added *furiata*, which
is also the vulg.). *ruebat* VR1.ra.
4. *vallibus* vulg. Hermann c. *callibus*.
5. *et dulci* Barth.
6. *Invascere* p. *Venerisque immitis* a2.f2., which Martell., Ulit.,
and Burm. approve. *Venerisque imbutus* VR1.raf1.π. Barth.
Veneris imbutus D1. *Venerique imbutus* PD2.3.R2.pβd2.bo. This
reading Wernsd. adopts, supporting it by Sil. Ital. 3, 64 : *Virgineis
juvenem taedis, primoque hymenaeo Imbuerat conjux. venerisque,
immitis uterque, Tum* Ulit.
7. Burm. c. *Dulcia tunc primum carpebant* or *capiebant*.
8. *iam nunc* PVD1.2.3.4.R1.2.ra. Ascens. gives *iam non*.
9. Heins. c. *Quis actae ter.* Burm. thinks we should read *et non p.
vota* (*Quis a. t. quinque*) *et primae c. iuv.* Haupt c. *cruda iuventa.*
11. *Quod non* PR1.raboπ. *Et non* D4.R2.d2.pf1.2.βa2.t. *trem
tenui* P. *sonaret* R1.2.raf1.boπ. *sonarent* d2.pβa2.tf2. Tit. c. *tenui
de filo.* Glaes. c. *tenui de filo voxque sonaret.*

1, 5 : *natura tenacissimi sumus
eorum, quae rudibus annis per-
cepimus.*
4. It is a favourite conceit of
the classical poets to describe girls
surprised by their lovers while
gathering flowers. Cf. Hor. C.
3, 27, 29; Ov. M. 4, 393; and
line 24 of this Eclogue.
Callibus. This is Hermann's
brilliant emendation for *vallibus*.
8. **Pueris,** &c., ' the boys had
wishes beyond their boyish years.'
9. ' Whose years numbered but
fifteen winters, and yet they had
the love pangs of early manhood,'
which is the period of life from

the twentieth to the fortieth year.
Anni is harsh, as **hiemes** really
stands for same idea, whence
Heinsius conjectures *actae*.
10. **Donacen . . . clausere.**
Cf. Hor. C. 3, 16, 1 : *inclusam
Danaen.*
11-13. These lines refer to Do-
nace, and, as Glaeser says, de-
scribe, 'Graviditatis signa, quibus
commoti parentes filiam incluse-
runt.'
11. 'Because the sound of her
voice was not of as fine quality as
before.' We use the word 'qua-
lity,' in reference to sound, much
in the same way as the Romans

Sollicitusque foret pinguis sonus, improba cervix,
Suffususque rubor crebro, venaeque tumentes :
Tum vero ardentes flammati pectoris aestus
Carminibus dulcique parant relevare querela,   15
Ambo aevo cantuque pares, nec dispare forma,
Ambo genas leves, intonsi crinibus ambo ;
Atque haec sub platano moesti solatia casus
Alternant, Idas calamis et versibus Alcon.
I. Quae colitis silvas, Dryades, quaeque antra Napeae, 20

---

12. D4. omits this line. *Sollicitumque foret linguis onus* R1. ; and
so, according to Wernsd., all editions, except f1.a1., in which *pin-
guis onus*. *Sollicitumque f. pinguis sonus* D1. *Sollicitamque f. lin-
guis honus* R2. Heins. c. *Insolitumque f. linguis onus*. Ulit. c.
Sollicitusque f. linguae sonus, which Burm. follows. Beck adopts
Sollicitusque f. pinguis sonus.
     15. *revelare* Ppβf1. pβ exhibit a similar transposition in VIII. 87,
giving *Fulmineos* for *Flumineos*.
     16. R2. seems to have had *animo* originally ; but the same hand has
corrected it to *aevo*. *aevi* P. *cantuque* d2.
     17. *genas lenes intonsi, crin.* D1. *genis* a2., adopted by Beck.
genae Ulit. *intonsis* Pd2.pβa2.f2. Beck has *nec intonsi*.
     18. *Atque hic sub* D1. Glaes. gives *Atque haec sub* from conjecture.
Atque sub hac vulg.

---

used *filum*, 'thread,' 'texture.'
Somewhat similar is the use of
filum in Cic. de Or. 2, 22, 93 :
*omnes etiam tum retinebant illum
Pericli sucum, sed erant paulo
uberiore filo.*
     12. 'And her voice was thick
and unsteady, and her neck coarse.'
For **improba cervix**, cf. XI. 35 :
fortia colla ; and Quint.11, 3, 160 :
*perfricare faciem et quasi impro-
bam facere.*
     15. For **dulci querela**, used
of the plaintive tones of a pipe ;
cf. Lucr. 4, 585 : *dulcesque quere-
las, Tibia quas fundit.* Hor. C.
3, 7, 30 : *sub cantu querulae . . .
tibiae.*

     16. Cf. Virg. E. 7, 4 sq. : *ambo
florentes aetatibus . . . et cantare
pares.*
     17. **Genas** is accusative of re-
spect, and **leves** is nominative in
agreement with **Ambo**.
     18. The text is Glaeser's con-
jecture. The vulgate reading, *sub
hac platano,* is an imitation of IV.
2, where the words occur in a
natural connexion ; while here,
where there is no further descrip-
tion of the tree, they betray the
clumsy imitator.
     19. Cf. line 53 and XI. 2.
     20. **Napeae**, 'nymphs of the
dells,' Greek ναπαῖος.

Et quae marmoreo pede, Naiades, uda secantes
Littora purpureos alitis per gramina flores,
Dicite, quo Donacen prato, qua forte sub umbra
Inveniam, roseis stringentem lilia palmis ?
Nam mihi iam trini perierunt ordine soles,   25
Ex quo consueto Donacen exspecto sub antro.
Interea, tamquam nostri solamen amoris
Hoc foret, aut posset nostros medicare furores,
Nulla meae trinis tetigerunt gramina vaccae

21. *ulla secantes* D2.3. *secatis Litt. purpureosque alitis* vulg. *secatis Litt. purpureos alitis* PR2. *uda secatis Gramina purpureosque alitis per littora* ψ.
23. *quo Donace prato* D1., probably should be *Donacē = Donacen. prato Donacen* vulg. *quo pacto* VR1.r.
25. *nam me iam trini petierunt* PVR1.2.rpβf1.va1.t. *Nam mihi iam tritam per.* P. *pepulerunt ordine* D3.
27. *solitamen* P.
28. *Hoc feret* P. *nostros* D1. *rabidos* vulg. *rapidos* PVD2.R1.rabo. *radios* D3.
29. *Nulla me* P. *Nulla mihi* ψ.

21. Uda secantes littora, 'cutting their way along the moist shore.' Though *aequor secare, aera secare,* and similar expressions are natural enough, *littora secare* is difficult. It seems to be modelled on *viam secare* Virg. A. 6, 899, and τέμνειν ὁδόν.
24. Roseis, &c., 'gathering lilies with her rosy hands.'
Roseis . . . palmis : cf. the Homeric epithet ῥοδοδάκτυλος.
25 sq. 'For I have now lost three successive days while awaiting Donace in our trysting cave.'
Trini. The distributive numeral used as an equivalent to the cardinal. *Trini,* in this case, is the correct form, not *terni,* which is found in some MSS. See Roby's *Latin Grammar,* vol. i. page 443.
Soles, 'days,' as in Lucr. 6,

1219 : *nec tamen illis solibus ulla Comparebat avis.*
26. Ex quo, sc. *tempore,* lit. 'since I have been awaiting.'
28. Medicare. This word, as well as the deponent form *medicari,* is found in poetry and post-Augustan prose for the classical *mederi.*
Furores, 'passion.' Perhaps the plural means 'transports of passion.' The word is used both in singular and plural of the passion of love. Cf. *Hamlet,* Act 2, scene 1 : *This is the very ecstasy of love.*
29 sq. Trinis . . . Luciferis, 'for three days,' 'within the space of three days.'
Lucifer = day, as in Ov. F. 1, 45: *Ne tamen ignores variorum jura dierum ; Non habet officii Lucifer omnis idem.*

Luciferis, nullo libarunt amne liquores :   30
Siccaque foetarum lambentes ubera matrum
Stant vituli, et teneris mugitibus aera complent.
Ipse ego nec iunco molli, nec vimine lento,
Perfeci calathos cogendi lactis in usus.
Quid tibi, quae nosti, referam ? scis, mille iuvencas   35
Esse mihi ; nosti numquam mea mulctra vacare.
Idas ille ego sum, Donace, cui saepe dedisti
Oscula, nec medios dubitasti rumpere cantus,
Atque inter calamos errantia labra petisti.
Heu heu, nulla meae tangit te cura salutis ?   40
Pallidior buxo violaeque simillimus erro.

---

30. *Nulloque libarunt* D1., whence Glaes. gives *nullo libarunt.*
nulloque biberunt vulg.   *nullos lamberunt* D3.   *nullo lamberunt*
PVD2.4.R1.2.rt.   Ulit. c. *nullos libarunt.*
31. *ferarum* Ppβ.   *labentes* P.
32. *atria complent* VR1.ra.   Ulit. c. *aethera.*
33. *nec iunco molli* D1.   *molli iunco* vulg.
34. *calamos* D4.R2.   *in usum* D4.   *lactis musum* R2.
35. De Rooy suggests *mille bidentes*, because *mille iuvencas* is incredible ; and Virg. E. 2, 21 gives *mille agnas.* Cf. ii. 68.
36. *multa* P.
40. P, according to Gebhard, has *En heu. n. m. te t. caussa ;* according to Barth., *En heu n. m. tangit te caussa.*   *tangit te* D1.   *te tangit* vulg.
41. *violisque* R1.r.   *molesque simill. erro* P.   *simill. euro* D4.
simillimus atre r.   *atrae (atris* written above) V.   *atrae* R1.abo.

---

30. **Libarunt**, 'sipped,' 'took a taste of.' Cf. Virg. G. 4, 54 : *(apes) flumina libant Summa leves. Libare* is used of cropping grass in vi. 52. The more common meaning is 'to pour out a libation.'
32. Cf. Virg. E. 6, 48 : *Proetides implerunt falsis mugitibus agros.*
Āĕră, distinguish *āĕră.*
33. **Vimine lento,** 'pliant osiers.'

34. **Cogendi,** &c., 'for the purpose of curdling milk.'
35. An imitation of iii. 65, but inappropriate here. See Introduction, page 17.
37 sq. Cf. iii. 55 sq.
41. **Buxo**, 'the pale, evergreen box-tree.'
Violae. Cf. Virg. E. 2, 46 : *Pallentes violas.* Hor. C. 3, 10, 14 : *tinctus viola pallor amantium.*
Erro. Cf. iii. 50.

Omnes, ecce, cibos et nostri pocula Bacchi
Horreo, nec placido memini concedere somno.
Te sine, vae misero, mihi lilia fusca videntur,
Pallentesque rosae, nec dulce rubens hyacinthus, 45
Nullos nec myrtus, nec laurus spirat odores.
At si tu venias, et candida lilia fient,
Purpureaeque rosae, et dulce rubens hyacinthus;
Tunc mihi cum myrto laurus spirabit odores.
Nam dum Pallas amat turgentes unguine baccas, 50
Dum Bacchus vites, Deo sata, poma Priapus,

42. Heins c. *noti. pocula vini* D1.
43. *nec blando* d2.
44. *me misero* pβf1.t. Ulit. c. *me miserum. lilia fusca vid.* D1.
lilia nigra vulg.
45. *rubensque* D1., doubtless by error from line 48, where D1. also
adds *que.*
46. This line and the two following are omitted in R1. *haec myr-
tus* f1.va1.t. *aspirat* f1.vt. *adores* R2. *Hunc mihi cum mirto laurus
spirabit odorem* (cf. line 49) D2.
47. *At si tu* D1. *At tu si* vulg.
48. *tunc dulce rubensque* D1.
49. *Hunc mihi c. m. l. sp. odorem* D2.
50. *Nam Dea Pallas amat* R1.r. *nam mea Pallas amat* V. *nam
cum Pallas amat* D1. *amet* vulg. *turgentes unguine* D1.d1.2.; this
was conjectured by Heins., but he afterwards approved of the vulg.
sanguine.
51. *Dum Bacchus uvas* D1. *vites deus, et sata poma* VR1.raf1.tboπ.
vites : deus et nova poma R2. *vites, Deus et sata, poma* Ulit., who
conjectures *vites, Ceres et sata* or *Tellus sata, poma.* Heins. c. *sua or
rata.* Burm. c. *Dum B. vites, meus, et sata poma.* Glaeser's conjec-
ture is given in the text. *Deo* (Δηώ), being misunderstood, gave place

43. Cf. Claud. Laud. Ser. 91:
si placido cessissent lumina somno.
44 sq. Cf. III. 51 sq.
45. Dulce rubens. Virg. E.
3, 63: *suave rubens.*
46. The myrtle and olive are
mentioned in connexion also in
Virg. E. 2, 54: *Et vos, o lauri,
carpam et te, proxima myrte, Sic
positae quoniam suavis miscetis
odores.*
48. Rosae, ēt. Observe hia-
tus.

**50. Turgentes unguine bac-
cas,** 'the berries swelling with
fatness,' i. e. the olive which was
sacred to Minerva.
51. Dēo = Δηώ Ceres, who was
the goddess of agriculture, and
especially of the culture of corn.
See Notes 1. This name occurs
in Theocr. 7, 3: τᾷ Δηοῖ γὰρ
ἔτευχε θαλύσια. The patronymic
Deois (Δηωΐς), the daughter of
Deo, i. e. Proserpine, occurs in
Ov. M. 6, 114.

Pascua laeta Pales, Idas te diliget unam.
Haec Idas calamis.   Tu, quae responderit Alcon
Versu, Phoebe, refer ; sunt aurea carmina Phoebo.

A.   O montana Pales, o pastoralis Apollo,   55
Et nemorum Silvane potens, et nostra Dione,
Quae iuga celsa tenes Erycis, cui cura iugales
Concubitus hominum totis connectere saeclis,
Quid merui ?   cur me Donace formosa reliquit ?
Munera namque dedi, noster quae non dedit Idas :   60
Vocalem, longos quae ducit, aedona, cantus ;

to *deus*, which was probably added as a marginal explanation, and *et*
was then inserted to satisfy the metre.
52. *te diligit* D1.R2.   *quoque diliget uvam* VR1.r.
53. *Poeta* is prefixed in VR1.rad2.pbo.
54. *sunt acirea* P.   Barth. c. *sint.*
58. *convertere* P.
59. *relinquit* VR1.rbo.
61. R1.Vra give *duceret* for *ducit*, doubtless regarding *aedona* as a
trisyllable ; so also d1. reads *quae non canit aedona.*

53 sq. Cf. Virg. E. 8, 63 sq. :
Haec Damon ; vos quae respon-
derit Alphesiboeus,   Dicite Pieri-
des ; non omnia possumus omnes.
    54. Aurea carmina. Cf. Lucr.
3, 12 : *Omnia nos itidem depasci-*
mur aurea dicta.
    55. Pales the tutelary deity of
shepherds is called **montana,** as
the upland pastures of shepherds
are called *montes.* See note on
II. 17.
    Pastoralis Apollo. See note
on VII. 22.
    56. Nemorum, Silvane, po-
tens, 'O Silvanus, ruler of the
groves.' He is represented in
sculpture with a tree in his hand.
He is called δενδροφόρος. Cf.
Virg. G. 1, 20 : *Et teneram ab*
radice ferens, Silvane, cupressum.
    Dione. This is properly the
mother of Venus, but is here used
of Venus herself, as in Ov. F. 2,

461. This line taken with the
following seems to show that the
poet was Sicilian.
    57. Eryx, now S. Giuliano, is
a mountain in the north-western
angle of Sicily, where was a fa-
mous temple of Venus, who was
hence called Erycina.
    59. Quid merui ? 'what fault
have I committed ?' lit. 'what
punishment have I deserved ?'
For *mereo* in a bad sense cf. Ov.
M. 5, 666 : *supplicium meruisse.*
    Formosa, 'beautiful.'
    60. Noster, ' my friend.'
    61. Plin. 10, 29 says of the
nightingale's song : *nunc continuo*
spiritu trahitur in longum, nunc
variatur inflexo, nunc distingui-
tur conciso, copulatur intorto.
    Aedona. For the hyperbaton
cf. Hor. S. 2, 1, 60 : *Quisquis erit*
vitae, scribam, color, on which pas-
sage see Professor Palmer's note.

Quae, licet interdum contexto vimine clausa,
Cum parvae patuere fores, ceu libera ferri
Norit et agrestes inter volitare volucres,
Scit rursus remeare domum tectumque subire, 65
Viminis et caveam totis praeponere silvis.
Praeterea tenerum leporem geminasque palumbes
Nuper, quae potui, silvarum praemia misi.
Et post haec, Donace, nostros contemnis amores ?
Forsitan indignum ducis, quod rusticus Alcon 70
Te peream, qui mane boves in pascua ducam.

62. *contexo* D1. Haupt. c. *clausae*, and removes the comma, on
the ground that the bird, if *clausa*, could not be said *libera ferri*. But
neither could *patuere* be used of the doors, if *clausae*. The wonder
described is that a 'caged bird' (*con. vim. clausa*), when the cage-
door was opened, could fly about just like a wild one, and yet was
willing to come back.

63. *patiere* R2. *potuere* P. *liberara ferre* D1.

64. All the books give *Novit*. Wernsd. c. *Norit*.

65. *Sicut rursus* R1.

66. Heins. c. *notis*.

68. *silvarum munera* R2.

69. *Tu* for *Et* R1.Vrabo.

71. *Te peream* D1. *Te cupiam* vulg. *qui mcine* R2. *in pascua
ducas* D1.

62. Contexto vimine, 'a
wicker cage,' expressed in line 66
by *viminis caveam*, where *vimi-
nis* is genitive of material. Cf.
Anthol. I, 60: λυγοτευχέα κύρ-
τον.

64. Norit. This is Werns-
dorf's correction for *novit*, which
is found in all the books, doubt-
less because of *scit* following in
the indicative. *Norit* of course
depends on *licet* in line 62.

69. Et. Frequent in indignant
questions : see Ov. M. 13, 6, and
my note on that passage.

Post haec sc. *mea munera.*
Cf. III. 9: *amatque novum post
tot mea munera Mopsum.*

70 sq. ' Perhaps you think it a
disgrace that I, the clownish
Alcon, should be desperately in
love with you.'

Forsitan, which in Cicero is
only used with the subjunctive, is
sometimes put with the indicative
in the poets and later writers, as
if it were the same as *fortasse.*

Dūcis, distinguish *dŭcis.*

Rusticus. Cf. Virg. E. 2,
56: *Rusticus es, Corydon,* ' you
are a clown, Corydon.' Theocr.
20, 3 : βουκόλος ὢν ἐθέλεις με
κύσαι, τάλαν ;

71. Te peream. Cf. Plaut.
Poen. 5, 2, 135: *earum hic alteram
efflictim perit.* See note on line 2.

Di pecorum pavere greges, formosus Apollo,
Pan doctus, Fauni vates, et pulcher Adonis.
Quin etiam fontis speculo me mane notavi,
Nondum purpureos Phoebus cum tolleret orbes,   75
Nec tremulum liquidis lumen splenderet in undis.
Quod vidi, nulla tegimur lanugine malas ;
Pascimus et crinem ; nostro formosior Ida
Dicor, et hoc ipsum mihi tu iurare solebas,
Purpureas laudando genas et lactea colla,   80

72. *Di* fɪ. *Di precor* Dɪ. *Dii precor pavere* R2.
73. *phauni nates* R2. *fauni, vates* fɪ. *vates Fauni* Dɪ. Ulit. c.
Faunusque pater.
    75. *dum tolleret orbes* Dɪ. *ortus* Rɪ.2.rafɪ.vaɪ.bo Barth.
    76. *lumen splenderet* Dɪ. *splenderet lumen* vulg. *lumine in*
pfɪ.βa2.t. *tremulo spl. lumine* cd. Titii.
    77. *tegimur perlanguine* Dɪ. *tegimus* Barth. *mala* D2.R2. *malis* d2.
    78. *Pascimur* R2.dɪ.2.pfɪ.nβψ. *crimen* D2.R2.d2.pβ. (Guid. in
Comm. corrects *Pascimus et crinem.*) *crines* bo.
    79. *iurare solebas* Dɪ. *narrare solebas* vulg. *narare* R2.

72. Apollo fed the cattle of Ad-
metus : see Tib. 2, 3, 11 : *Pavit et
Admeti tauros formosus Apollo.*
    73. **Doctus**: sc. *calamis ac ver-
su*, which words are expressed,
XI. 2. Pan is called *doctus* from
his musical skill, as the Greeks
called poets σοφοί.
    Fauni vates. Plural. 'The
oracular Fauns.'
    Pulcher Adonis. Cf. Virg.
E. 10, 17 : *Nec te poeniteat pe-
coris, divine poeta ; Et formosus
ovis ad flumina pavit Adonis.*
Theocr. 1, 109 : ὡραῖος χὥδωνις,
ἐπεὶ καὶ μάλα νομεύει.
    74. Quin etiam, 'nay even.'
Here, as often, to mark a climax.
    Fontis speculo, 'a fountain's
mirror.' Cf. Phaed. 1, 4, 2 sq. :
*Canis per flumen, carnem dum
ferret, natans, Lympharum in
speculo vidit simulacrum suum.*
Cf. II. 88 : *fontibus in liquidis
quoties me conspicor.*

Virgil E. 2, 25, less suitably
makes the shepherd see his reflec-
tion in the sea, although that
mirror is appropriate enough in
Theocritus' description (6, 34) of
the Cyclops, who actually entered
the sea.
    75. Orbes, 'disk.' Cf. Cow-
per's Winter Morning Walk :
'*Tis morning : and the sun with
ruddy orb Ascending, fires the
horizon.*
    76 sq. Cf. Tasso's *Aminta*, 2, 1 :
*Non son io Da disprezzar, se ben
me stesso vidi Nel liquido del
mar, quando l'altr'ieri Taceano
i venti, ed ei giacea senz'onda.*
    77. Quod vidi, 'as far as I
saw.'
    78. Pascimus et crinem, 'I
let my hair grow.' Cf. Hor. S. 2,
3, 35 : *sapientem pascere barbam.*
    79. Repeated from III. 62.
    80. Laudandŏ. See note on
VIII. 53.

Atque hilares oculos et formam puberis aevi.
Nec sumus indoctis calamis : cantamus avena,
Qua divi cecinere prius, qua dulce locutus
Tityrus e silvis dominam pervenit ad urbem.
Nos quoque te propter, Donace, cantabimur urbi, 85
Si modo coniferas inter viburna cupressos
Aut inter pinos corylum frondescere fas est.
Sic pueri Donacen toto sub sole canebant,
Frigidus e silvis donec discedere suasit
Hesperus, et stabulis pastos inducere tauros. 90

---

82. *indoctis calamis* D1. *indocti calamis* vulg. *indocti. calamis cantamus avenae* PVR1.rabo. *indocti. calamis* p. *cantare et avenae* nd1.2. (in the last *cantamus avene* is added). Heins. c. *indocti calamos.*
83. This line is omitted in VD2.4.R1.2.rd1.2.na. *Qui divi* p. Ulit. c. *Quae.*
84. *in urbem* Barth.
85. *Donacen* D2. *donacē* R2. *cantabimur* aπBarth.Burm. *cantabimus* R1.2.d2.b, and so the other editions.
86. *corniferas* D3.R2. edit. Aurel. *carniferas* P. *consertas* d1.2. *inter iuburna* d2. *inter urbana* pβ (Guid. corrected to *viburna*).
87. *Aut inter* f1.βπ Barth. *At inter* p. *Atque inter* D3. vulg.
88. *Poeta* is prefixed in R1.rapf1.a1.bod2. Tit. edits *tosto sub* in f2., from a certain MS.
89. *discedere* R1.2.raboπ Barth. *descendere* pβd2.f1.a2.f2ψ, and so the later editors.
90. Burm. c. *includere tauros.*

---

81. Hilares oculos. Cf. VI. 15 ; *ridens oculis.*

82. Cantamus, &c. Cf. Virg. E. 2, 23 : *Canto, quae solitus, si quando armenta vocabat, Amphion Dircaeus.*

84. Tityrus i.e. Virgil. Cf. IV. 64 and 161.

85. 'I too will be celebrated by the city on your account, O Donace.' Cf. Ov. Am. 1, 3, 25 : *Nos quoque per totum pariter cantabimur orbem.* Wernsdorf is inclined to read *cantabimus* i. e.

through desire to please you I will attempt loftier themes so as to win fame in the city.

86. Cf. Virg. E. 1, 26 : *Quantum lenta solent inter viburna cupressi* (sc. *efferre caput*). Id. A. 3, 680 : *coniferae cyparissi.*

88. Toto sub sole, 'as long as it was daylight.'

89. Discedere. For this Wernsdorf reads *descendere* = *abire :* cf. Virg. A. 11, 450 : *Tyrrhenamque manum totis descendere campis.* Compare the ending of Virgil's sixth Eclogue.

ECLOGA DECIMA.

(NEMESIANI III.)

PAN.

THREE lads surprise Pan sleeping under an elm, and endeavour to play on his pipe, which they find suspended on a neighbouring branch. Their unskilful attempts waken the god, and he thereupon volunteers a song himself, taking as his subject the praises of Bacchus, whence this Eclogue is entitled *Bacchus* in many editions.

The scene is laid in Arcadia on Mount Maenalus. See lines 14 and 66.

The poem is modelled on Virgil's sixth Eclogue, in which Silenus is 'caught napping,' and, apparently nothing loath, pays the penalty of a song.

Conington observes that the praises of Bacchus are much more appropriate in the mouth of Silenus than of Pan.

Wernsdorf mentions several extant gems, the carvings on which illustrate the various scenes described in this Eclogue.

Nyctilus atque Mycon nec non et pulcher Amyntas
Torrentem patula vitabant ilice solem,
Cum Pan venatu fessus recubare sub ulmo
Coeperat, et somno lassatas sumere vires :
Quem super ex tereti pendebat fistula ramo.   5
Hanc pueri, tamquam praedam pro carmine possent
Sumere, fasque esset calamos tractare deorum,
Invadunt furto : sed nec resonare canorem
Fistula, quem suevit, nec vult contexere carmen ;

In hac Ecloga (a adds *decima*), *Pan inducitur cantare laudes ac munera dei Bacchi, Nyctilo et Mycone audientibus cum Amynta* R1.ra (in a *Loquitur primus poeta* is added). *Bacchus* ‖ *Pan trium puerorum impulsu modulatur* f1.va1.tπ. This Eclogue is commonly inscribed *Bacchus*, but *Pan* in a2.sf2.

1. *Poeta* is prefixed in R1.rd2.af1.vpβbo. *Nictylus* R1. *Nitulus* D1. *Nyctilos* vulg.

4. *Ceperat* b. *Coeprat* s. *Ceparat* R1. Glaes c. *se parat. lassatas* VD1.2.3.R1.rabo and Guid. from some texts ; the rest give *lassatus. lassatus resumere* ψ. Barth. c. *lassus resumere ! summere* R1.f1. *sonno lassatus summere vires* R2. Heins. c. *laxatas sumere.* Burm. c. *ex somno lapsas* or *lapsasque resumere.*

6. Tit. Barth. and Burm. c. *praedem. carmine poscunt* d1.2. Gud. c. *per praedam carmina possent. Hanc . . . dam pro carmine possent . . . fasque* D1.

8, 9. *Invadet* D1. *canorem* D1.2.3. *canorem Fistula quem suevit* R1. Guid. from an old copy, rabοπ Barth. *quem suerat* D2.d1.2. *canorem Fistula quem fuerat* R2. *canorum F. quem suevit* f1.vt. *fuerat* D3. Heins. c. *canorum F. ceu suerat. canorum* (understand *tam*) *F. quam suerat* Ulit. *canorem F. quem suerat* has been the reading since Burm.

1. Nec non et, 'likewise,' also.' Cf. Virg. A. 1, 707 : *nec non et Tyrii.* This use is confined to poetry and late prose. The connexion is different in such passages as Cic. Fin. 4, 22 : *nec hoc ille non vidit, sed verborum magnificentia est et gloria delectatus.*

2. Cf. v. 2.

3. Cf. Theocr. 1, 15 sq.: οὐ θέμις, ὦ ποιμάν, τὸ μεσαμβρινὸν οὐ θέμις ἄμμιν συρίσδεν· τὸν Πᾶνα δεδοίκαμες· ἦ γὰρ ἀπ' ἄγρας τανίκα

κεκμακὼς ἀμπαύεται· ἐντὶ δὲ πικρός.

6. Hanc sc. *fistulam.*

Praedam is preferred to the reading *praedem* by Wernsdorf, on the ground that the latter reading is less appropriate with the following words : *invadunt furto.*

8 sq. Sed nec, &c., 'but neither would the pipe resound with its wonted melody, nor weave a wreath of song.'

9. Contexere carmen. For

N 2

Sed pro carminibus male sibila dissona reddit.   10
Tum Pan excussus sonitu stridentis avenae,
Iamque videns, Pueri, si carmina poscitis, inquit,
Ipse canam ; nulli fas est inflare cicutas,
Quas ego Maenaliis cera coniungo sub antris.
Iamque ortus, Lenaee, tuos et semina vitis   15
Ordine detexam : debemus carmina Baccho.
Hoc fatus coepit calamis sic montivagus Pan :

10. *male sibila dissona* D1.2.4.R2.a2.f2. *mala sibila* D3.pβd1.2.
vulg.
11. *Cum Pan* D1. Lines 11-16 are accidentally omitted in β.
12. *Pan* is prefixed in R1.rapf1.d2.bo.
14. *cera compingo* d1.2.   This line is wanting in D3.
15. D1. reads *tuus* for *tuos*. *Iamque, ego, Bacche, tuos ortus* vulg.
Ulit. c. *Iamque ego Baccheos ortus*. Tit. c. *orsus et stamina*.
16. In D1. after this line follows : *Atque ilares oculos et formam*
pulchrior aevi, which seems to be borrowed from IX. 81.
17. *Hoc coepit fatus* D1. *Hoc* PD3. *Haec* vulg. Glaes. c. *Occoepit*
fatus.

the metaphor cf. Pindar, N. 2, 2,
where the Homerids are called
ῥαπτῶν ἐπέων ἀοιδοί.
   10. **Male dissona**, 'wretch-
edly discordant,' as *male rauci*,
'miserably hoarse.' When joined
to an adjective *male* more usually
has a negative meaning, as Virg.
A. 2, 23 : *statio male fida carinis*,
i.e. 'unsafe.'
   11. **Excussus**, 'startled,' sc.
somno.
   Stridentis avenae, 'piping
reed.' Cf. III. 60 : *acerbae stridor*
avenae.
   12. **Videns**, sc. Myconem et
Amyntam, or, as Wernsdorf ex-
plains, seeing his pipe had been
taken from him.
   In Virg. E. 6, 21, the words
jamque videnti are used of Silenus
just roused from sleep, and Ser-
vius explains *videnti* by *vigilanti*,
a meaning for which Conington
observes there does not seem to

be a parallel. This note of Ser-
vius, perhaps, gives the true
explanation of the present pas-
sage : 'and now with his eyes
wide open', 'wide awake.'
   Si carmina poscitis, 'if you
call for a song.' *Posco* is often
used in this connexion, especially
in passive, e. g. Hor. C. 1, 32, 1 :
Poscimur : ' we are called on for
a song'; and the same expression
occurs in Ov. M. 5, 333.
   14. **Maenaliis.** Maenalus was
a mountain range in Arcadia,
extending from Megalopolis to
Tegea, and sacred to Pan.
   16. **Detexam**, 'unfold,' 'de-
scribe'; cf. Poet. ap. Auct. Her.
2, 27, 42 ; *te ab summo jam*
detexam exordio.
   Debemus carmina Baccho,
i. e. because wine inspires song.
Cf. Tib. 1, 8, 37 : *Ille liquor do-*
cuit voces inflectere cantu.
   17. **Montivagus Pan.** This

Te cano, qui gravidis hederata fronte corymbis
Vitea serta plicas, quique udo palmite tigres
Ducis odorato perfusus colla capillo,   20
Vera Iovis proles ; iam tunc post sidera coeli
Sola Iovem Semele vidit Iovis ora professum.
Hunc pater omnipotens, venturi providus aevi,

18. *gravidus* D1. *gravidis* vulg. *fronde* D3.R2. *Pan* is added in
f1.a.
19. *plicans quique udo palm.* D1. *quique udo* is approved by Burm.
and Wernsd., and adopted by Beck. *qui quando* is found in almost
all the old MSS. and editions. *qui qñ palm.* R1.2. *qui comptos
palm.* aboπ Barth. Ulit. *comptas* a Burm. Wernsd. Ulit. c. *qui
ovantes (qui* not being elided) *palm.* Burm. c. *pando* or *lento palm.*
Hoeufft. c. *qui quasso palm.* or *comptus,* if *comptos* had MS. authority.
20. *odoratis — capillis* f1.va1.tπ Barth. *odoratu profusus* P.
21. Burm c. *nam tunc.* Glaes. c. *quoniam post. post fulmina*
abo. *coelo* R1.d2.
22. *Semel* D1.
23. Beck and Klausen give *futuri providus.*

ending may be paralleled from
Virgil, but not from Calpurnius.
See Introduction, page 16. Cf.
ὀρειβάτης.
18. Gravidis, &c., 'the clus-
ters of berries hanging heavy on
thy ivy-wreathed brow.' Cf. de-
scription of Bacchus, Tib. 1, 7,
45 : *varii flores et frons redimita
corymbis.* Cf. Homeric Hymn
25, 1 : Κισσοκόμην Διόνυσον, ἐρί-
βρομον, ἄρχομ' ἀείδειν, Ζηνὸς,
καὶ Σεμέλης ἐρικυδέος ἀγλαὸν υἱόν,
ὅν τρέφον ἠΰκομοι Νύμφαι, παρὰ
πατρὸς ἄνακτος δεξάμεναι κόλποισι,
καὶ ἐνδυκέως ἀτίταλλον, Νύσης ἐν
γυάλοις· ὁ δ' ἀέξατο πατρὸς ἕκητι
ἄντρῳ ἐν εὐώδει, μεταρίθμιος ἀθα-
νάτοισιν.
19. Udo, 'soaked in wine.'
Cf. Stat. Theb. 4, 758 : *uda mero
lambunt retinacula tigres.*
20. Odorato, &c., 'with per-
fumed hair flowing over your
neck.'
21 sq. Post sidera coeli, &c.,

'Semele alone after the stars of
heaven (i. e. except the gods
above) saw Jove under the form
of Jove'. For *profiteri,* 'display,'
'make a show of,' cf. Ov. A. A.
3, 433 : *Sed vitate viros cultum
formamque professos.*

Semele is said, at the insti-
gation of Juno, to have asked
Jupiter to appear to her in the
same majesty in which he ap-
peared to Juno. Her request was
granted, but she was consumed
by the lightning which accom-
panied the manifestation. Jupiter
saved her son Bacchus, and sewed
him up in his thigh until he
reached maturity. Cf. Nemesia-
nus, Cynegetica, 16 sq.: *Quis non
Semelen, ignemque jugalem Leta-
lemque simul, novit de pellicis
astu ? Quis magno recreata tacet
cunabula Baccho? Ut pater omni-
potens maternos reddere menses
Dignatus, justi complerit tempora
partus ?*

Pertulit, et iusto produxit tempore partus.

Hunc Nymphae, Faunique senes, Satyrique procaces,   25
Nosque etiam Nysae viridi nutrimus in antro.

Quin et Silenus parvum veneratus alumnum
Aut gremio fovet, aut resupinis sustinet ulnis,
Evocat aut risum digito, motuque quietem
Allicit, aut tremulis quassat crepitacula palmis.   30
Cui deus arridens horrentes pectore setas

24. *Pertulit* D1., which was conjectured by Burm. and adopted by Beck. *Protulit* vulg. *iusso* D1.

25, 26. Glaes. places these lines as in the text; Wernsd. and Beck invert the order. *Vosque etiam — nutrimus* D1. *Nosque etiam nymphae* D2.3. *Vos etiam et Nysae v. nutristis* pf1.βa2.f2. Wernsd. observes that the words *Nymphae* and *Nysae* were confused together.

27. *parvus* R1. *veneratur* R2.

28. *sonet* P. *resupinis* R1.raf2.a2.sboπ Barth. Ulit. Burm. d2. *resupinus* D4.R2.d1.2.pβf1.a1.

29. *Aut evocat risum* D1. *Evocat adrisam* R2. Glaes. says we should certainly read as in the text : he, however, follows the vulg. in printing *Et vocat ad risum*. Glaes. c. *motuve*, but gives in his text *motumque*, probably by a printer's error, for *motuque*. *quietum* a.

30. This line is wanting in PVD2.3.4.R1.2.rd1.2.a.

31. *Qui deus* D4.R2.

24. Pertulit not *protulit*, as the latter would be tautological with *produxit*.
Pertulit = gessit foetum ad maturitatem partus. Cf. Plin. 7, 13, 11, 57 : *quaedam non perferunt partus.*
26. Nysae. Wernsdorf and Adelung say that Diodorus Siculus places Nysa in Arabia Felix. There was a city of the same name in India on Mount Meros, which also claims to be the birthplace of Bacchus. If the name of the mount were confused with the Greek μηρός it would explain the origin of the myth referred to in the note on line 21.

27. Alumnum, ' his nursling,' i. e. Bacchus.
28. Resupinis sustinet ulnis, ' cradles him in his arms.'
29. Motuque quietem Allicit, 'and courts sleep by rocking him to and fro.'
30. Tremulis, ' shaking,' no doubt through intoxication.
Crepitacula, ' rattles.' Adelung compares Arnobius 2 p. 70 : *tum ad silentium pavidae nutricis motibus, et crepitaculis adducerentur auditis.*
31. ' Smiling on whom the god pulls out the hairs which bristle on his breast.'

Vellicat, aut digitis aures astringit acutas,
Applauditve manu mutilum caput, aut breve mentum,
Et simas tenero collidit pollice nares.
Interea pueri florescit pube iuventus,   35
Flavaque maturo tumuerunt tempora cornu.
Tum primum laetas ostendit pampinus uvas ;
Mirantur Satyri frondes et poma Lyaei.
Tum deus, o Satyri, maturos carpite foetus,
Dixit, et ignotos, pueri, calcate racemos.   40
Vix haec ediderat, decerpunt vitibus uvas,

32. *Vellitat aut digitos* R2. *astrigit* D1. *aures astringere acutas*
pβ (Guid. cites *astringit* from an old MS.). *adstringit* R1.r. *sub-
stringit* D4.R2.
33. *Aut plauditve* D1. *Applauditque* R1.rabova1.d2. *Aplaudit
ve m. rutulum c. a. breve m̄bum* R2. *breve mentum* R1.raπ. *leve* all
others acc. to Wernsd. *multum caput* D3. *mutum* P. *rutilum* D4.
34. *Et simas* f1.va1.π. *Et summas* D2.3.R1.2.rbd2. *Aut summas t.
sustulit poll.*, with *sustollit* written above V. *Aut simas* Barth.
subducit poll. abo. *collidit podice* R2. *collidit police* p.
35. Burm. c. *puero. iuventus* D1. *iuventa* vulg. Heins. c. *iuventas.*
36. *timuerunt* R1.2.r.
37. *leves* D4. *primus leves ostentat* R2. *lenes* d2.pβa2.f2. Burm.
c. *foetas.*
38. *dona liei* R2. *dona Lycaei* pβ.
39. *cupite* D3. *foetus* D1. *fructus* vulg.
41. *ediderant* R2. *audiderant* f1. *audierant* VR1.rava1.bod2.

32. **Aures . . . acutas.**
'pricked-up ears'. Cf. Hor. C.
2, 19, 4.
Astringit, 'pulls.'
33. **Applaudit,** 'pats.' Cf.
Silius Pun. 16, 357 : *nec qui cer-
vicis amaret Applausae blandos
sonitus.* Virg. G. 3, 186: *plausae
sonitum cervicis amare.*
Mutilum. Hardly ' bald,' as
Wernsd. after Heins. explains.
Silenus was represented with
short horns, and the allusion is
probably to this : ' with cropped
horns,' ' short stumpy horns'. Cf.
Ov. A. A. 3, 249 : *Turpe pecus
mutilum.*

34. **Simas . . . nares,** 'snub
nose.'
Collidit, 'pinches.'
36. The representation of Bac-
chus with the horns of a ram or
bull is found chiefly on coins but
never in statues. See Smith,
Class. Dict.
40. **Ignotos . . . racemos ;**
because he was the first to teach
their use. A similar expression
is used with regard to Osiris in
Tib. 1, 7, 32 : *Pomaque non notis
legit ab arboribus.*
41. ' Scarcely had he said this
when they gather grapes from the
vine.' The clause following that

Et portant calathis, celerique elidere planta
Concava saxa super properant ; vindemia fervet
Collibus in summis, crebro pede rumpitur uva,
Rubraque purpureo sparguntur pectora musto.   45
Tum Satyri, lasciva cohors, sibi pocula quisque
Obvia corripiunt ; quod fors dedit, arripit usus.
Cantharon hic retinet, cornu bibit alter adunco :
Concavat ille manus, palmasque in pocula vertit :
Pronus at ille lacu bibit, et crepitantibus haurit   50

42. *Et poterat* R1. *elidere* D1. *illidere* VR1.raf1.bo𝜋 vulg. *illudere* pβa2.f2.d2.
43. *Con cuia saxa* D1. *super ponunt* b. *superponunt* o. *fervent* R2.
45. *Rubraque* D1. *Nudaque* vulg. *Udaque* R1.rabo.
46. *Cum satyri* D1. *lasciva chori* D2.
47. *corripuit* pβa2.f2.d2. (in the last—*iunt* is added), *quod fors dedit, arripit usus* D1. *sors* vulg. *hoc capit usus* vulg. Heins. c. *hoc capit unus* or *hic capit urceum*. Ulit. c. *occupat usus*.
49. *Convocat* d1.2. (in the latter corrected to *concavat*) pβ (Guid. corrects *concavat*). *que* after *palmas* is omitted in PD4.R2.
50. *Pronus ac* d2. Tit. cites *Prorsus ac* on line 43.

with *vix* usually begins with *cum* in prose, with *et* in verse. The ellipsis, as here, however, is not uncommon, e. g. Ov. F. 5, 278 : *Vix bene desieram, rettulit illa mihi.*

42. Elidere, 'crush.' Cf. Propert. 4, 6, 73 : *Vinaque fundantur prelis elisa Falernis.*

43. Vindemia fervet. Cf. 1. 3, and Virg. G. 2, 6 : *spumat plenis vindemia labris.*

44. Crebro pede, &c., ' the grape is crushed with many a foot.'

45. 'And the breasts (of those who are treading the grapes) are red, spattered with the fresh purple wine.' **Rubra** is proleptic, 'spattered so as to become red.'

46 sq. ' Then the wanton Satyrs snatch each the goblets that come in their way ; what chance offers their requirements seize upon.'

48. Cantharon. The Greek form for *cantharum*, on account of the metre. The *cantharus* was a large drinking vessel, with handles, especially used by Bacchus and his followers. Hence Marius was censured because, after the conquest of the Cimbri, he drank from the *cantharus* like a triumphing Bacchus.

Cornu . . . adunco, ' from a crooked horn.'

49. Cf. Propert. 4, 9, 36 : *et cava suscepto flumine palma sat est.*

50. Pronus, &c., 'but another, stooping down, drinks from the wine vat.'

Musta labris : alius vocalia cymbala mergit,
Atque alius latices pressis resupinus ab uvis
Excipit ; at potis saliens liquor ore resultat,
Spumeus inque humeros et pectora defluit humor.
Omnia ludus habet, cantusque chorique licentes.   55
Et Venerem iam vina movent ; raptantur amantes
Concubitu Satyri fugientes iungere Nymphas,
Iam iamque elapsas hic crine, hic veste retentat.

51. *aluis vocalia cymbala vertit* R2. *vocalia cymbia* Titii cdd. d2.
(with *cymbala* written on margin) pβfi.2.a2. *Multa l.a. vocabula
cimbula* D1. *venalia cymbala* VR1.rabo. Some read *venalia
cymbia.*
52. In all the old books this line is placed after the following one.
a2. or g seems to have been the first to arrange as above. *pressus*
D1.pβfi.v. *aluis presset r. abuvis* R2.
53. *potis* D1. *ac potus* VR1.rad1.2.pβfi.boπ. *ac potu* R2. Heins.
c. *ac poto. Excipit ad potus* Barth. Ulit.
54. *Spumeos* R1.r. *Spumeus* b. *Evomit inque* D1. Glaes. c.
Evomis (i. e. *spumeus*) *inque. defluit* PD1.2.3.4.R1.2.rabo. *difluit*
Vpβt Ulit. *diffluit* a2.f2.π Barth. Burm. Wernsd.
55. *corique* D1. whence Glaes. edits as in text. *habet : cantusque
chorosque licentes Et Venerem* vulg.
56. *iam una monent* R2.
57. *Concubitum* D1. Heins. c. *Satyris* or *Satyros.*
58. *hic veste hic crine retentant* Barth.

Et crepitantibus, &c., 'and
takes a draught of the fresh wine
with smacking, noisily sucking
lips.'
51. *Labrum,* 'a lip,' has the
first syllable common; *labrum,* 'a
basin,' always has the first syllable
long.
Alius, &c., 'another plunges
in the sonorous cymbals.'
52. Resupinus, 'lying on his
back.'
53. At potis, &c., 'but when
they are drunk, the liquid, welling
up, overflows from their lips.'
54. 'And the foaming fluid

streams over their shoulders and
breasts.'
55. Chorique licentes, 'wan-
ton, riotous dances.' Cf. Stat.
Silv. 1, 6, 93 : *jocos licentes.*
56. Et Venerem, &c., 'and
now wine awakens love.'
Raptantur . . . . jungere.
A Grecism : raptim discurrunt
apprehensuri Nymphas fugien-
tes ut concubitu sibi jungant.
Wernsdorf. In Hor. C. 3, 18, 1 :
Faunus is called *Nympharum
fugientum amator.*
58. 'And as they are on the
very point of escaping, one (Satyr)

Tum primum roseo Silenus cymbia musto
Plena senex avide non aequis viribus hausit. 60
Ex illo venas inflatus nectare dulci
Hesternoque gravis semper ridetur Iaccho.
Quin etiam deus ille, deus Iove prosatus ipso,
Et plantis uvas premit, et de vitibus hastas
Ingerit, et lynci praebet cratera bibenti. 65
Haec Pan Maenalia pueros in valle docebat,
Sparsas donec oves campo conducere in unum

59. *primum* R1.raf1.va1.boπ. *primam* Barth. *Tu primus* R2.
primus D2.3.pβa2.f2.d2. *roseo sileneus tibia musto* D1. *cimbala* R2.
62. *Externoque* D2.
63. *prosatus ipso* R1.rf1.π. *prosatus ab* D1. *pronatus* D2.4. *pro
natus ipso* R2. *natus ab ipso* PD3.apβa2.f2.bo. *natus ab illo* d2.
(with *prosatus ipso* in margin).
64. *Ex plantis* D2. *vitibus haustas* d1.2. *haustus* cd. Titii.
65. *Integit et* D1. which Glaes. adopts. *Ingerit et* vulg. *luci* D3.
clatera D1. *videnti* D4.d1.
66. *Poeta* is prefixed in R1.rd2.apf1.vbo.

holds them back by the hair, another by the dress.'
60. Non aequis viribus, 'with strength not equal to the draught.' Wernsdorf following Burmann says Silenus had not the same drinking powers as the Satyrs. Cf. Virg. A. 2, 724: (*Ascanius*) *sequitur patrem non passibus aequis*, i. e. with steps not equal to those of Æneas, not keeping pace with him. Nemesianus himself in his Cynegetica 189 sq. uses the very expression of the text : *His* (*sc. catulis*) *leporem praemitte manu, non viribus aequis, Nec cursus virtute parem*, i. e. when training young dogs give them a hare to hunt that is not of equal strength with themselves.
61. Ex illo, sc. *tempore*.
62. Hesterno . . . Iaccho, ' yesterday's debauch.' Cf. Virg.

E. 6, 15: *Inflatum hesterno venas, ut semper, Iaccho.*
63. 'Nay, even that god (sc. Bacchus), a god sprung from Jupiter himself.'
Prosatus is found also in Auson. Idyll. 7, 1.
64. De vitibus hastas, i. e. the thyrsi made of wands of vine wood twined with vine leaves and ivy. Cf. Ov. M. 3, 667: *Pampineis agitat velatam frondibus hastam.*
65. Ingerit, 'hurls,' 'throws.' Cf. Stat. Theb. 9, 708: *saevas miserantibus ingerit hastas.* Virg. A. 9, 763 : *hinc raptas fugientibus ingerit hastas In tergus.*
Et lynci, &c. There is a Mosaic at Pompeii, representing a wine genius riding a panther and holding a goblet in his hand.
66. See note on line 14.
67 sq. ' Until night bid them

Nox iubet, uberibus suadens siccare fluorem
Lactis, et in niveas astrictum cogere glebas.

68. *uberius* fı.vaı. *liquorem* VRı.raboπ Barth. Ulit. Burm.
fluorem R2.fı.2.pβd2. (*liquorem* added in margin) a2. Wernsd.
Beck. *flurorem* D3. Haupt says that Dı. also supports the reading
fluorem.

drive together the sheep scattered
over the plain.' Cf. Virg. E. 6,
85 : *Cogere donec oves stabulis
numerumque referri Jussit et
invito processit Vesper Olympo.*
**68. Uberibus . . . siccare
fluorem,** hypallage for *ubera
siccare fluore* as in Hor. C. 1, 31,
10 : *aureis mercator exsiccet cu-
lullis vina.* For *fluorem lactis*

cf. Nemesianus Cynegetica 227 :
*Mox lactis liquidos sensim super-
adde fluores.*
69. Et in niveas, &c., 'and
curdle and thicken it into snow-
white clots ' : i. e. make the milk
into cheese, which was done before
sunrise, and after sunset. See
v. 34 and 65.

ECLOGA UNDECIMA.

(Nemesiani IV.)

LYCIDAS, MOPSUS.

THIS Eclogue is appropriately entitled *Eros*. Two shepherds, Lycidas and Mopsus, lament the cruelty of their respective loves, Iollas and Meroe.

Without adopting the dictum of Barthius, that this Eclogue, though last in order is first in merit of all the Eclogues (he attributes the eleven to Calpurnius), we must admit that the poem possesses much grace and beauty, especially in the description of rural sights and sounds.

This is the only Eclogue by Calpurnius or Nemesianus which contains a recurring burden, a feature which is probably imitated from the Φαρμακεύτρια of Theocritus and from Virgil's eighth Eclogue, which bears the same name.

Populea Lycidas, nec non et Mopsus in umbra,
Pastores, calamis et versu doctus uterque,

In hac Ecloga [a adds *undecima*] *Lycidas et Mopsus amores suos querelis desperati prosequuntur, Meroes Mopsus, et Lycidas Iolle* [a adds *pueri. Loquitur primus* poeta] R1.rad2. *Aegloga undecima* is added in pβa2.s, although in these editions the four Eclogues are attributed to Nemesianus. *Commentaria Dion. Guidalotti Bononiensis in quartam et Ultimam Nemesiani Aeglogam. Mopsus et Lycidas Interlocutores aegloga undecima* β. *Eros* (h. e. *Amatorius* or *Amor* Tit.) is prefixed in f1.va1.π and the succeeding editions up to Wernsdorf. *Nemesiani Ecloga* iv. vulg. before Wernsd.
1. *Poeta* is prefixed in d2.pabo.
2. *calamis et versu* D1. *ac versu* vulg.

2. Cf. IX. 82 : *nec sumus indocti calamis.*

Nec triviale sonans, proprios cantabat amores.
Nam Mopso Meroe, Lycidae crinitus Iollas
Ignis erat, parilisque furor de dispare sexu   5
Cogebat trepidos totis discurrere silvis.
Hos puer ac Meroe multum lusere furentes,
Dum modo condictas vitant in vallibus ulmos,
Nunc fagos placitas fugiunt, promissaque fallunt
Antra, nec est animus solitos alludere fontes.   10

3. Scriver. c. *Nil triviale.*
4. Heins. on Ov. H. 16, 102, quotes *formosus Iolas.*
5. Heins. c. *Ignis erant. parilique* D4.
6. In pβa2.sgf2. this line is followed by line 13, *Inque vicem,* &c.
7. *Flos puer ac mero multum* R2.   *luxere parentes* or *furentes* D1.
Glaes. c. *lusere paventes.*
8. *conductas* VD1.2.3.4.R1.2.r.   Mod. cites *condictas v. in v.*
ornos.
9. *Hunc fagos* R2.   *placidas* VR1.2.raβf1.bo.   *praemissaque* D1.
10. *est amnis* D1.   *amnus* R2.

3. Nec triviale sonans, 'singing no common-place strain.' Cf. I. 28.

Proprios = suos. Cf. Hor. Ep. 1, 7, 51 : *Cultello proprios purgantem leniter ungues.*

5. Ignis. This word is used by the poets of a beloved object, as we sometimes use 'flame.' Cf. Virg. E. 3, 66 : *At mihi sese offert ultro, meus ignis, Amyntas.* In line 11 *ignis* means the fire of love, the glow of passion.

6. Trepidos, &c., 'to wander restlessly through the groves.' Cf. III. 50 : *tabidus erro,* and Virg. E. 2, 3.

7. Lusere, 'made sport of, deceived.' Cf. Hor. C. 3, 4, 5 : *auditis, an me ludit amabilis Insania?* Tib. 1, 6, 9 : *Ipse miser docui, quo posset ludere pacto Custodes.*

8 sq. Modo . . . nunc, 'at one time . . . at another,' as in Ov. M.

13, 922 sq. *Modo . . . modo* is the usual combination; but instead of the second *modo,* we find not only *nunc,* but also *aliquando, interdum, nonnunquam, saepe, rursus.*

Condictas . . . ulmos, 'the trysting-place, the rendezvous under the elms.' Cf. Ov. M. 4, 95 : *dictaque sub arbore sedit. Condicere* implies a mutual agreement.

9. Fagos placitas, 'favourite beech-trees.'

Promissa . . . antra. Cf. IX. 26 : *antrum consuetum.*

Fallunt, 'do not keep their appointment at the promised cave.'

10. Nec est, &c., 'nor have they a mind, inclination, to play by the wonted springs.'

Est animus. Cf. Virg. A. 4, 639 : *Sacra Jovi Stygio . . . Perficere est animus.*

For the accusative with **allu-**

Tum tandem fessi, quos lusus adederat ignis,
Sic sua desertis nudarunt vulnera silvis,
Inque vicem dulces cantu luxere querelas.
M. Immitis Meroe, rapidisque fugacior Euris,
Cur nostros calamos, cur pastoralia vitas 15
Carmina? quemve fugis? quae me tibi gloria victo?
Quid vultu mentem premis, ac spem fronte serenas?
Tandem, dura, nega : possum non velle negantem.

11. Barth. c. *Dum. durus adederat* D1. *lusus dederat* R1. *lusus ederat* D4.R2.pa2.sf2. *luxus ederat* PD2.f1.va1. Mod. cites *lusus et ederat.* *lusus et edit et ignis* d1.abo. *adederat* vulg.
12. *vellera* V (with *vulnera* written over) R1.ra.
13. *dulces luxere* D1. *dixere* vulg. *duxere* PD2.R2.
16. *vincto* R2. *victor* D4. Burm. c. *spreto*, or *luso*, or *quaenam t. gloria, ficto Si vultu.*
17. *vultum veniens premis* VD4.R1.2.rad1.2.f1.va1.botψ Barth. *vultu venientem premis* P. Gebhard, however, quotes *veniens premissis* from P, whence Glaes. c. that there were two Palatine MSS. Gebhard c. *Voltum scaenis* or *poenis premis.*
18. *nega* D1., whence Glaes. gives the arrangement of the text. *fronte serenans Tandem dura negas? possum* vulg. *possum non velle* PVD1.4.R1.2.rf1.va1.tψ Wernsd. *non possum non velle* pβ. (Guid. says the first *non* should be erased). *non possum nolle* ad2. (corrected to *possum non*) ca2.f2.boπ Barth. Ulit. Burm. Ulit. c. *possum nunc velle.*

dere cf. Cat. 64, 66 : *Omnia quae, toto delapsa e corpore passim, Ipsius ante pedes fluctus salis alludebant.* The dative is found IV. 67.
11. Quos, &c., 'whom the oft-deceived fire of love had consumed.' Cf. Virg. A. 4, 2 : *caeco carpiter igni.*
12. The disappointed lovers desire solitude. Cf. Propert. 1, 18 : *Haec certe deserta loca et taciturna querenti.*
13. Dulces . . . querelas, 'sweet,' because they soothe sorrow, according to Wernsdorf, or perhaps 'tuneful.' Cf. IX. 15 : *Carminibus dulcique parant relevare querela.*

Luxere, 'wailed forth their sweet complaints.' From *lugeo.*
14. Rapidisque, &c. Cf. Ov. M. 13, 807 : *ventis volucrique fugacior aura. Fugax* is a common epithet of coy maidens.
16. Quae me, &c., 'what glory will you have in conquering me?' **Me . . . victo,** abl. abs., 'if I am conquered.'
17. Spem fronte serenas, 'show cheerful hope on your brow.' Cf. Virg. A. 1, 209: *spem vultu simulat:* ib. 4, 477 : *spem fronte serenat:* Silius, Pun. 11, 369 : *tristia fronte serenant.*
18. 'At length hard-hearted one refuse me; I may perhaps

Cantet, amat quod quisque ; levant et carmina curas.
L. Respice me tandem, puer o crudelis, Iolla.　　20
Non hoc semper eris : perdunt et gramina flores,
Perdit spina rosas, nec semper lilia candent,
Nec longum tenet uva comas, nec populus umbras.
Donum forma breve est, nec se quod commodat annis.
Cantet, amat quod quisque ; levant et carmina curas.　　25
M. Cerva marem sequitur, taurum formosa iuvenca,
Et Venerem sensere lupae, sensere leaenae,

21. *Nonhaec* D2. *herit—et germina* D1. *Nec hoc semper eris, nec semper lilia candent* (the intervening words being omitted) D4. *Hoc hoc semper eris : nec semper lilia candent Perdit spina rosas : perdunt et gramina flores* R2.
22. Glaes. follows D1. in reading *Perdunt spina,* and says 'forma *spinum* Calpurnio propria : cf. I. 57, *discordium,* II. 44, *oleastrum.*' Haupt approves of the vulg. *Perdit spina,* rejecting the reading of D1., which he says was introduced from the preceding line *perdunt et gramina.*
24. Glaes. gives *nec se quod,* following D1., which, however, has *annus* instead of *annis. nec se tibi* vulg. *annis* PR2.d2.pf1.βa2.f2.tψbo Wernsd. *annus* aπ Barth. Ulit.
26. *Cerva matrem* R1.
27. p gives *Mo.* before this line instead of the preceding.

cease to wish for you if you refuse me.' For *volo,* followed by accusative of person, cf Mart. 1, 9, 6 : *Nolo virum, facili redimit qui sanguine famam : Hunc volo, laudari qui sine morte potest.*
19. Cf. IX. 15. Hor. C. 4, 11, 35 : *minuentur atrae Carmine curae.* Similar refrains are found in Theocr. 1 and 2, and Virg. E. 3.
Curas, 'the pain or anxiety of love,' as often.
20 sq. Cf. Herrick's Counsel to Girls : *Gather ye rosebuds while ye may, Old Time is still a-flying; And this same flower that smiles to-day, To-morrow will be dying. Then be not coy, but use your time, And while ye may, go*

marry ; *For having lost but once your prime, Ye may for ever tarry.*
21. Cf. Theocr. 23, 28 sq. : καὶ τὸ ῥόδον καλόν ἐστι, καὶ ὁ χρόνος αὐτὸ μαραίνει· καὶ τὸ ἴον καλόν ἐστιν ἐν εἴαρι, καὶ ταχὺ γηρᾷ· λευκὸν τὸ κρίνον ἐστί, μαραίνεται, ἁνίκα πίπτει· ἁ δὲ χιὼν λευκά, καὶ τάκεται, ἁνίκα παχθῇ· καὶ κάλλος καλόν ἐστι τὸ παιδικόν, ἀλλ' ὀλίγον ζῇ.
22. See Notes, 1. Glaeser, reading *Perdunt,* takes *spina* as neut. pl., a form not found elsewhere.
24. 'Beauty is a short-lived gift, nor one that lends itself to advancing years,' or ' nor one that adapts itself to years.'
26. Cf. Virg. E. 2, 63.

Et genus aerium, volucres, et squamea turba,
Et montes silvaeque, suos habet arbor amores.
Tu tamen una fugis, miserum tu perdis amantem.   30
Cantet, amat quod quisque ; leuant et carmina curas.
L. Omnia tempus alit, tempus rapit : usus in arcto est.
Ver erat, et vitulos vidi sub matribus istos,
Qui nunc pro nivea coiere in cornua vacca.
Et tibi iam tumidae nares, iam fortia colla,   35
Iam tibi bis denis numerantur messibus anni.
Cantet; amat quod quisque ; levant et carmina curas.
M. Huc, Meroe formosa, veni ; vocat aestus in umbram.

28. *volucrum et sua mea turba* D1.   *et si quamea* D3.   *squammea*
pβa2.sf2.
29. Burm. c. *suosque habet.*
30. *ima fugis* R2.   *fugas* d1.2. (in the latter corrected *-is*).   Burm.
c. *spernis,* or *pellis.*
32. *in arcto est* R2.apβf1.a2.bπ Barth. Ulit. Beck.   *in arte es*
VR1.r.
33. p gives *Lyc.* before this line, instead of the preceding.
34. Barth. Advers. 47, 6, cites *coiere in praelia.*
35. *Quod tibi* P.   *timidae* D3.a.   *mares* D1.   *nares infortia* R1.
Tit. in lemm. mentions *iam fortiora,* which he corrects *tam fortia.*
36. *Iam tribus denis* D1.   *deni—mensibus* D3.P.   *tibi bis deni n.*
m. agni R2.   *agni* D4.   *missibus anni* s.   This line is wanting in
d1.2.
38. *in umbra* VD4.R2.r.

28. Squamea turba, 'the finny
tribe, or throng.'
29. Cf. Claud. nupt. Hon. 66 :
Vivunt in Venerem frondes, om-
nisque vicissim Felix arbor amat :
nutant ad mutua palmae Foe-
dera, &c. Cf. also Plin. 13, 4,
7, 31.
30. Miserum, &c., 'you de-
stroy your unhappy lover.' Cf.
Hor. C. 1, 8, 2 : *Sybarin cur*
properes amando Perdere.
32. Omnia tempus alit, tem-

pus rapit. Cf. Tennyson's Love
and Duty : *The slow, sweet hours*
that bring us all things good ; The
slow, sad hours that bring us all
things ill.
Usus in arcto est, 'enjoy-
ment is short-lived.'
33. Sub matribus, sc. *lac-*
tentes.
34. Coiere in cornua, ' butt
each other with their horns.'
35. With these signs of ma-
turity compare IX. 11 sq.

Iam pecudes subiere nemus, iam nulla canoro
Gutture cantat avis, torto non squamea tractu   40
Signat humum serpens : solus cano. Me sonat omnis
Silva, nec aestivis cantu concedo cicadis.
Cantet, amat quod quisque ; levant et carmina curas.
L. Tu quoque, saeve puer, niveum ne perde colorem
Sole sub hoc ; solet hic lucentes urere malas.   45
Hic, age, pampinea mecum requiesce sub umbra,
Hic tibi lene fluens fons murmurat, hic et ab ulmis
Purpureae foetis dependent vitibus uvae.
Cantet, amat quod quisque ; levant et carmina curas.
M. Qui tulerit Meroes fastidia lenta superbae,   50

39. *subire nemus* PR2. *subiire* D2. *subeunt* D1. Glaes. c. *sub-
eunt nemus, et iam.* *iam nulla* aboπ. *nam nulla* (with *iam* writ-
ten above) V. *nam nulla* R1.rf1.va1.t. *non illa* D3. *non ulla*
D2.R2.pβa2.f2.d2. *canora* a.

42. *tantum concede* (-*do* written above) V. *tantum concede* R1.r.

44. *scaeve* D4.β. *nactum ne* VR1.r. *natum* PD2.3.R2. *notum*
ad1.2. *calorem* R2. Tit. cites from two MSS. *O formose puer, niveo
ne crede colori.*

45. *s'de sub* R1. *sed et hic lucentes vertito malas* R1.2.D4.rd2.
sed et hic VD2.3. *sed et huc* a. *sed te huc luc. vertito* d1.c. *luentes*
D1. Heins. c. *liventes.* *Sed et huc lucentis urere malas* bo.

46. *Dic age* D2.

47. *leve fluens* PD2.π. *hic et abundas* D1., whence Glaes. c. *hic et
ad undas.*

50. Lines 50 to 55 are omitted in D4.R2. *fastidia lenta* D1. *longa*
vulg.

39. **Pecudes subiere**, &c. The
flocks have sought shelter from
the sun under the trees.
Jam nulla, &c. The birds
cease to sing in the extreme heat,
only the cicadae are then heard.
40. **Tractu**, 'the serpent's trail.'
42. **Nec aestivis**, &c., ' nor
do I yield to the summer tree
crickets in singing.' For the simile
cf. Hom. Il. 3, 150 : ἀγορηταὶ
ἐσθλοί, τεττίγεσσιν ἐοικότες. See

also VIII. 2.
45. **Hic**, sc. *sol.* ' It (i. e. the
sun) is wont to burn fair cheeks.'
46. Cf. Virg. E. 10, 42 sq. :
*Hic gelidi fontes, hic mollia
prata, Lycori, Hic nemus ; hic
ipso tecum consumerer aevo.*
47. **Lene fluens**, 'soft-flowing.'
48. **Foetis** is used of the fruit-
ful **vitibus**, just as *gravidis* is
used of *corymbis* in X. 18.
50. **Tulerit**, ' put up with.'

Sithonias feret ille nives Libycosque calores,
Nerinas potabit aquas, taxique nocentis
Non metuet succos, Sardoaque gramina vincet,
Et iuga Marmaricos coget sua ferre leones.
Cantet, amat quod quisque ; levant et carmina curas.   55
L. Quisquis amat pueros, ferro praecordia duret,
Nil properet, discatque diu patienter amare,
Prudentesque animos teneris non spernat in annis,
Perferat et fastus. Sic olim gaudia sumet,
Si modo sollicitos aliquis deus audit amantes.   60

52. *Nerinas* D1.2.R1.r.   All the other old books, according to
Wernsd., give *Nerines*. In Virg. E. 7, 37, we find *Nerine Galatea*.
53. *Sardoaque gramina* aboπ.   *Sardorum gramina* Pd2. (in latter
que is written over *Sardorum*) pβa2.f1.2.tψ.   *salebrosaque gram.*
VR1.r.   *metuat Sardoi germina* D1.   *vincent* PD2. Heins. c. *iunget.*
54. *Et iuga marmoricos coget sua* D1., whence Glaes. gives as in
text.   *Et sua Mar. cog. iuga* vulg.   *perstringet virga leones* d1.2. (in
the latter *coget sua* is added).
56. Lines 56 to 61 are wanting in VR1.r.   *praecordia dives* P.
57. *discatque diri* D1.   *lubens potienter* a.
58. *spernat in nanis* R2.
59. *Proferat* D4.R2.

51. Sithonias, i. e. Thracian.
52. Nerinas . . . aquas, 'sea-water.' The adjective *Nerinus*
is equivalent to *Nereius*, 'of
or belonging to the sea-god Ne-reus.'
Taxique nocentis. The same
epithet is applied to the yew-tree
in Virg. G. 2, 257. The yew was
considered poisonous.
53. Sardoaque gramina. Cf.
Virg. E. 7, 41 : *Immo ego Sar-doniis videar tibi amarior herbis.*
Conington says this acrid plant
was celery-leaved crowfoot.
54. Marmaricos. Marmarica
was the country lying between

Egypt and the Syrtes, now
Barca.
56. Ferro praecordia duret,
'steel his heart.' Cf. Tib. 1, 1,
77 : *praecordia ferro vincta.*
57. Of. Ov. Her. 20, 88 : *Ipsa
tibi dices, Quam patienter amat.*
Id. A. A. 3, 565 sq. : *Ille vetus
miles sensim et sapienter amabit,
Multaque tironi non patienda
feret.*
59. Olim, 'one day,' 'here-after.' Cf. Virg. A. 1, 203 : *for-san et haec olim meminisse juva-bit. Olim* also means ' formerly'
(the most common meaning) and
' at times.'

Cantet, amat quod quisque ; levant et carmina curas.

M. Quid prodest, quod me pagani mater Amyntae
Ter vittis, ter fronde sacra, ter ture vaporo
Lustravit, cineresque aversa effudit in amnem,
Incendens vivo crepitantes sulphure lauros,   65
Cum sic in Meroen totis miser ignibus urar ?
Cantet, amat quod quisque ; levant et carmina curas.
L. Haec eadem nobis, quae versicoloria fila,
Et mille ignotas, Mycale, circumtulit herbas,

63. *Ter victis* D4.fi.vai. *vitis* di.2.p. *viciis* H. *vitiis* π (Pithoeus
corrected *vittis*). *ter fronte sacra* d2. *ter frondes* D1. *ture vaporem*
P. *ter fonte vaporem* R1.r. *fronde vaporem* V. *thure vaporo*
R2.d2.pβfi.2.a2.sbo Barth.
64. *lustravit mireque adversa* D4. *cinereque adversa* R2. *aversa*
R1. Haupt transposes this and the following line.
65. *Incendes* D1. *Incedens* b Ulit. *Incendens vino* P.
66. Heins. and Broukh. c. *Meroe.* *totis miser ossibus* ψ Barth.
ignibus urat D1. Glaes. gives *urar* from conjecture. *ignibus arsi*
vulg.
68. *versicoloria* Ppβfi.2.a2.tψd1.2. *vericoloria* D2.4.R2. *varie-
que coloria* VR1.raπ Barth. Ulit. Burm. *nobis quidquid versicoloria*
D1. Glaes. c. *nobis, quid* or *quin versicoloria.*
69. *herbas* R1.2.rafi.boπ. *artes* Ppβa2.f2.d2.

62. For the following lines com-
pare the 'Pharmaceutria' both of
Virgil and of Theocritus.
  Pagani, 'of our village.'
  63. Three and multiples of
three were regarded as sacred
numbers. Virgil E. 8, 76, gives
as the reason *numero deus impare
gaudet.* Cf. Virg. E. 8, 65 sq. :
*Effer aquam, et molli cinge haec
altaria vitta, Verbenasque adole
pinguis et mascula tura.*
  64. Cineresque, &c. Cf. Virg.
E. 8, 102 sq. : *Fer cineres, Ama-
rylli, foras rivoque fluenti Trans-
que caput jace ; nec respexeris.*
Haupt transposes this and the
following line, thus making the
reference in **cineres** intelligible.
  Aversa, 'with averted face.'

  66. In Meroen . . . urar,
' burn for Meroe.'
  Totis . . . ignibus, 'with all
the fire of love.' Cf. Hor. C. 1;
19, 9 : *In me tota ruens Venus.*
  68. Haec eadem nobis . . .
Mycale . . . cantavit, 'Mycale
has performed these same incan-
tations for me.'
  Versicoloria fila. Cf. Virg.
E. 8, 78 : *Necte tribus nodis ter-
nos, Amarylli, colores,* which Con-
ington explains ' make three knots,
each of a thread with à different
colour.' Ib. 74 : *Terna tibi haec
primum triplici diversa colore
Licia circumdo.*
  69. Ignotas . . . herbas.
Probably 'foreign herbs.' Cf.
Virg. E. 8, 96 sq. : *Has herbas*

Cantavit, quod luna timet, quo rumpitur anguis,　　70
Quo currunt scopuli, migrant sata, vellitur arbos;
Plus tamen ecce meus, plus est formosus Iollas.
Cantet, amat quod quisque; levant et carmina curas.

70. *tumet* D1. *colubrina tumet* VR1.r. Burm. c. *quo luna tumet.*
quod luna timet vulg., which last I retain, as corresponding better to
the parallel from Virgil quoted in Notes 2. Glaes. reads *quo Luna
tumet*, regarding *Luna* as a proper name.
71. *Quod currunt* D2. *Qui currunt* v. *Concurrunt* R1.ra. *magice
sata* Vra. *magice sacra* R1.
72. *fastuosus Iol.* ψ.

*atque haec Ponto mihi lecta venena
Ipse dedit Moeris; nascuntur plu-
rima Ponto.*
　　Circumtulit. Carried round
for purposes of incantation, or
purification. Cf. Virg. A. 6, 229:
*Idem ter socios pura circumtulit
unda*, which Lewis and Short say
is a poetical construction for *un-
dam circum socios.*

70. Cf. Virg. E. 8, 70 and 72:
*Carmina vel coelo possunt dedu-
cere Lunam. Frigidus in pratis
cantando rumpitur anguis.*
　　72. The meaning is that these
charms, despite their power, fail
to free Lycidas from love for
Iollas, whose beauty is more effi-
cacious to hold him fast.

APPENDIX

ON ECLOGUE VII.

MERIVALE, Gibbon, and other writers assume that the description in this Eclogue refers to the Flavian amphitheatre, commonly called the Colosseum. This theory must, of course, be abandoned if Calpurnius wrote his Eclogues during the earlier part of Nero's reign (see Introduction, page 2 sq.), since the Colosseum was commenced by Vespasian about A.D. 77, while the *quinquennium Neronis* terminated in A.D. 59. The internal evidence of the Eclogue points to the same conclusion. In line 23 sq., Corydon, describing the amphitheatre, says that it almost looked down on the Tarpeian Rock (*spectacula . . . Tarpeium prope despectantia culmen*), a statement which could hardly be made of the Colosseum, for the Tarpeian Rock is part of the Capitoline, while the Colosseum is at a considerable distance from the Capitoline, and would be more naturally said to overlook the Palatine. Moreover, had the Flavian amphitheatre been before the poet's mind he would, doubtless, have made more definite allusion to its solid stone-built character. Line 23 suggests that wood formed an important part of the building, and the only allusion to more solid materials is in line 49, where the barrier between the spectators and the wild animals is described. The most striking feature in the Colosseum, even after the depredations of ages, is its ponderous solidity, and the words *trabibus spectacula textis* would form a singularly infelicitous description of the blocks of travertine and pillars of marble, whose massive grandeur Burn compares to the Pyramids and the Taj Mahal of Agra. Corydon's account, however, would exactly apply to the vast amphitheatre of wood erected by Nero in A.D. 57. Suetonius (Nero 12) and Tacitus (A. 13, 31) describe this building as *amphitheatrum ligneum* and *molem amphitheatri trabibus exstructam*, though, unfortunately, they considered a detailed account of the structure more suitable for the daily papers (*diurnis urbis actis*) than for their own dignified narrative. They tell us, moreover, that it was situated in the Campus Martius, and it might therefore have easily been so near the Capitoline as to justify the words of Corydon, *Tarpeium prope despectantia culmen.*

In support of this view Professor Ridgeway has called my attention to Strabo 5, 236 : πλησίον δ' ἐστὶ τοῦ πεδίου τούτου (i. e. the Campus Martius) καὶ ἄλλο πεδίον καὶ στοαὶ κύκλῳ παμπληθεῖς καὶ ἄλση καὶ θέατρα τρία καὶ ἀμφιθέατρον καὶ ναοὶ πολυτελεῖς καὶ συνεχεῖς ἀλλήλοις. This was written before 21 A.D., and it is possible that there may have been a permanent site, which was fitted up with temporary scaffolding, as occasion might require, just as is done for the Ober-Ammergau Passion Play at the present day.

At the exhibition given by Nero in this building, Suetonius (l. c.) says that there was no loss of human life, but that wild beasts were killed, and that there was a naval combat with monsters swimming in sea-water. This falls in with the fact that Corydon says nothing of men being slain, but makes frequent reference to the wild beasts, and expressly says that he saw not only the monsters of the forest, but also seals (*aequoreos vitulos*) and the hippopotamus. Suetonius adds that Nero, who at first courted privacy by using a kind of private box, afterwards viewed

the games from the open balcony (*podio adaperto*); and this
corresponds to line 28, where there is an incidental allu-
sion to the best seats being under the open sky (*quaecun-
que patent sub aperto libera coelo*).

Corydon's description of the amphitheatre is not as full
as could be wished, yet it throws considerable light on the
general structure of the building, on the arrangements for
the spectators, and the character of the exhibitions.

The form of the Amphitheatre was in this, as in all
cases, oval (*ovum*, line 34), probably because the first
building of the kind, that which C. Scribonius Curio
(Plin. 36, 15, 24, 117) made of two wooden theatres re-
volving on pivots, was composed of two segments of
circles, each greater than a semicircle. The shape may
have also been affected by the elongated form of the
circus, which was adopted for convenience in racing. To
secure the safety of the spectators a solid wall of marble
(*marmoreo muro*, line 49) ran round the arena. The top of
this wall (*podium*, Juv. 2, 147, and Suet., l. c.) was wide
enough to contain two or three rows of seats, and, as af-
fording far the best view of the sports, was reserved for
the emperor, the senators, and magistrates, or other per-
sons of distinction (line 29, *aut eques aut nivei tribuni*). Its
nearness to the arena, however, rendered this position one
of some danger (Lipsius, De Amph. ch. 12, says, *In Podio,
id est, in ipso ostio orci*) as well as honour, and it was pro-
bably no unnecessary precaution to fence the wall with the
revolving cylinders and the net-work mentioned in lines
50–56. A veneering of ivory (*sternitur ebur*) adorned the
cylinder, whose easy revolution was intended to baffle and
throw back the wild beasts that endeavoured to climb up
among the spectators, while nets of gold wire (*auro torta
retia*) lent brilliancy to the scene (*refulgent*), and were no
less an object of wonder than the elephants' tusks, from
which they were suspended, and which projected over the

arena (lines 48–56). Behind the *podium* the seats rose in tiers (*gradus*, line 25 ; *spectaculorum gradus*, Tac. A. 14, 13), connected by gentle inclines (*clivos lene jacentes*), which ran transversely to the direction of the seats, and divided the latter into wedge-shaped blocks (*cunei*). The several tiers of seats were divided into stories (*maeniana*) by walls, which ran completely round the amphitheatre, like a belt, and which were hence called *baltei*, or *praecinctiones*. In front of each of the walls was a terrace, likewise called *balteus*, or *praecinctio*, which facilitated access to the tiers of seats below it, and could also be used as a standing-place by those who were unable to secure seats. These terraces were sometimes called *praecinctionis itinera*, to distinguish them from the dividing walls, as appears from Vitruvius 5, 3, where, speaking of a theatre, he says : *Praecinctiones ad altitudines theatrorum pro rata parte faciendae videntur, neque altiores quam quanta praecinctionis itineris sit latitudo.* The faces of the walls formed a conspicuous object, and were often richly ornamented (line 47, *Balteus en gemmis*, &c.). When the term *balteus* or *praecinctio* is used the context must decide whether reference is made to the perpendicular face of the wall, or to the terrace at its foot. For instance, in line 47 the reference is evidently to the face of the wall. It would be absurd to suppose that the terrace along which the spectators walked to reach their seats was covered with gems ; but if the face of the wall, which rose above the seats in each story, was so decorated, it would add much to the brilliancy of the scene. The meaning terrace, or passage, is required in Tertullian de Spectaculis 3 : *Nam apud spectacula et in via statur; vias enim vocant cardines balteorum per ambitum, et discrimina popularium per proclivum.* Allusion is here made to the fact, that when all the seats were taken the spectators used to stand on the terraces at the foot of the dividing walls, and in the inclines (*clivos*) mentioned above, both of which were called *viae*, or passages. Both meanings of *praecinctio* occur in the passage quoted above from Vitruvius. The expression *cardines balteorum* is explained by Currey from Pliny 18, 33, 76, 326, where it is said that if a line be drawn from north to south across a field *qui ita limes per agrum currit, cardo vocatur.* Hence *cardo* was used for a principal line of division, and the *cardines balteorum per ambitum* were the terraces, which ran round the amphitheatre, and divided it into stories, while the *clivos* of Calpurnius (line 25), which ran in a cross direction from the top of the building towards the bottom, and divided the seats into *cunei*, are called *discrimina popularium per proclivum*, i.e. the gangways, or divisions, between the seats of the populace sloping down the incline.

The *gradus spectaculorum* were not properly the seats, but the series of elevations rising one above another, on which the seats were placed, as appears from Vitruvius 5, 6, where he says, in reference to a theatre, *gradus spectaculorum ubi subsellia componantur.*

At the top of the building rose the *porticus*, or covered colonnade, from which alone women and the lower orders were allowed to view the games (line 26 sq.: *Venimus ad sedes ubi pulla sordida veste Inter femineas spectabat turba cathedras*). This portion of the building was often gilded (line 47, *illita auro*), and vied with the *balteus* (line 48, *Certatim radiant*) in the splendour of its decoration.

The white toga (*nivei tribuni*, line 29) was *de rigueur* in the better seats, and Corydon (line 81) complains that his shabby attire and unfashionable buckle (*pulla paupertas et adunco fibula morsu*) relegated him to the top gallery, among the women and the dingy crowd of the poor (line 26 sq., already quoted).

It has been observed above, that in the account of the exhibition described in this Eclogue there is no mention of a loss of human life. The exhibition was a *venatio*, and

the more ferocious kind of animals were not produced
(unless, indeed, *Mantichoram* be read in line 59, and
explained 'tiger': see note on the passage), notwith-
standing Corydon's boast, that he had seen every kind of
wild beast (line 57, *vidi genus omne ferarum*). The animals
mentioned are white hares, boars (58), elks (59), Syrian
bulls (60), bisons (61 sq.), seals, bears (65), the hippopo-
tamus (66), with regard to all which see the notes on the
several lines. Besides the animals mentioned by Calpur-
nius, elephants, lions, panthers *(Africanae)*, crocodiles,
giraffes, the rhinoceros, ostriches *(passer marinus)*, cranes,
zebras (ἱππότιγρις), hyenas *(crocotta)*, and many other crea-
tures were at times exhibited, for a detailed account of
which see Friedländer's *Sittengeschichte*. From lines 69 sq.
it appears that these animals were sometimes introduced
into the arena from subterranean caverns within its circuit,
whence also at times an artificial grove arose as by the
touch of a magician's wand. (See the notes on the lines
referred to, and also the Introduction, page 7).

The persons who fought with wild beasts were called
bestiarii, and are to be distinguished from the *gladiatores*,
who fought with one another.

I am indebted to Professor Ridgeway for a further proof
that Nero is the emperor of this Eclogue. The *nivei le-
pores*, which may be Arctic hares, the bears fighting with
seals, and the elks savour of the north, and we learn from
Pliny that a Roman knight was actually sent to the north
to procure amber for use at Nero's games. The fact that
this amber was obtained in large quantities, and profusely
used in decorating the amphitheatre, may account for the
brilliancy of the scene described by Calpurnius (*Balteus en
gemmis*, &c.), and it is possible that the northern animals,
which were unfamiliar even to the old citizen who patro-
nized Corydon, may have been brought to Rome at the
same time. The passage of Pliny referred to is 37, 3, 11,

45 : *Sexcentis M. pass. fere a Carnunto Pannoniae abesse litus id Germaniae, ex quo invehitur* (sc. *sucinum*, amber), *percognitum nuper, vivitque eques Romanus ad id* (i. e. amber) *comparandum missus ab Juliano curante gladiatorum munus Neronis principis, qui et commercia ea et litora peragravit, tanta copia invecta ut retia coercendis feris podiumque tegentia sucinis nodarentur, arma vero et libitina totusque unius dies adparatus in variatione pompae singulorum dierum esset e sucino.*

For further information on the amphitheatre and its games, Friedländer's *Sittengeschichte*, Burn's *Rome and the Campagna*, Tertullian *de Spectaculis*, the articles in Smith's *Dictionary of Antiquities*, and the chapter on Amphitheatres in Middleton's *Ancient Rome in* 1885, may be consulted.

INDEX.

Roman numerals refer to the Eclogues. Arabic numerals, when preceded by a Roman numeral, refer to the lines of the Eclogues; otherwise they refer to the pages.

P

THE END.